PENGUIN BOOKS

Real Fast Food

Nigel Slater is the author of a collection of bestselling books including the classics *Real Fast Food* and *Real Cooking*, and the award-winning *Appetite*. He has written a much-loved column for the *Observer* for over a decade. His autobiography *Toast: the story of a boy's hunger*, won six major awards, including the British Book Awards Biography of the Year. His latest book is *The Kitchen Diaries*.

Also by Nigel Slater:

Real Fast Food
Real Fast Puddings
The 30-Minute Cook
Real Cooking
Nigel Slater's Real Food
Appetite
Thirst
Toast: the story of a boy's hunger
The Kitchen Diaries

NIGEL SLATER

Real Fast Food

350 recipes ready-to-eat
in 30 minutes

PENGUIN BOOKS

PENGUIN BOOKS

Published by the Penguin Group
Penguin Books Ltd, 80 Strand, London WC2R ORL, England
Penguin Group (USA) Inc., 375 Hudson Street, New York, New York 10014, USA
Penguin Group (Canada), 90 Eglinton Avenue East, Suite 700, Toronto, Ontario, Canada M4P 2Y3
(a division of Pearson Penguin Canada Inc.)
Penguin Ireland, 25 St Stephen's Green, Dublin 2, Ireland
(a division of Penguin Books Ltd)
Penguin Group (Australia), 250 Camberwell Road, Camberwell, Victoria 3124, Australia
(a division of Pearson Australia Group Pty Ltd)
Penguin Books India Pvt Ltd, 11 Community Centre, Panchsheel Park, New Delhi – 110 017, India
Penguin Group (NZ), cnr Airborne and Rosedale Roads, Albany, Auckland 1310, New Zealand
(a division of Pearson New Zealand Ltd)
Penguin Books (South Africa) (Pty) Ltd, 24 Sturdee Avenue, Rosebank, Johannesburg 2196, South Africa

Penguin Books Ltd, Registered Offices: 80 Strand, London WC2R ORL, England

www.penguin.com

First published by Michael Joseph 1992
Published in Penguin Books 1993
This re-set edition published 2006
6

Set in 9.25/13.75 pt PostScript TheSans Light
Typeset by Rowland Phototypesetting Ltd, Bury St Edmunds, Suffolk
Printed in Great Britain by Clays Ltd, St Ives plc
This edition produced for The Book People Ltd, Hall Wood Avenue, Haydock, St Helens WA11 9UL

ISBN-13: 978-0-141-02950-4
ISBN-10: 0-141-02950-1

For Michael

Contents

Introduction

This is a book of ideas for everyday eating. A collection of recipes for simple food that is easy to prepare and quick to cook. It is written for anyone who enjoys good food eaten informally, and should particularly appeal to those who lack the time to cook it. Most of the recipes are based on fresh food with as little as possible done to it. There are no complicated procedures, no dithering around with affected arrangements on oversized plates, and no effete garnishes. It is a set of straightforward recipes for fast food with bold flavours, cooked in minutes and served without pretension.

There are three types of fast food I think worth eating. Firstly, there is street food, such as the crisp Indian *samosas*, sold hot from their pans of crackling fat, or the robust and smoky Greek *souvlakia*, grilled over charcoal and wrapped in comforting pitta. Then there is take-away food, some of which can be very fine indeed. What can beat a crisp-based and deeply savoury Italian pizza or a fillet of fresh fish fried in light, rustling batter with home-made chips?

Thirdly, there is fast home cooking, the sort of food you throw together when you come home tired and hungry. At its worst this can come from the '101 ways with condensed mushroom soup' school of cookery, or be a bland ready-made supper chucked in the microwave, but at its best fast home cooking can mean fresh food, bright flavours and relaxed eating. That is what this book is all about.

The recipes are easy and within the grasp of all but the most ham-fisted of cooks. While most of the recipes included here are fast, I make no claims for five-minute feasts or ten-minute dinner parties. I think that good food can be measured only by its flavour and freshness, not by a stop-watch. That said, most of the recipes in this book can be completed in under 30 minutes, which is, after all, the time it takes a supermarket cook-chill supper to heat through. Many of them take just half that time. The ingredient lists are short and most of the recipes require only one or two fresh ingredients that can be bought on the way home. I like the idea of buying one ingredient that looks particularly good, then mixing it with some storecupboard staples and seeing what happens.

The ideas behind the recipes are a hotchpotch of the original, the borrowed and the stolen. It would be an arrogant writer indeed who suggested that all his recipes were his own. Many of the recipes here are classics whose origins are obscure, if not totally lost, to all but the most thorough of food historians. Some of the recipes are mine (whatever that may mean), some have been adapted from others, and a few have been previously published in another form in *marie claire*.

There are a few indulgences. I stand accused of using some things to excess: extra virgin olive oil, Parmesan cheese, garlic, basil, olives and bitter salad leaves. I will accept criticism too for my overuse of berries, fruits and soft fresh cheeses, and I might as well admit addictions to anchovies and to dark, bitter and absurdly expensive chocolate, though thankfully not together.

If there is one thing I hope will emerge from this book it is that fast food is not just about pizzas, hamburgers and noddles, good though they can be (and they are all here); fast food can also mean a slice of truly ripe Charentais melon eaten with a hunk of salty Feta cheese and a few black olives, or perhaps a juicy white peach sliced and dropped into a glass of chilled deep yellow wine.

Think of a piece of chicken brushed with aromatic herbs and lemon, then char-grilled and stuffed into a crisp roll slathered with garlic mayonnaise, or a comforting bowl of porridge with blackberries and heather honey. Imagine shredded peppery basil leaves stirred into buttery mashed potato, a slice of pork pan-fried with fennel or a plate of purple-yellow muscat grapes and ripe figs. All this is fast food.

Whether it is Mrs David's immortal omelette and a glass of wine, a hot bacon sandwich when you return from the pub on a cold night, or a plate of pasta with slices of soft white goat's cheese and leaves of pungent fresh thyme, there is nothing like real, fast, food.

A Few Notes for the Fast Cook

Most of the recipes are enough for two. I know this is slightly unusual, but I am certain that more people eat this sort of food in twos than in fours. Although four is a popular number for dinner parties, it is less practical for everyday eating, with different members of the same family eating at different times. But it is easy to double the recipes in order to serve four. Those traditional complicators of recipe multiplication, such as gelatine and cornflour, have no place in this book. I also believe that many of us eat alone, particularly the young and elderly, and it is easier to halve a recipe successfully than to quarter it.

The dietary balance of the recipes in this book is based on the World Health Organisation's recommendations; the bulk involve fresh vegetables and fruit, and most main dishes are accompanied by a salad (the WHO suggests we eat 400g [14oz] of these per day). A good number of the recipes include starches in the form of bread, pasta and potatoes. (The WHO recommendation is that they should provide 50–70 per cent of our energy.) The remaining recipes using red meat, cream and high-fat cheeses should provide no more than 30 per cent of your daily food intake. Over two-thirds of the recipes are suitable for non-meat eaters, and the majority of them are distinctly frugal in meat quantities.

These recipes are not definitive. I should hate to think of anyone following them slavishly. I would prefer that they are used as a starting-point, a springboard if you like, for your own ideas. I cook in a relaxed way that would probably raise eyebrows with the house-proud or the more efficient of cooks. I believe that no recipe should appear in a book until it has been tested, but I should add that I rarely enjoy the triple-tried-and-tested style of cooking where recipes have been tested to death. They may be guaranteed to work but have more often than not lost their heart and soul along the way.

Timings

The majority of these recipes can be on the table within 30 minutes or less. If waiting even that long is beyond you there is a section of storecupboard Quick Fixes at the end of the book. It is difficult to give accurate timings for recipes. Everybody works at a different pace, cookers do not have identical thermostats, and one person's idea of a minute can differ from the next's (even with one eye on the clock). My timings therefore should be taken as approximate. All recipes point to a clue other than just time whether a dish is ready or not, that is, firm to the touch, tender to the point of a knife, black round the edges and so on, which is a more reliable guide than the clock.

Accompaniments

Many of the snacks in this book can become a complete meal by serving them with a salad and following with cheese and fruit. I cannot think of a fish or meat dish that I would not accompany with a salad of various green leaves.

Although most of the recipes will stand up for themselves as a light meal, I have included suggestions with some recipes for accompanying dishes should you wish to combine them in a more traditional fashion. This particularly applies to the meat sections where some hearty eaters may find my ubiquitous accompaniment, 'a salad of baby green leaves', insufficient.

Ingredients lists

The lists of ingredients that precede the method of each recipe are generally quite short. I have tried to include no more than one or two that you will need to go out and buy while the rest of the list is made up of things you will probably have hanging around anyway: lemons, mustard, spices, herbs and the like. Some recipes include nothing that is not in a reasonably well-stocked cupboard. And by that I mean an average household cupboard as opposed to a country house larder or a student's windowsill.

When listing ingredients I have attempted to be as helpful as possible, that is, extra virgin olive oil or groundnut oil rather than just 'oil'. Likewise I have stated waxy or floury, wholemeal or *ciabatta*, or cherry or plum rather than simply potatoes, bread or tomatoes. My suggestions, though, are probably the ideal rather than a necessity, for example, 4 medium cloves of garlic is not a world away from 2 plump cloves. I have put 2 large ones because they are easier to peel and sometimes both fresher and sweeter. Just use the best you can get hold of.

I have tried to find a balance between the practical and the absurdly pernickety. If, for instance, I have listed English or Dijon or tarragon mustard in the ingredients, then that is what I consider to be right for the recipe; if I have just said 'mustard' then the type is of less importance to the finished dish. Use what you have to hand.

When I say butter, I mean unsalted. When I say flour I mean plain, and when I say salt I mean sea salt. By butter I do not mean margarine or a low-fat spread. And stock comes fresh in cartons from the supermarket or from a wine bottle or, if there is no other aromatic liquid around, the tap. Never a cube. If you will not take my advice, then at least try Marigold Swiss Vegetable Stock Powder, to my taste the least offensive.

Herbs

When I list herbs in the recipes you can take it I mean fresh ones. Dried herbs, with the possible exception of oregano, are of little use to the quick cook as they need slow cooking in order to give up their flavour to the dish. Many dried herbs, in particular parsley, chervil and basil, are a complete waste of time and money, though I will concede that thyme and rosemary have their uses – but not here.

Measurements

I have to admit to rarely measuring anything. My cooking is not so finely tuned that a *soupçon* more or less of anything will cause much grief. If I am cooking for myself I forget all about scales and tablespoons and just go with whatever tastes and looks right. If you were to use this book as a stepping-stone to adopting the same method I would be a very happy man.

In measuring ingredients I have tried to be accurate; generally speaking, tablespoons are lightly heaped unless it says otherwise, and are proper measuring spoons. A glass of wine means a normal Paris goblet, about 100ml / 4fl oz). 'A small bunch of' means the size of a child's posy, and 'a handful' refers to the amount that can comfortably be held in the palm and fingers of the average hand. Where I feel scrupulously accurate measurements are essential to the balance of flavours then I have said so; if not, then a gram or an ounce either way is unlikely to end in tears. But I wouldn't take any of it as gospel. I have given both Imperial and metric measurements, so choose whichever you prefer, but stick to one or other throughout the recipe as they are not interchangeable.

Shopping

Be prepared
I have mentioned before that many of the ingredients listed in each recipe are probably to be found in a reasonably stocked kitchen cupboard. It is worth spending a little time every now and again to stock up on oils, spices, dried pasta, rice and condiments such as soy and chilli sauces.

Daily food shopping can then be cut to a minimum; a few fish fillets, a green vegetable or some fruit. Shopping, however limited your time, becomes less of a hassle if most of the heavy stuff is already at home, giving you time to find the ripest fruit and the pick of the vegetables.

A word about prepared food. Supermarkets stock an increasing number of prepacked labour-saving ingredients. Some of these I approve of: fillets of fish (though I wish they would put a few bones into the pack for stock) and washed potatoes, for instance. Bags of ready-washed spinach and salad leaves save time, and despite the fact they appear expensive, I find them cheaper than keeping several different types of leaves and herbs in the fridge or rinsing spinach fifty times. I draw the line at sliced vegetables, though. Can anyone really be too busy to slice a courgette?

Organic foods

I want food that is as fresh and as pure as possible. My first stop in any supermarket is the organic section. Food labelled 'organic' has been produced without the use of chemical pesticides, herbicides and fungicides normally used in today's intensive farming methods. These chemicals can leave residues in the food about which the long-term effects on the body are not known. Some of the big food chains are taking the organic movement seriously and there are often available potatoes, tomatoes, mushrooms and wonderful green-topped carrots.

Food grown in this natural way is more expensive because the farmers' yields are lower and less reliable. Organic farming is a massive growth area and given encouragement from the consumer it will go from strength to strength.

Quality

The better quality an ingredient the more use it is to the cook whose time is short. By quality, I mean flavour and freshness. After a couple of decades when food quality seemed to be on a downward spiral, I think it is safe to say that the choice has never been better. Where some greengrocers, grocers and fishmongers are still reluctant to offer us anything new, there are many who set a shining example, stocking all manner of interesting things. I look to these people first, before I tackle the supermarkets as I think it would be sad to see our local foodshops (or bookshops and stationers for that matter) disappear in favour of the big chains.

The supermarkets, though, are responding quickly to consumer interest in good food. Among buyers, flavour, rather than yield, reliability and shelflife, is the buzzword. Some chains work directly with the growers and farmers to produce a better product; for instance, one chain has been rekindling interest in old English apple varieties, and done sterling work to find a tomato with a good balance of sweetness and acidity. Things are looking up.

How to speed up your Cooking

Check the ingredients
It is worth spending a couple of minutes checking that you have all the ingredients before you start cooking. Many times I have found that the butter I 'knew' I had has mysteriously disappeared. If you get halfway through a recipe and find that the crucial ingredient is missing, then you must experiment or starve. Improvisation is a wonderful thing. It is how cookery moves forward.

In the kitchen
It really does help to assemble all the ingredients first. I do not mean measuring out the tablespoons into twee little bowls like some demonstration cook, but bringing the olive oil to the cooker, grating the cheese and rummaging through the spices for the fennel seeds will save some time. When you have to chop and sweat an onion I suggest you do that first and then prepare the other ingredients while it cooks.

A place for everything
I am as suspicious of a tidy kitchen as I am of a tidy desk. I hate the sort of kitchen (they are usually white) that if you so much as turn the egg-timer over will look like a bomb has hit it. But I have to admit that everything in my kitchen has its place. This is not due to some manic do-it-and-dust-it side of my nature, but partly because my kitchen is so small. The oils, vinegars and mustards all live in the same place, and the salt and pepper haven't changed place in years.

This is a great boon when time is short. It can take for ever to locate the coriander seeds if they are not put back in the same cupboard each time.

The right tools

I hardly even need to mention that sharp knives and good quality heavy-based pans make cooking quicker, safer and more enjoyable. You know that. But I shall point out that it is useless, not to mention dangerous, to throw those sharp knives in the washing-up water. I also cannot resist saying that I recommend Le Creuset enamelled cast-iron pans. I have had mine for years and swear by them rather than at them. The best woks, incidentally, are the thin, one-handled ones from Chinese shops, rather than the designer numbers from kitchen shops.

Get on with it

There is little point in standing over a pot or constantly peering into the oven. Unless a recipe insists that you should keep an eye on the food while it cooks, or that something requires constant stirring, you can do something else while it cooks, such as toss the salad, finish the crossword or brush the cat.

Taste, taste, taste

I suggest you taste your cooking at every stage. If you like the taste of a dish before you are supposed to add the cream or the lemon juice then stop right there. Try adding salt and pepper only after tasting the dish first, as some foods, cheese for one, can vary enormously in saltiness. Remember that many of us eat too much salt so try to cut back a bit as it is not always necessary; in fact, quite a few of the recipes in this book do not contain it at all. Taste continuously, and use your finger – it's quicker.

The table

Good food is good food, and no amount of pretentious table settings will make it taste any better. My motto is the less fuss the better, but little things do make a difference. A white linen napkin and a fruit knife can turn eating an apple (if it is a good one) into a special occasion. But if I have time to spare I use it to cook with rather than to starch napkins. Flowers on the table are delightful, but I think they are far more beautiful when naturally arranged (for which read 'plonked'). Flower arrangers have a great deal to answer for.

Food looks much more appetising on a plain white plate (preferably with a deep rim to hold any pan juices or sauce) than on some artful designer number. The Italians and the French make good sturdy ones for everyday eating. The fickleness of fashion means that heavy deep-bowled white plates are now available in the designer shops.

Ignore anyone who tells you that every meal should be a 'performance' and be suspicious of those who tell you they iron a tablecloth and arrange the flowers when they come in from work, exhausted, at eight o'clock. They are trying to hide something. Probably the food.

And remember that any fast food, be it a sandwich eaten while standing in the kitchen, or a sauté of chicken with olives and herbs, tastes even better with a glass or two of wine.

The Fast Foodies' Storecupboard

It was Patience Gray and Primrose Boyd who pointed out, in their delightful little book *Plats du Jour*, that the main object of the storecupboard is: 'to provide meals at short notice without shopping, and, equally important, to leave one free to select the piece of beef for *gulyas or bœuf à la mode* without having to search at the last moment for paprika pepper or a handful of juniper berries.'

To the quick cook a sufficiently stocked storecupboard is not just a time-saver but a source of inspiration. On countless occasions I have come home and made a meal from the contents of the kitchen cupboards. *Pappardelle* cooked with olive paste from a jar, tinned salmon fish cakes and bottled peppers char-grilled, then served warm with a drizzle of olive oil and scattered with garlic, have all been the results of rummaging through the cupboards.

I have a small kitchen. It has probably less room than most larders. Cupboard space is at a premium, and large bottles of olive oil and vinegar tend to migrate to the already cluttered work surfaces. Rolling out pastry or making bread demands that everything be relocated to the floor. This is not my dream kitchen.

My storecupboard is lean and restricted to essentials rather than groaning with all manner of 'things that may just come in useful'. I am ruthless about just how many jars and bottles I have open at one time, so there are perhaps three different mustards and pickles on the go rather than the five or so I really wish for. I have no facilities for hoarding 'little bits in bags', and will have no truck with unfamiliar ingredients that glare accusingly at me every time I open the cupboard door. Not for me the packets of rock crystal sugar or Christmas-pudding-flavoured tea that clutter so many shelves for months, even years, on end.

If I had to choose only three ingredients for my desert island storecupboard, and assuming that a few staples such as rice, dried pasta and some potatoes had been washed ashore with me, they would probably be lemons, olive oil and Parmesan cheese. Allowed to take six and I would probably add anchovies, dried mushrooms and then agonise over a block of fine dark chocolate or a wooden box of rose or lemon Turkish Delight. I detail below some key ingredients that will form a strong backbone to the fast cook's kitchen. I have kept it short and somewhat personal, knowing that this list has worked for me for years.

Oils I have three, sometimes four, oils open at once: two olive oils, one bland and one fancy nut oil. I like a light olive oil for general cooking – the French James Plagniol brand is one I like – and a smart fruity extra virgin oil from Italy for pouring over salads and vegetables. I prefer a bland groundnut oil for frying and stir-frying, using the deeply fragrant walnut and hazelnut oils, bought in small tins and bottles, for mixing with lemon juice for dressing salad leaves and goat's cheeses. Toasted sesame oil is good for finishing stir-fries, but I can live without it.

Vinegar I use wine vinegar, red or white, for almost everything (I like the *Badia a Coltibuono* one available in good delis). I have both sherry and cider vinegar for salad dressings and I have paid a king's ransom for rich, mellow balsamic vinegar to which I am becoming addicted. Forget the cut-price supermarket blends and go for broke.

Mustard I have three jars open at once, all from Dijon. A great favourite both for spreading on sandwiches and cooking with is a smooth tarragon mustard from any of the leading French importers. A jar of grainy French mustard made crunchy by the inclusion of seeds or the smooth yellow variety are types I also find invaluable. I avoid the fancy mustards, the old English ones with honey and heaven knows what, as I find a straightforward mustard hard to beat.

Dried Pasta Lots. Something flat such as *fettuccine* or, better still, the wider *pappardelle*. A variety for picking up copious quantities of sauce such as shell-shaped *conchiglie* or corkscrew-shaped *fusilli* and a vacuum bag of *gnocci* are pretty much essential. Look out for brands such as de Cecco.

Salt, Peppercorns and Spices Maldon salt with its large flat crystals is my first choice. Black peppercorns are the most essential spice; it is hard to think of cooking without them. I rarely use hot white peppercorns, preferring the aromatic black ones, and grinding them as I need them in a wooden peppermill. Other spices to have handy include dried chillies, whole coriander, chilli powder, ground cinnamon, ground cumin, a good proprietary curry powder or your own ground and stoppered, and ground paprika.

Dried herbs are rarely used in quick cooking as they do not keep well and rarely bear any resemblance to the fresh thing. They can be used to good effect in casseroles when the slow cooking time can extract their flavour.

Bottled Sauces These are useful when you have no time to make your own or to visit the deli for freshly-made ones. Creamed artichoke, pesto and black and green olive pastes for pasta, hot red *harissa* for cous cous, and dark soy for stir-fries and light soy as a condiment.

Tinned Foods Some things survive the canning process well enough to be included in the storecupboard. Chick peas, tomatoes and sardines in olive oil are obvious contenders. Some flageolet and white haricot beans can be okay, though they lose the bite of the dried ones when cooked. Salmon is quite sufficient for fish cakes and bakes, and tuna even better. The sardines in tomato sauce in my cupboard belong to the cats, who will not eat any other sort.

I use little flour in my cooking so buy it in small bags, stocking large amounts only when I am going through one of my baking sprees. When I do, I buy organic stone ground plain flour from Doves

Farm, which is available in many health food shops. Jordans is another brand I like and is more accessible. I have been caught without sugar in the house many times but I try to remember to keep a small bag of caster for sprinkling on pancakes and making *brûlees*. I always have a box of French *A la Perruche* cane sugar cubes for coffee.

A Few Extras I mention some ingredients I keep for instant snacks in Quick Fixes on page 314 but here are a few other foodstuffs which are hardly essential but I like to have them in the cupboard if possible. They are: tapenade for spreading on toasted rounds of French bread. Salty *anchoïade* for smearing thinly on toast. Sun-dried tomatoes for snacking on straight from the jar. High fruit, low sugar jams are becoming popular and make a satisfying sweet snack when spread on French bread or stirred into yoghurt. Apricot and greengage are usually the most successful for keeping a true fruit flavour. Unfiltered flower honey and Marmite for spreading on soldiers and thick, crunchy peanut butter for sandwiches.

1

Bakery Goods and *Drinks*

I find something intrinsically 'right' about eating food while holding it in my hands. It is as if this is how food was meant to be eaten all along, with knives, forks and chopsticks being part of a parlour game that somehow got out of hand. I certainly enjoy the feel of the food in my fingers and no doubt aspire to the primitiveness of it all.

Hand-held food is not just for the street and the picnickers' meadow, but an established alternative to eating at table. For comfort and convenience most of it is enclosed in an edible wrapper. Sometimes warm, sometimes not, but almost invariably dough-based.

The snatched sandwich of a working lunch, the croissant stuffed with melted cheese for a light supper, even the soft chapati used to mop up a spicy stew, are instances of how a starchy envelope is used to cradle the scorchingly hot and the rich and messy. Examples can be found in almost every culture. The Chinese have their sweet pork stews wrapped in thick balls of steamed dough, and the Mexicans their tacos. The Cornish choose a strong pastry case for the traditional pasties in a miners' lunch, while within the pitta pockets of the Middle East lurk all manner of savoury things. The Greek souvlakia, the French baguette and the Indian samosa share a raison d'être with both the American hamburger and the Russian blini with its precious freight of caviar.

I love the idea of swapping fillings and wrappings to suit my mood and what is available at the time of my hunger. I can see no reason why the fluffy apples and thick cream of a French crêpe cannot sit in an English muffin, or why the moist and fragrant tikka-spiced chicken of India should not lie between bread from a British farmhouse loaf (indeed it does, just look at Marks & Spencer).

I did not know that strawberries and cream were better suited to a flaky French croissant than a substantial English scone until I tried it. Neither was I aware of how perfectly Chinese spiced pork sat in a floury Scottish bap. But those bound by tradition and prejudice will no doubt disagree.

The sandwich, bagel, muffin and pitta fillings that follow are merely suggestions. Chop and change to suit your predicament. But do not skimp. The dainty triangular sandwich, with its scraping of marg and thin line of wet ham, makes an uncomfortable bedfellow alongside the generously-filled flat bread of the Middle East, stuffed to bursting with its hot and spicy cargo. Only the generous can make a sandwich worth eating.

BREAD

Bruschetta

Bruschetta is garlic bread. Not the sort made from French bread and dripping with garlic butter, but the Italian version made with slices from a coarse-textured country loaf and thick, unctuous extra virgin olive oil.

Grill a slice of coarse-textured white bread on both sides. You can do this over a charcoal grill, under a standard domestic one, or bake it in a very hot oven. Loath to heat my oven for a piece of toast, I often just zap it on my preheated, ridged Le Creuset grill pan.

When crisp on both sides, cut a juicy clove of garlic in half and rub it over one side of the bread. Drizzle the bread with olive oil. Use your best oil, something deep green and fragrant.

Bruschetta al Pomodoro

FOR 2

4 slices of white bread, cut from a crusty loaf, 1cm / ½ inch thick

1 clove of garlic, peeled

4 ripe tomatoes, roughly chopped

salt

freshly ground black pepper

extra virgin olive oil

Grill the bread on both sides. Cut the garlic clove in half and rub the cut edge all over one side of the toasted bread.

Spread the tomatoes over the garlic toast and sprinkle a little salt and a grinding of black pepper. Trickle olive oil over the tomatoes and eat the toast while still hot.

A few good things to put on *Bruschetta* or *Crostini*

Crostini are small rounds of bread toasted and then brushed with olive oil much as in *bruschetta*.

Aubergine, Feta and Mint

Spread the oiled and garlicked bread with aubergine purée from the deli, crumble over some salty Feta cheese and scatter with a little chopped fresh mint.

Creamed Eggs and Grilled Onions

Brush trimmed spring onions with olive oil and grill till golden, about 3 minutes on each side. Scramble eggs with a little butter in a pan, then fold in a spoon or two of *fromage frais*. Place the grilled onions on hot *bruschetta*, and spoon the creamed eggs on top. Serve hot.

Gorgonzola

Mash an equal quantity of Gorgonzola cheese and softened unsalted butter. Mix in a little brandy and spread over the hot toast.

Grilled Radicchio and Goat's Cheese

An idea from Frances Bissell. Cut a head of radicchio into thick slices, about 4 per large head. Brush each slice with olive oil, season and place under a preheated medium hot grill, turning it occasionally. Top each slice with a round of goat's cheese and grill till bubbling.

Pain Perdu

FOR 2 AS A SNACK

4 slices of white bread, crusts removed
150ml / ¼ pint milk

2 tablespoons sugar
1 small egg, beaten
butter, for frying

Cut the bread into triangles. Sweeten the milk with the sugar. Dip the bread into the milk, then the egg and fry it on both sides in hot butter till crisp, which will take around 3 minutes on each side. Remove, sprinkle with sugar and eat hot.

Mozzarella in Carrozza

FOR 2 AS A SNACK

175g / 6oz Mozzarella cheese, sliced 5mm / ¼ inch thick
4 slices of white bread, 5mm / ¼ inch thick, crusts removed
2 tablespoons milk
a little flour, seasoned with salt and freshly ground black pepper
1 small egg, beaten
fresh breadcrumbs
groundnut oil, for deep-frying

Place the sliced Mozzarella on two of the slices of bread and top with the remaining slices to make two large cheese sandwiches. Brush the sandwiches on both sides with the milk, then dust with flour. Dip into the beaten egg, followed by the breadcrumbs. Fry in hot oil, about one finger's depth, till crisp, about 3 minutes on each side. Cut into quarters and serve.

Toasted Cheese and Ham

I make this snack from time to time, sometimes omitting the onion, and occasionally adding chutney instead of mustard.

FOR 2 AS A SNACK

4 slices of bread, cut thick
English or other hot mustard
75g / 3oz / 1 loosely-packed teacup cooked ham
1 spring onion, trimmed and finely chopped
½ teaspoon Worcestershire sauce
75g / 3oz grated cheese, whatever you have

Toast the bread on one side. Spread the untoasted side meanly with mustard. Mix the other ingredients and spread on top. Place under the preheated grill for a couple of minutes till the cheese has melted.

Sandwich Jambon de Pays

A good ham sandwich is a rare thing. I have found more of them in France than in Britain. But then, the French have a knack of getting the simple things right.

A ham sandwich can be good when only ham and bread are used, so long as both are the best of their type. It does not require mayonnaise, tomatoes, chutney or lettuce, though I really do think a fine spreading of hot mustard enhances the ham. The bread should be cut from a thin baguette. It must have a crackling crust that shatters when you bite. The ham must be carved from the bone and not, absolutely not, peeled from a packet of wet, pink, rectangular slices. I do not believe that fine, sweet ham can come out of a packet.

Choose roast or boiled ham, with a cure that suits you. Ask to taste the ham before you buy, just as you taste cheese. Get the assistant to carve it thinly; it is much better sliced thin and piled high. Spread just a little mustard on to the bread, a hot English one rather than a mild French variety. Pile on the ham in slender, small pieces, then top with the second half of the bread.

Some good things to put in a Ham Sandwich

However good your bread and ham may be, you may want to gild the lily a little. Perhaps in order to turn a snack into supper:

* Cover the ham with creamy scrambled egg (see page 31) into which you have stirred a spoonful of fresh chopped chives

* Toast the bread and spread it with tapenade, the olive and anchovy paste. Cover that with the ham, then add thin slices of good melting cheese, such as Gruyère or Mozzarella. Flash it under the grill till the cheese melts

* Shred some radicchio leaves. Toss them in olive oil and grill till

they start to wilt. Return them to their bowl, and while still warm toss them with the thin slices of ham. Pile on to the bread

* Toss the ham with sliced bottled artichokes that have been drained and grilled till tender and browned

* Brush baby leeks with olive oil and grill till they are soft and lightly browned. Sprinkle with grated Parmesan cheese and grill a little more till the cheese smells savoury. Lay them on top of the ham

* Toss the ham with bottled red pimientos, cut into strips, which have been grilled till sweet and browned at the edges

* Sauté dandelion leaves till they wilt, toss in a few pine nuts and slightly fewer raisins. Pile on to the bread and top with the ham

Italian Prosciutto Sandwich

Prosciutto is dry-cured Italian ham. Parma is the most famous variety. It is usually sliced very finely, and has a generous proportion of fat around the edge. Its flavour is piquant and as with most cold meats it is best sliced just before it is bought, rather than ready-sliced and vacuum-packed.

I prefer an open-textured bread with ham sliced this thinly. A French baguette is good enough, but the best is Italian *ciabatta*, which has a floury crust and huge holes. It is becoming easier to find now.

* One of my favourite sandwiches is a split piece of *ciabatta*, spread with a little mayonnaise, then stuffed with alfalfa sprouts, watercress sprigs and Parma ham

* A substantial sandwich I made recently consisted of an open-textured bread, split and spread with black olive paste from a jar. I then filled it with baby rocket leaves tossed with lemon and olive oil, and thin slices of Taleggio cheese. Topped with a slice of prosciutto and a handful of black olives it satisfied both my addiction to olives and my love of cheese and bitter leaves

The Hot Dog

Frankfurter sandwiches, better known as hot dogs, are an American institution. Like all such things, feelings run high about how they should be eaten. Apparently, the frankfurter was born in the 1850s, when a German butcher stuffed a long roll with a smoked sausage in honour of his pet dog. The idea went to America in the 1860s with one Charles Feltman, who sold them in the street from a charcoal stove on Coney Island, Brooklyn.

Purists insist that the sausage be grilled over charcoal or boiled, then stuffed into a long soft roll. Mustard is piped along the entire length of the frankfurter. These views apart, I think hot dogs make a fine late supper, especially after a film. Buy them in tins or vacuum packs. Split the roll in half, it should be a bit longer than the sausage, and soft. Stuff it with warm sauerkraut, which you have transferred from its tin to a pan and heated gently. Spread a little mild mustard on a hot grilled frankfurter and push it inside the roll. Eat with a cold beer.

Bacon Sandwich

Feelings run high about bacon sandwiches. White bread or brown, toasted or untoasted, smoked bacon or green back, butter or not. Then there's the ketchup question. For me the bread should be white, and untoasted. Somehow it is better made with factory-made 'plastic bread'. I like the bacon to be smoked streaky, cooked just short of crisp. The bread should be dunked in the hot bacon fat. I tend to give the ketchup a miss.

Our love of the bacon sandwich is looked on with amazement by Americans, who, of course, have their sublime BLT (see below). But the bacon sandwich remains the quintessential after-pub nosh. Like Chinese take-aways, it only really comes into its own when you are slightly drunk.

For each sandwich:

4 rashers of smoked streaky bacon
a little fat if the bacon is lean
2 rounds of medium-sliced white bread

Fry the bacon, in a little fat if the bacon is very lean, until it starts to show signs of crisping. I think the edges should be just turning golden. Push the rashers to the side of the pan. Dunk one side of each slice of bread into hot bacon fat. Sandwich the rashers between the bread and eat while still very hot.

Pastrami on Rye

Pastrami on rye is the most chic of all sandwiches. Pastrami is a wood-smoked brisket of beef that has been first cured with sugar, salt and several spices. Garlic, ginger and pepper are the most obvious, but the recipes vary. They are almost always secret. All that really matters is that the spiced pink meat is juicy and very garlicky.

As I understand it, the definitive pastrami on rye is made with hot beef (it is steamed to keep it moist) and light rye bread. There should be mustard, but no butter, and a garnish of a lightly pickled cucumber.

To make the authentic Manhattan-style kosher sandwich at home is difficult. Good pastrami is difficult to find outside London's East End and is expensive. (I am not keen on the British commercial brick-shaped blocks with their paprika coating, preferring the original peppercorn-coated variety.) To buy a block of it large enough to steam and slice would be very expensive.

The next best thing is to eat it cold. Secure a quarter-pound of pastrami per sandwich. You will find it, apart from at kosher delis, in good food halls and delicatessens. Make sure it is moist before they slice it for you, particularly important as you are eating it cold. Cut slices from a light rye loaf, no thicker than 5mm / ¼ inch. Spread them with English mustard and pile on thin slices of pastrami. Add a second slice of mustard-spread bread and serve a pickled cucumber on the side.

The Club Sandwich

A true feast that the late American writer James Beard described as one of the 'great sandwiches of all time'. Surprisingly, this Gargantua among snacks was not of the monstrous proportions we are now led to believe, as it was traditionally made with only two rather than the assumed three layers. Here is a reasonably authentic version, saved from being definitive only by my suggestion of wholemeal toast, which will no doubt ruffle a few feathers. Butter a crisp piece of toast cut from a white or light brown loaf. While this is still warm layer crisp lettuce, long oval-leaved Cos for preference, with slices of tomato, cooked sliced chicken and rashers of bacon with mayonnaise. Finish with a second piece of toast.

A few rules that one is wise, but not obliged, to bow to: the toast and bacon rashers should be crisp, the chicken moist from a freshly-roasted bird, and the mayonnaise home-made or Hellman's at the very least. The peculiar condiment known as Salad Cream has no place here, or anywhere else for that matter. You can garnish the sacred sandwich with little green olives without offending anyone.

Cold Roast Pork Sandwiches with Pickled Walnuts and Crackling

My father liked pickled walnuts, cold roast pork and its crackling almost more than anything else. This is for him.

1 teaspoon mild mustard

2 tablespoons mayonnaise

7.5cm / 3 inches or so of pork
  crackling, crushed into
  fragments

a small handful of white or red
  crisp cabbage, finely shredded

2 rounds of soft wholemeal,
  granary or nut bread

2 slices of cold roast pork, about
  as thick as pound coins

salt

1 large pickled walnut, sliced
  into rounds

Mix the mustard into the mayonnaise, tasting and adding more mustard as you wish. Fold in the crushed crackling and the shredded cabbage. Spread half of the cabbage on to one round of bread. Lay a slice of pork on top. Add a little salt and the sliced pickled walnut. Lay the second slice of pork on top and cover with the remaining dressed cabbage. Top with the second piece of bread.

Spiced Tuna on Rye

Have you noticed how celery seems to be *de rigueur* in tuna sandwiches?

MAKES 2 SANDWICHES

1 × 250g / 8oz tin line-caught
  tuna, drained

4 tablespoons mayonnaise

2 tablespoons finely-diced celery

1 tablespoon finely-chopped
  sweet onion

a clove of garlic, crushed to a
  pulp

pinch / ¼ teaspoon paprika

¼ teaspoon cayenne pepper

1 teaspoon lemon juice

salt

a bunch of watercress, fresh
  and green, trimmed

4 rounds of rye or white bread

Flake the tuna, not too finely, with a fork. Mix with the mayonnaise, celery, onion, garlic and spices. Stir in the lemon juice. Taste and add salt if necessary. Pile between the bread with sprigs of watercress.

* There has been a lot of fuss about tuna. Rightly so. Some tuna are

netted causing the dolphins, which are sometimes picked up with them, to be killed. Check that any tuna you buy is line caught, and save a dolphin.

Hot Sandwiches

Pan-fried Anchoïade *and Camembert Sandwich*

SERVES 1

2 slices of white bread
olive oil
2 teaspoons *anchoïade* or
   tapenade

50g / 2oz Camembert, thinly
   sliced
freshly ground black pepper

Brush the bread on both sides with olive oil. Spread one side of each piece with *anchoïade* or tapenade and one with sliced Camembert. Season with pepper. Heat a little olive oil in a frying pan. Place one piece of bread on top of the other and fry in the hot oil over a low heat till golden, turning once. The sandwich is ready when both sides are golden brown and the cheese is oozing.

Grilled Tofu with Cheese and Chilli Sandwich

SERVES 1

150g / 5oz pressed tofu, cut into
   1-cm / ½-inch cubes
2 slices of wholemeal bread

½ teaspoon chilli spread
75g / 3oz good melting cheese
   such as Gruyère, grated

Fry the tofu in a non-stick pan till golden on all sides. Toast the bread on one side only under a preheated hot grill. Slather with the chilli spread, using a little more if you like things really spicy. Cover with the cubes of tofu and scatter with the grated cheese. Grill till bubbling, then cut into fingers.

Pan-fried Mushy Pea and Bacon Sandwich

SERVES 1

4 slices of white 'plastic' bread
2 rashers of streaky bacon,
  crisply fried

75g / 3oz mushy peas (from a
  tin or the local chippy)
salt
freshly ground black pepper

Fry the bread in the bacon fat till crisp on one side. Warm the mushy peas in a small saucepan, stirring so that they do not burn. Spread the untoasted sides of two of the slices of bread with the mushy peas, top each with a bacon rasher, season and cover with the remaining slice, cut into rectangular halves.

A FEW SWEET SANDWICHES

French Bread with Goat's Cheese and Fruit
Split a baguette in half, spread with a creamy soft goat's cheese and top with whole and sliced summer berries.

Toasted Chocolate Panettone with Hot Prunes and Armagnac
Chocolate *panettone* and fruits bottled in alcohol are treats stocked by Italian delicatessens and good grocers at Christmas.

Toast a flat round slice of *panettone* under the grill, then drizzle with a little Armagnac or alcohol from the bottled fruits. Warm the prunes in a small pan. Pile on prunes, which you will of course have first stoned, and eat while warm. Have a ball of vanilla or coffee ice cream on the side.

Peanut Butter and Banana Sandwich
White bread, spread thickly with crunchy peanut butter (the one with the bits in), and covered with sliced bananas. Top with a second slice of bread. To be taken with a glass of milk.

Malt Loaf with Warm Fig Jam and Clotted Cream
4 slices of malt loaf, such as Harvo
6 tablespoons Turkish or French fig jam
clotted cream

Warm the jam in its jar in a small pan with enough water to come halfway up the side of the jar. Very lightly toast the bread, just enough to heat it and heighten the flavour. Spoon the warm jam over the slices of malt bread and add a dollop of thick, yellow clotted cream at the side of the plate.

PITTA

A few good things to stuff into Pitta Bread

Fried Potato with Spices and Basil Vinaigrette
Fry a couple of spring onions, chopped fine, in a little butter. When they are soft stir in 2 leftover boiled potatoes, chopped into 1-cm / ½-inch cubes. Cook till the potatoes are golden. They will probably break up a little. Add a tablespoon of lemon juice, a teaspoon of *garam masala* and a pinch of cayenne. Fry for 1 minute, then pile into the warm pitta with finely-shredded fennel or white cabbage dressed with vinaigrette to which you have added half-a-dozen or more shredded basil leaves. Enough for 1.

Deep-fried Courgettes with Turkish Tarator Sauce
To make the tarator sauce, which is a Middle Eastern garlic and nut sauce, dunk a thin slice of white bread in water and squeeze dry. Crumble it and whizz slowly in the blender with 2 cloves of garlic and either 50g / 2oz pine nuts or walnuts. Add salt, a good ½ teaspoonful, and 4 tablespoons olive oil. Taste, and sharpen with a tablespoon lemon juice or wine vinegar. Slice each of 2 plump medium courgettes into three lengthways. Dust them with flour and

deep-fry in very hot groundnut or sunflower oil till crisp. Drain on kitchen paper and pile into the warm pitta with generous drizzles of the tarator sauce.

Cauliflower and Bacon with Coriander Cream Sauce

Grill or fry 4 rashers of streaky bacon till crisp. Steam a handful of cauliflower florets until quite tender (about 6 minutes). Whizz a handful of fresh coriander leaves with 100ml / 4fl oz single cream, 3 tablespoons groundnut oil and a tablespoon Dijon mustard in a blender. Taste and add lemon juice, salt and freshly ground pepper. Snap the bacon into pieces and mix with the hot cauliflower. Dress while hot with the coriander cream sauce. Pile into the warm pitta. Enough for 2.

Labna Balls with Aubergine and Chilli

Labna balls are bought in jars from delicatessens and are a Middle Eastern speciality made from strained sheep's yoghurt. Slice a small aubergine into discs as thick as pound coins. Fry them in groundnut oil till soft and golden, about 4 minutes on each side. Drain. Toss them with 2 sliced labna balls and a tablespoon of dressing from the jar, a crushed clove of garlic, and a little finely-chopped fresh chilli pepper. Toss with shredded Cos lettuce and stuff into the hollow warm pitta.

Hot Mackerel, Tomato and Sweet Onion

Place a mackerel fillet on a buttered ovenproof dish, season with salt and freshly ground pepper, and bake, skin side up, in a preheated hot oven, 220°C/425°F (gas mark 7), for 6 minutes till golden and crisp. Break the hot fish into large chunks and pile into the warm pitta with sliced tomatoes, sweet onion rings and finely-shredded crisp lettuce, which has been tossed with lemon and a little olive oil. Enough for 1.

A few more good things to stuff into Pitta Bread

* The Cod, Parsley and Warm Potato Salad on page 54

* The Fresh Plum *Tabbouleh* on page 193 with slices of cold roast duck or chicken.

* The Sautéed Chicken Livers on page 230 with a handful of baby spinach leaves and the pan juices from the livers

* The Spiced Lamb Kofta with Pine Nuts and Red Cabbage on page 241

* Softly-scrambled eggs, and melted butter in which you have fried a teaspoon good-quality curry powder

MUFFINS, CRUMPETS AND PIKELETS

I am delighted by the knowledge that a 'muffin-worry' is a colloquialism for an old ladies' tea party. The expression conjures up fireside gossip of scandalous goings-on in the neighbourhood. English muffins are the soft doughy baps that you split in half, a crumpet is thinner and full of little holes, while a pikelet is a flatter, larger version of a crumpet.

Muffins make sound bases for poached, scrambled or fried eggs, and for melted cheese and baked beans. There is a certain etiquette concerning muffins and their toasting. But we are not obliged to follow it. In her *Book of Breakfasts*, Marian McNeill writes, 'The correct way to serve them is to open them slightly at their joint all the way round, toast them back and front and butter the insides liberally. Serve hot.'

I can find no reason for not splitting the muffin first and toasting it in the toaster. You will get a different texture, of course, with the dough toasted crisp, but I like that very much. Crumpets and pikelets

I prefer toasted and smothered, absolutely smothered, in butter. You may like to consider these toppings.

* Thick orange blossom honey and thickly-sliced bananas

* Blackcurrant jelly and *fromage frais*

* Cottage cheese with chopped fresh mint and sliced fresh apricots

* Blue cheese such as Beenleigh Blue or Stilton and pan-fried apple slices

* Squares of the darkest, bitterest chocolate you can find placed on the toasted bun and allowed to melt ever so slightly

Hot Cheese Muffins

My mother died when I was quite young. My father was left with the daunting task of feeding a somewhat finicky child. Apart from vast quantities of fruit and vegetables (even spinach) there was very little I would eat. His greatest, and possibly only success was this simple dish. Needless to say he soon gave up and installed a house-keeper, of whom I shall say no more.

FOR 2 AS A SNACK

a walnut-sized knob of butter	**175g / 6oz Cheddar cheese,**
the whites of 2 small spring	**grated**
onions, trimmed and	**2 hot toasted English muffins,**
chopped	**split**

Melt the butter in a small heavy-based pan over a gentle heat. Add the chopped onions and fry till soft and slightly golden in colour. Stir in the grated cheese and let it melt slowly over a low heat. Slide the whole lot on to toasted muffins and eat while still very hot.

* Spread the muffin with home-made pickle or chutney before you coat with the molten cheese

* Sandwich the muffins together with streaky bacon, grilled to a crisp

THE BAGEL

The bagel is different from other bread rolls in that it is both baked *and* boiled. It is the brief boiling, or more often steaming, which gives the bread its chewy texture. Bagels are round, about 10cm / 4 inches across, with a hole in the centre. They originated in Austria, where *beugeln* means ring.

The close-textured bread rolls landed in America with the first Jewish immigrants, and at first were rarely known outside the Jewish community. Now they are found all over, eaten warm and stuffed with all manner of unorthodox things. I buy mine at Brick Lane in London's East End. The queues are long, but the shops are open 24 hours a day, and at least you can watch the dough being prepared and the bagels being baked.

A few good things to put in a Bagel

Lox and Cream Cheese
Smoked salmon, cut thicker than usual, and a generous spreading of cream cheese is the most famous filling for a bagel. If I fill them at home I always add a little lemon juice.

Smoked Mackerel
Creamy smoked mackerel works well with the close-textured bread. A pickled gherkin, chopped finely, can be added if you wish.

Cinnamon and Raisins
Split and toast the bagel, then spread with butter, and dust with ground cinnamon. Scatter over a few raisins and a dollop of cream cheese.

THE CROISSANT

A really flaky, buttery croissant is satisfying enough to eat on its own, but can be stuffed quite successfully for a more substantial snack. In Paris they are to be found warm, filled with thin slices of ham and melted cheese.

The supermarket variety, which are often not as flaky as they might be, crisp up well under a hot grill. Slice the croissant in half horizontally, losing as few crumbs as possible. Fill with any of the following.

Fromage Frais, *Thyme and Sun-dried Tomato*
Remove the tomato from its oil and slice it thinly. Season the *fromage frais* with a little freshly ground black pepper and fold in some chopped leaves of fresh thyme. Spoon on mounds of the *fromage frais* on the bottom half, dot with slices of sun-dried tomato and top with the other half.

Roquefort and Walnut
Crumble the Roquefort and pile on to the bottom half of the croissant, scatter over a few broken walnuts and grill, with the top half, till the cheese has just melted and the nuts are fragrant. Do not overcook, the cheese should just start to ooze. Eat hot.

Apple Purée and Crème Fraîche
Warm the croissant gently under the grill. Split carefully and spoon on a layer of apple purée, scented with cinnamon if you like. Cover with dollops of unctuous, very cold *crème fraîche* and top with the other half. Eat while the pastry is hot, and cream has just started to run.

PIZZA BASES

A home-made pizza base, given character with rye flour and made light and crisp by its two provings, is a fine thing. But it is not a serious contender in the fast food stakes. Commercially-made, vacuum-packed pizza bases are not so bad. They store well, and can be filled, baked and on the table in 15 minutes.

Artichoke and Green Olive Pizza

Tinned or bottled globe artichokes in oil can be found in Italian delicatessens. Often sold by weight from a bowl, they make the finest of all pizza toppings. Not to mention the quickest.

FOR 2

450g / 1lb preserved globe
   artichokes
½ lemon

50g / 2oz green olives, stoned
fresh parsley
1 pizza base

Drain the artichokes from the oil that comes with them. Sharpen the oil with the lemon juice and brush over the pizza base. Slice the artichokes and their soft stems in half, and lay over the pizza. Dot with green olives and bake in a preheated oven, 220°C/425°F (gas mark 7), for about 20 minutes, till the outer rim of the pizza base is golden and crisp. Scatter parsley over as it comes from the oven and eat while hot.

Good things to put on a Pizza Base

Char-grilled Red Pepper, Aubergine and Goat's Cheese Pizza
Brush the base with olive oil. Cover with quarters of red pepper (grilled till sweet and slightly charred, then peeled), grilled slices of aubergine and thick wedges of goat's cheese. Brush with olive oil again and bake in a preheated oven, 220°C/425°F (gas mark 7), for

about 20 minutes. Top with a large spoonful of chopped black olives and flat-leaf fresh parsley.

Cheese Garlic Pizza
Mozzarella is traditional and melts smoothly, but other cheeses are interesting too. I often use up ends of cheese, grating or slicing anything from goat's cheese to Gorgonzola. Brush the pizza base with olive oil and crushed garlic, then add grated cheese, mixed or in separate sections. Cook as above.

Salami and Black Olive Pizza
Cover the pizza base with a thin layer of tomato sauce – home-made or from a jar – the thicker the better, leaving just 2.5cm / 1 inch of rim bare. Top with a layer of thinly-sliced salami and scatter over a handful of black olives. Drizzle with oil. Bake as above.

Four-tomato Pizza
Over a layer of thick tomato sauce, home-made or from a jar, arrange sliced plum tomatoes, whole cherry tomatoes and sliced sun-dried ones. Brush with oil and bake as above. Scatter with torn fresh basil leaves and coarse-ground black pepper.

Pissaladière
A quick version of the famous Provençal tart. Brush the base with garlic oil, then cover with sautéed onions, anchovy fillets, chopped tomatoes and black olives. Drizzle with oil and bake as above.

TACOS

Tacos, the crisp Mexican corn pancakes, are just the job for holding a slightly sloppy cargo such as beans in a spicy sauce or minced beef with chillies. The idea is to pile the wet filling into the taco wrapper, then top it with grated cheese, yoghurt and a spiced sauce.

Minced Beef Tacos with Salsa Cruda

Fay Maschler is now the London *Evening Standard*'s restaurant critic, but before that she wrote the daily recipe column. Just as my collection of her cuttings was becoming too sticky to read she cleverly issued them all in book form. The result, *Eating In*, has since become one of my most used books, sitting with half-a-dozen others next to the cooker. This recipe is from her book.

FOR 4

1 large onion, finely chopped
2 cloves of garlic, finely chopped
a little vegetable oil
450g / 1lb minced beef
1 teaspoon ground cumin or cumin seeds
1 teaspoon dried oregano

pinch of chilli powder or 1 fresh chopped chilli pepper or 1 teaspoon chilli sauce
dash of soy sauce
salt
freshly ground black pepper
pinch of sugar

FOR THE SAUCE:

4 tomatoes
2 teaspoons wine vinegar
½ onion, finely chopped
2–3 tinned chilli peppers, chopped

pinch of fresh oregano
salt
12 taco shells, reheated in a moderate oven for 2–3 minutes

Fry the onion and the garlic in the vegetable oil. Add the beef and stir until browned. Season with cumin, oregano, chilli and a dash of soy. Season with salt, pepper and sugar. Keep warm.

To make the salsa cruda, grill the tomatoes until the skins blister and can be removed, then blend the flesh with the wine vinegar, chopped onion and peppers, oregano and salt. Put out the heated taco shells, a bowl of the spiced beef and another of the sauce alongside bowls of shredded lettuce, grated cheese, ripe avocado mashed with a peeled, seeded and diced tomato, lemon juice and chilli sauce, yoghurt or soured cream. Assemble your own tacos with the constituent parts.

Black Bean Tacos with Tomato Chilli Salsa

A non-meat alternative filling for tacos which takes about half an hour to prepare. Add a chopped avocado to the salsa if you have one ripe.

FOR 4

2 × 400g / 14oz tins black
    beans, haricot beans or
    black-eyed beans, drained
    and well-rinsed
3 tablespoons olive oil
1 bay leaf
2 onions, sliced
2 plump cloves of garlic, finely
    sliced
2 teaspoons ground paprika

½ teaspoon cayenne pepper
2 × 400g / 13oz tins chopped
    plum tomatoes
1 tinned jalapeño chilli pepper,
    seeded and finely chopped
salt
freshly ground black pepper
approximately 2 teaspoons
    white wine vinegar

FOR THE TOMATO CHILLI SALSA:

3 large tomatoes
2 cloves of garlic, finely chopped
1 large or 2 medium tinned
    jalapeño chilli peppers, finely
    chopped

1 tablespoon fresh coriander
    leaves, roughly chopped
12 taco shells
1 lime, to serve
100g / 4oz grated cheese,
    anything hard will do

Put the rinsed beans in a pan with a tablespoon of the oil and the bay leaf and cover with water. Bring to the boil and simmer for 10 minutes. Warm the remaining oil in a shallow pan, add the onions and cook till soft and golden. Add the garlic, paprika and cayenne and cook till the garlic is soft, about 4 minutes. Add the tomatoes and their juice and chilli and simmer for 10 minutes. Drain the beans, and add to the sauce. Taste and season with salt, pepper and wine vinegar. Simmer rapidly till thick, about 10 minutes.

To make the tomato chilli salsa, chop the tomatoes roughly, include their skins and seeds but not their cores. Dump them in the food processor or blender with the garlic and the chillies. Whizz briefly to produce a rough sauce, then stir in the coriander leaves. Warm the taco shells for 3 or 4 minutes in a hot oven, or for 2 under the grill, then fill them with the bean stew and spoon over the salsa, squeeze over a drop of lime, and top with cheese.

DRINKS

There are a few drinks that are sustaining enough to call a snack in a glass. A spicy Bloody Mary, a rich dark Hot Chocolate or a Banana Milk Shake. I have also added a couple of fruity yoghurt drinks, one made with orange juice, the other with puréed mangoes.

Bloody Mary

Sunday morning is my usual time for one of these. Made with love it can be substantial enough to be considered a snack. At the risk of sounding pathetic, I actually prefer it without the alcohol, when it should really be known as a Virgin Mary.

FOR 1

25ml / 1fl oz vodka	**Tabasco sauce**
200ml / 7fl oz tomato juice	**2 teaspoons lemon juice**
Worcestershire sauce	

Mix the vodka and the tomato juice. Season with the spiced condiments and lemon juice to taste. Serve chilled, over ice cubes.

Mango Lassi

One sniff of mango and yoghurt and I am immediately transported back to Goa, and the palm hut on the virtually deserted beach where I took breakfast and lunch almost every day during my stay there.

FOR 1

225ml / 8fl oz natural plain yoghurt	**100g / 4oz peeled ripe mango flesh, chopped, juice reserved**
225ml / 8fl oz chilled water	**a little salt**
2 teaspoons lemon juice	

Whizz together all the ingredients, apart from the salt, in the blender. Salt to taste.

Hot Chocolate

Real hot chocolate made with the finest, darkest chocolate is far removed from the sweetened powdered stuff. Real hot chocolate is very rich, and is best served in small cups rather than mugs. This recipe is based on one by the Chocolate Society, which like me, suggest that Valrhona chocolate is the most suitable.

ENOUGH FOR 4 CUPS
75g / 3oz good-quality dark chocolate, such as Valrhona Manjari
100ml / 4fl oz single cream
600ml / 1 pint milk

Break the chocolate into bits, put in a small saucepan and allow to melt in the cream over a medium heat. Bring the milk to the boil and pour over the melted chocolate. Whisk lightly to prevent a skin forming and drink while hot.

Meal-in-a-Glass

Whizz equal quantities of natural plain yoghurt and orange juice, freshly squeezed if possible, in the blender with 1 egg yolk and 1 peeled banana per 300ml / ½ pint liquid. Stir in a few ice cubes and a teaspoonful of wheatgerm if the idea grabs you.

Banana Milk Shake

250ml / 8fl oz milk
1 banana, peeled and sliced

4 tablespoons double cream
squeeze of lemon juice

Whizz all the ingredients in a blender till really smooth. Pour over ice cubes and serve cold. A scoop of vanilla ice cream would be a divine way to gild the lily. The shake should be very cold and very smooth; there is nothing more difficult to swallow than a warm and lumpy banana milk shake.

2

Eggs

*T*he egg must be the most convenient of all foods. A couple
of eggs and a few storecupboard staples and you have a
meal. Add butter to make an omelette, herbs to produce oeuf en
cocotte, a red pepper and a few tomatoes to make chakchouka or
pipèrade and you have a feast.

Eggs are possibly the ultimate fast food because they have to
set only rather than actually cook. It takes less than five minutes
to make scrambled eggs with potted shrimps, and little more to
make a version spiked with Eastern spices. Those who do not
have the time to cook can toss an egg yolk into fruit juice and
yoghurt for an instantly nourishing drink.

Unless otherwise marked eggs are gathered from a battery
unit, in which birds are stored in cages, so small the creatures
can hardly turn around. They are fed automatically and spend
their lives in total confinement. Having seen such an operation,
it amazes me that people are still prepared to buy eggs produced
in this way, so patently cruel the system and artificial the birds'
existence.

Eggs marked free range come from birds that do have a certain
opportunity to roam. Usually there is a warm hen house and
reasonable access to a meadow outside. Unfortunately, the laws
regarding 'free-range' egg production can be misinterpreted, and

it is not always the case that the birds want to leave their cosy house to peck around outside.

When looking for free-range eggs it is worth reading the label on the box carefully. Some producers give quite a lot of detail about the birds' welfare, feed and living conditions. All the egg recipes in this book were developed for size 3 free-range eggs (actually, Martin Pitt's eggs at Levitts' Farm), unless a larger egg is otherwise specified.

* Eggs keep surprisingly well. Most egg boxes now have sell-by dates on them and tell you in which week they were packed. It is worth checking these thoroughly. I rarely keep eggs longer than a week

* Eggs should be stored with the most pointed end of the egg downwards and in a cool place. Although many refrigerators have special egg compartments, the humid air inside a fridge could possibly damage the eggs' natural protective coating

* To test an egg for freshness just drop it into a glass of water. If it sinks it is fresh. The less fresh the egg is, the more likely it is to float

* Brown eggs look so wholesome, especially the small 'Welsummer' eggs, that it is sad to report they taste little different from a pale egg. The brown eggs simply come from another breed of bird

* You may occasionally come across perchery or barn eggs. These are eggs from birds that, though not caged, are still confined indoors

A Plain Boiled Egg

Allow 2 very fresh, large eggs per person, and make sure that they are not too cold, or they will crack in the water.

Bring a large pan of water to the boil. Carefully slide in the eggs, cover the pan, and simmer for 3½ minutes. They will have a barely set white and a runny yolk. Eat them straight away with soldiers of brown toast.

Scrambled Eggs

At their best, scrambled eggs should form soft, creamy curds, barely set. This is quite easy to achieve if you cook them slowly over a low heat and ignore any interruptions. Friends and family must wait for their scrambled eggs, not, most emphatically not, the other way round.

FOR 2 AS A SNACK

4 eggs	freshly ground black pepper
salt	25g / 1oz cold butter

Break the eggs into a bowl, add a little salt and 3 or 4 twists of the peppermill. Beat with a fork for a few seconds just to mix the yolks and the whites.

Melt most of the butter in a small saucepan or frying pan. Pour in the eggs. Stir with a wooden spoon, scraping the bottom of the pan and bringing the outside edges to the middle. Continue this for 2 minutes, remove from the heat, don't stop stirring (the eggs are still cooking), and check to see if they are done. If some of the egg is runny return the pan to the heat, slowly stirring for another minute till just set.

Remove the pan from the heat, drop in the remaining cold butter to arrest the cooking and tip gently on to a warm, but not hot (which would allow the eggs to continue cooking) plate.

Scrambled Eggs with Swiss Cheese

As an apprentice, one of my jobs in the kitchen was to prepare various 'reductions', usually of wine and herbs, to be added to sauces. Any of the concentrated liquid that was left over usually found its way into midnight feasts such as these cheesy scrambled eggs.

FOR 2

1 wineglass of dry white wine	salt
1 large or 2 small cloves of garlic	freshly ground black pepper
4 healthy sprigs of fresh tarragon	a knob of butter, about the
3 large eggs	size of a walnut
50g / 2oz Emmenthal or Gruyère cheese, coarsely grated	2 rounds of toast

Pour the wine into a small saucepan, preferably one with a heavy base, and place it over a medium heat. Flatten the garlic clove(s) with the flat of a knife blade and drop it, with the tarragon, into the wine. Leave to simmer for 5–7 minutes at quite a pace, until half has evaporated. Remove from the heat.

Break the eggs into a bowl, stir them about a bit with a fork to break them up, then stir in the grated cheese. Season with a good quarter-teaspoon of salt and several turns of the peppermill. Remove the garlic from the wine and beat the wine into the egg mixture with a fork. Throw away the garlic and tarragon.

Tip the mixture into the saucepan you reduced the wine in, add the butter, and cook over a gentle heat, stirring gently with the fork. The eggs will start to set. When they are creamy and still a little liquid, tip them over the toast.

Scrambled Eggs with Potted Shrimps

Potted shrimps are sold in little waxed cartons similar to the ones in which you buy ice cream at the theatre. They freeze well and are handy to have around. Use the butter in which they are potted to cook the eggs.

2 cartons of potted shrimps	salt
4 eggs	freshly ground black pepper

Remove the butter from the top of the shrimps, reserving half and melting the other in a small heavy-based pan. Break the eggs into a small bowl, season with salt and pepper and beat them for a few seconds with a fork.

When the butter has melted pour in the beaten eggs and stir with a wooden spoon, scraping the bottom of the pan and bringing the outside edges to the middle.

Cook the eggs for 2 minutes, then toss in the shrimps, remove the pan from the heat and keep stirring while the shrimps warm through in the creamy egg. If any of the egg is still liquid, then return it to the heat for a minute till just set. Drop in the remaining shrimp butter to stop the eggs cooking and tip gently on to warm, rather than hot, plates.

Parsee Scrambled Eggs

These spiced eggs are made all over India. I have been offered them for breakfast there, but chickened out. I usually prefer my morning kick-start to come from espresso rather than chillies. This makes an exceedingly good supper dish, though.

FOR 2 AS A PRINCIPAL DISH

2 tablespoons melted butter, oil or clarified butter or ghee	½ teaspoon ground turmeric
	½ teaspoon ground cumin
1 small onion, finely chopped	1 tomato, seeded and chopped
1-cm / ½-inch piece of fresh root ginger, peeled and finely chopped	4 eggs, beaten with 2 tablespoons milk
	salt
1 fresh hot green chilli pepper, about 5cm / 2 inches long, seeded and chopped	freshly ground black pepper
	1 tablespoon fresh coriander leaves, chopped

Melt the butter, oil or ghee in a deep-sided frying pan and cook the onion, ginger and chilli until the onion is golden, about 5 minutes.

Add the turmeric and cumin and fry for 2 minutes. Add the tomato, cook for 2 minutes longer, then add the egg and milk mixture. Season with salt, pepper and coriander and stir gently until the eggs start to set in places – probably 30 seconds or less. While the eggs are still creamy and with a tinge of runniness to them, slide them on to warm plates. Serve with toast or fried bread.

Scrambled Eggs with Cheese and Chives

Any cheese that melts well is good for this, in particular Gruyère, Emmenthal or Edam. I have had success, though, using up scraps of assorted cheeses, grated and mixed together.

FOR 2

75g / 3oz good melting cheese, grated

a large knob of butter-

salt

freshly ground black pepper

3 large eggs

1 tablespoon chopped fresh chives

3 English muffins, split and toasted

In a small heavy-based saucepan cook the cheese and butter with the seasonings over a low heat until the cheese has melted.

Beat the eggs with a fork, add the herbs and pour into the cheese. Cook over a low heat, stirring continuously. The mixture will become creamy and start to thicken. Serve it with the toasted muffins.

Good things to add to Scrambled Eggs

* A tablespoon of juices from the roasting pan

* A spoonful of mustard, a crunchy one full of seeds

* Fresh tarragon, chopped and stirred into the eggs before beating

* Green olives, stoned and chopped

* Fresh leaf coriander and a splash of chilli sauce

* A spoonful of bottled or home-made basil pesto sauce

* Shredded smoked salmon, chopped fresh dill, a generous grinding of black peppercorns and sea salt

* Watercress, wilted in a frying pan with a drop of olive oil, sprinkled with a drop or two of sweet rich vinegar, such as balsamic or sherry

* A handful of cooked brown or green lentils and a spoonful of chopped fresh parsley

* Dark-green Savoy cabbage, shredded very finely and steamed for 30 seconds, then dressed with a splash of olive oil

Creamed Eggs and Asparagus

My variation of Jane Grigson's recipe from *English Food* for scrambled eggs with asparagus.

225g / 8oz fresh asparagus tips	**salt**
4 slices of wholemeal bread	**freshly ground black pepper**
a large knob of butter	**2 tablespoons double cream**
8 eggs	

Cook the asparagus tips in boiling salted water. Drain and keep warm. I find the best way to do this is by wrapping them in a tea towel.

Toast the bread and butter it. Put it, buttered side up, in a warm dish. Beat the eggs with salt and pepper and melt the butter in a small solid saucepan. Tip the eggs into the pan and scramble them, stirring to stop the egg sticking round the edges of the pan, until soft, creamy and still slightly liquid. Stir in the cream.

Place the asparagus tips on top of the toast and spoon over the creamed eggs. Eat immediately.

Pipèrade

I spent part of my wandering apprenticeship in the West Country, with Kenneth Bell at Thornbury Castle. This dish, originally from the Basque region of France, was something he mastered when at The Elizabeth restaurant in Oxford, and it appeared from time to time on the menu at Thornbury. Diners generally came to the castle for something slightly grander, and the dish became a favourite for the staff midnight suppers.

FOR 2

2 tablespoons olive oil
2 red peppers, cored, seeded
   and cut into narrow strips
2 small onions, finely sliced
2 cloves of garlic, chopped
1 × 225g / 8oz tin plum
   tomatoes, drained, seeded
   and chopped

4 large eggs
salt
freshly ground black pepper
fresh basil leaves
chopped fresh parsley

Heat the oil in a frying pan and add the peppers and onions. Cook them over a moderate heat, until they are tender and the onions golden, about 5–7 minutes. Add the garlic and cook a minute or two longer. Tip in the tomatoes and simmer the mixture until it thickens.

Beat the eggs, season them, and pour them into the mixture, stirring as you would for scrambled eggs. Shred the basil leaves and stir in with the chopped parsley. Serve while the eggs are creamy.

Parmesan and Anchovy Eggs

Good though this is by itself, it makes a more substantial snack on toast or toasted English muffins.

4 eggs
freshly ground black pepper
50g / 2oz butter
2 tablespoons grated Parmesan
   cheese

8 anchovy fillets, drained of
   their oil and chopped

Break the eggs and beat them gently with a little freshly ground pepper. Melt half the butter in a small solid saucepan, turn down the heat and pour in the seasoned, beaten eggs.

Stir the eggs with a wooden spoon making sure that you get round the edges of the pan. While the eggs are still slightly liquid, remove the pan from the heat and stir in the remaining butter. Stir in the grated Parmesan and chopped anchovies. Serve immediately, on toast.

A Plain Omelette

3 eggs
salt
freshly ground black pepper

20g / scant 1oz butter, cut into
   small chunks

Break the eggs into a small bowl, add a teaspoon cold water, the salt and pepper and half of the butter. Beat them a little with a fork.

Melt the rest of the butter in a small frying pan, or omelette pan if you have one. It will start to sizzle and then to foam; just as the butter starts to smell nutty, swoosh in the egg.

Quickly stir the egg three or four times with the fork, it will start to set on the bottom of the pan. Lift the edge of the omelette nearest the handle with the fork, tilting the pan as you do, and gently flip one half of the omelette over the other. Slide out the finished omelette on to a warm plate.

Cold Omelette with Vinaigrette

If you have made and eaten an omelette, then I suggest that you make another while you are still in the mood. Keep it in the fridge, it will come to little harm overnight, then eat it cold, with a strong chive dressing.

FOR 1, OR 2 WITH SOME SALAD ON THE SIDE

a cold omelette, brought to room temperature

1 shallot, finely diced

1 tablespoon and 1 teaspoon red wine vinegar

4 tablespoons extra virgin olive oil

2 teaspoons chopped fresh chives

salt

freshly ground black pepper

Put the omelette on a serving plate. Mix the shallot and the vinegar in a small bowl and pour in the olive oil. Whisk gently with a fork, stir in the chives and season with salt and pepper.

Pour the dressing over the omelette. Slice the omelette into thick diagonal strips and eat with a fork, pushing the slices round the plate to soak up the chive dressing.

Good things to put in an Omelette

* Wine, or better still, balsamic vinegar

* Onions, fried in butter till golden and slightly caramelised, moistened with a drop or two of wine vinegar

* Leeks, sliced into thin rounds, steamed for a few minutes and sprinkled with chopped fresh tarragon

* Cubes of bread, fried in butter, hot from the pan

* Sorrel leaves, softened for a couple of minutes in butter

* Feta cheese, crumbled and mixed with fresh thyme leaves

* Fresh flat-leaf parsley, roughly chopped with a rinsed anchovy fillet, stirred into the beaten egg

* Tinned globe artichoke hearts, drained and rinsed, sliced and dressed with a little olive or walnut oil and lashings of chopped fresh parsley

* Sun-dried tomatoes, patted dry of their oil, and sliced thinly

* Goat's cheese, crumbled with a few chopped fresh thyme leaves

* Basil leaves, torn into shreds and stirred into the beaten egg

* Nasturtium leaves and flowers, shredded and dressed with a squeeze of lemon juice

* Rocket, roughly chopped, then wilted in a spoonful of oil over a gentle flame

* Broad beans, steamed till tender and (if you have the time and patience) peeled of their papery outer skins

* Blue cheese, such as the exquisite French Fourme d'Ambert, a creamy Italian Gorgonzola or a melting Irish Cashel Blue, sliced into soft chunks and tossed with toasted walnut halves

* Unsmoked bacon, fried to a crisp and crumbled

* Or, if you know your supply and are feeling brave, quiveringly fresh raw mussels, torn straight from the shell

Frittata

A *frittata* is an Italian omelette. Unlike its soft and creamy French cousin, a *frittata* is cooked slowly over a very low heat. It is sautéed on both sides and cut into wedges like a cake. This is the basic recipe, flavoured with grated cheese and a generous grinding of black pepper. Like the omelette, though, it can be filled with almost anything that takes your fancy.

6 large eggs
salt
freshly ground black pepper

a large handful of grated
   Parmesan and / or Gruyère
   cheese
50g / 2oz butter

Beat the eggs in a bowl, with a fork, for 20 seconds or so, until just mixed. Beat the salt, pepper and cheese into the eggs. Melt the butter in a large frying pan, at least 25.5cm / 10 inches in diameter. When the butter starts to froth tip in the eggs. Turn down the heat, as low as it will go. Leave the eggs to cook gently for 15 minutes, or until the underneath is set. The topside should still be runny.

Have ready a hot grill. Remove the eggs from the heat and put under the grill for 1 minute to set, but not brown, the surface. Slide a palette knife under the *frittata* to free it from the pan. Slide it out on to a warm plate, cut into wedges and serve.

Caramelised Onion and Parsley Frittata

A deeply savoury dish, this. Let the onions cook for as long as you have time for, do not worry when they blacken around the edges, it's just the natural sugar in the onions caramelising with the heat. Suitable for lunch or supper, this dish is good warm or at room temperature.

FOR 4 AS A PRINCIPAL DISH WITH SALAD

450g / 1lb onions, finely sliced
4 tablespoons olive oil
5 large eggs
a good handful of fresh parsley,
   coarsely chopped

50g / 2oz grated Parmesan
   cheese
salt
freshly ground black pepper
a generous knob of butter

Put the onions in a shallow pan with the olive oil and cook over a medium to high heat until the onions are golden and tinged with dark brown and almost blackened at the edges. This will take about 15 minutes, stirring occasionally.

Break the eggs into a bowl and beat them thoroughly with a fork. Remove the onions from their pan with a draining spoon and stir them into the eggs. Season with the parsley, Parmesan cheese, salt and pepper.

Heat the butter in a shallow, heavy-based pan, about 25.5cm / 10 inches across, that does not stick. Tip in the egg, onion and parsley mixture. Turn the heat to the lowest setting and cook until the *frittata* has set on the bottom but the surface is still runny, about 15 minutes.

Flash the pan under a preheated hot grill to set the uppermost surface. Loosen with a palette knife, then slide out on to a warm plate. Cut into wedges and serve.

Good things to add to a *Frittata*

A *frittata* is cooked more slowly than other eggy things like omelettes and scrambled eggs. This means that any additions to the basic mixture can be in slightly larger pieces, giving this substantial dish a certain rusticity. Fry all of the following ingredients in a little olive oil before pouring over the egg mixture:

* Small aubergines, sliced as thick as pound coins, seasoned with crushed garlic

* Red pimientos from a tin or bottle, cut into strips, sautéed until they smell sweet and have crisped slightly along their cut edges

* Courgettes, sliced, fried with a diced onion and scattered with chopped fresh parsley

* Diced or grated potatoes seasoned with fennel seeds

* Freshly-ground curry spices or your favourite curry powder, cooked in a little clarified butter till fragrant, then tossed with leftover cooked new potatoes, cut in half if large

A Plain Poached Egg

Poached eggs take about 3 minutes to cook. Use the freshest eggs to ensure that the whites hug the yolks rather than waft around in the cooking water like ghosts. Bring two eggs' depth of water to the boil in a shallow pan. Turn off the heat and gently break the eggs into the water. Cover tightly with a lid and leave for 3 minutes. Lift the lid: if the eggs are shrouded by an opaque white then they are ready. Lift out each egg gently with a perforated spatula (called the 'holy spoon' in my house), then drain carefully for a second or two on kitchen paper to get rid of any water. Serve while hot, on buttered toast.

Spinach with Poached Eggs and Bacon

A rather substantial salad. Use any green leaves, curly endive, *frisée* or soft, floppy lettuce leaves instead of the spinach if you like. Use slices of garlic sausage instead of the bacon too, if you have some.

FOR 2

2 large handfuls of small spinach leaves, carefully washed

2 eggs

4 rashers of streaky bacon, cut into 2.5-cm / 1-inch long pieces

2 slices of white bread, cut into large dice

4 tablespoons virgin olive oil

4 teaspoons red wine vinegar

2 teaspoons grain mustard

salt

freshly ground black pepper

Divide the spinach leaves between two plates. Poach the eggs for 3 minutes, drain and then put them into cold water to stop them cooking.

Fry the bacon till crisp, lift it out with a slotted spoon and scatter it over the spinach leaves. Fry the bread cubes in the bacon fat, adding a little oil if there is not enough, till golden and crisp. Scatter them over the spinach.

Mix the oil, vinegar, mustard and salt and pepper in a small bowl. Remove the eggs from the cold water – they will still be slightly warm – then place one in the centre of each plate. Pour the dressing into the hot pan, it will sizzle and spit, then knap it quickly over the eggs and spinach.

Poached Eggs with Herbs

A lovely idea from Elizabeth David that first appeared in her book *French Country Cooking* in 1951. Tarragon has a magical affinity with eggs, but chives are good too; snip them into 1-cm / ½-inch lengths.

FOR 2

50g / 2oz butter
4 poached eggs, drained

2 tablespoons chopped fresh herbs, such as parsley and tarragon
lemon juice

Melt the butter in a shallow pan such as an omelette or small frying pan. When the butter starts to bubble, slide in the eggs and sauté them without letting the butter burn.

Sprinkle in the herbs and squeeze over a few drops of lemon juice. Serve immediately.

Fried Eggs

Olive oil, and the richer the better, is the only thing in which to fry eggs. Try one of the Spanish oils, which will impart some of its characteristic spiciness to the egg.

olive oil
allow 2 large eggs per person

Pour a finger's depth of olive oil into a frying pan and heat until you see a little smoke rise. Break each egg into a cup. Tilt the pan and slide the eggs, one at a time and no more than two in the pan together, into the hot oil.

Splash some of the hot oil over the egg with a spoon, frying it quickly, until the white is set and the yolk runny. Remove carefully with a draining spoon and eat with brown bread.

Stir-fried Eggs

Yan Kit So tells us in her *Classic Chinese Cookbook* that the idea of stir-frying eggs originates from Whampoa, a port near Canton. A stir-fried egg's consistency should be soft and only just set, rather like a cross between a scrambled egg and an omelette. Use a frying pan if you do not have a wok.

FOR 2 AS A SNACK OR QUICK BREAKFAST
Beat 4 eggs with a pinch of salt and a tablespoon groundnut or vegetable oil until well mixed.

Heat a wok or frying pan until it starts to smoke. Add a finger's depth of groundnut oil and carefully tip the pan to cover the sides of the pan with oil. Pour all but a couple of tablespoons of the oil into a heatproof container (that is, not back into the bottle).

Heat the oil until it starts to smoke. Slowly pour in the beaten egg while stirring it with a metal spatula. Drizzle over a tablespoon more of the oil, stirring and folding the egg over on itself at the same time. After 1 minute the egg will start to set in pieces. Slide the egg out on to warm plates and eat while hot.

Stir-fried Eggs with Spring Onions

FOR 2

4 eggs	2 bunches of spring onions,
2 teaspoons sesame oil	trimmed
	2 tablespoons vegetable oil

Beat the eggs in a small bowl and add the sesame oil. Cut the spring onions on the diagonal into small pieces. Heat a wok or frying pan until it is hot, before the pan starts to smoke, add the vegetable oil and the spring onions. Cook, stirring the onions and tossing the pan, till the green shoots start to wilt – about 30 seconds to 1 minute.

Pour in the eggs and stir-fry, moving the contents of the pan around quickly, until they start to set, about 1 minute. The texture is similar to that of a runny omelette. Slide on to a warm dish and serve immediately.

Buttered Eggs

A very quick dish, cooked in a matter of minutes. Use any good vinegar to sharpen the butter, ordinary red wine vinegar would be good enough, mellow sherry vinegar even better.

FOR 1

Melt a good 50g / 2oz butter in an omelette pan. Use a small frying pan if you do not have one. Break 2 eggs and slide them, without breaking the yolks, into the bubbling butter.

As soon as the whites are set, scoop the eggs out of the butter with a draining spoon and slide on to a warm plate. Return the pan to the heat, turn up the heat until the butter starts to brown and smell nutty. Sprinkle a few drops of vinegar into the butter and knap quickly over the eggs.

Oeufs en Cocotte

The simplest form of this dish uses nothing more than fresh eggs and a little butter.

Brush the inside of a china ramekin with butter. Do this with generosity. Break a large fresh egg and let the yolk and white delicately slide into the ramekin, grind over a little black pepper and sprinkle with a very small pinch of salt.

Place the dish inside a larger one, say a gratin dish, and pour enough hot water in to come two-thirds of the way up the sides. Place a large knob of butter on top of the yolk and bake in a preheated oven, 190°C/375°F (gas mark 5), for 7–10 minutes. The egg is cooked when a thin, opaque film has appeared over the yolk. The texture must be soft and wobbly. Eat at once, with toast.

Oeufs en Cocotte – *A Different Way*

A grander version of *Oeufs en Cocotte* can be made by adding cream, asparagus, sliced mushrooms or even truffles. Cream and Parmesan cheese are probably the best way to gild this lily.

FOR 4

100ml / 4fl oz double cream
salt
freshly ground black pepper

2 tablespoons freshly grated
  Parmesan cheese
4 large fresh eggs

Pour the cream into a small saucepan and warm it with a little salt and pepper. Stir in the cheese and pour the mixture into 4 buttered china ramekins. Break an egg into each one and place the dishes in a gratin dish and pour enough hot water to come two-thirds of the way up the sides. Bake in a preheated oven, 190°C/375°F (gas mark 5), for 7–10 minutes, until the eggs are just set. Eat straight away.

Eggs Baked with Meat Juices

Now is the time to use up that cup of gravy or meat juices that is lurking in the fridge.

FOR 2

butter, for greasing
4 large eggs
salt
freshly ground black pepper

4 tablespoons gravy or meat
  cooking juices
50g / 2oz mature farmhouse
  cheese, grated

Butter 4 heatproof, thick china cups. Use little ramekin dishes if you have them. Be generous with the butter.

Break an egg into each cup. Grind the peppermill over each one and sprinkle a little salt over each egg. Spoon a tablespoon of the meat juices into each cup, dribbling it over the egg yolk. Divide the grated cheese between the cups.

Boil the kettle. Put the cups into a gratin or roasting dish. Pour in enough boiling water to come halfway up the cups or ramekins. Place the whole thing carefully into a preheated oven, 200°C/400°F (gas mark 6). Bake for 10–12 minutes, until the eggs are set.

Chakchouka

A classic North African egg dish, quite substantial enough to serve for supper. This is my adaptation of Meg Jump's recipe from *Cooking with Chillies*.

FOR 2 AS A MAIN DISH

2 tablespoons olive oil
1 onion, finely sliced
4 tomatoes, chopped
1 large or 2 medium red
    peppers, seeded and
    chopped

1 small hot fresh green chilli
    pepper, seeded and finely
    chopped
salt
freshly ground black pepper
4 eggs

Heat the oil in a medium frying pan, add the onion and fry for 3 or 4 minutes, until the onion has softened. Add the tomatoes, peppers and the chilli and let them simmer, covered, and seasoned with salt and pepper, until they soften.

After 15 minutes or so, taste the mixture, and add more salt and pepper if necessary and a drop of water if it is sticking to the pan. When the vegetables are slushy make 4 little hollows in which to cook the eggs. Break the eggs, sliding them carefully into the hollows. Cook over a gentle heat until the eggs are just set, about 3 or 4 minutes.

I first cooked this simplified version of *Chakchouka* when I had even less time in the kitchen than usual.

Chop 6 medium tomatoes into rough pieces about as big as shelled walnuts. Cover the base of a small frying or omelette pan with olive oil and colour a finely-chopped clove of garlic in it for a minute or so.

Before the garlic turns brown and bitter add the chopped tomatoes and cook for a couple of minutes. Turn up the heat to evaporate some of the liquid and concentrate the flavours, then smooth them out over the base of the pan.

Crack 4 eggs carefully into the pan, in order not to break them. Cook until the eggs are set, about 3 or 4 minutes. Scatter over some fresh herbs if you have them, parsley or coriander would be nice, basil even better. Season with some coarse black pepper and serve.

Baked Eggs with Tarragon and Garlic

FOR 4 AS A SNACK

150ml / ¼ pint double cream

2 cloves of garlic, squashed flat with the blade of a knife

3 sprigs of fresh tarragon

4 eggs

Pour the cream into a small pan, drop in the garlic cloves and the tarragon, and bring slowly to boiling point. Remove the pan from the heat, cover with a plate and leave in a warm place for 10 minutes for the garlic and herbs to perfume the cream.

Butter 4 cocotte dishes or heatproof cups, break an egg into each one, and bake them for 8 minutes in a preheated oven, 170°C/325°F (gas mark 3). Strain the cream through a sieve and pour over each egg, return to the oven for 2 minutes. Eat straight away.

Stracciatella

Although I have eaten this simple soup in Tuscany it is more often found in Rome. It is most important that the stock is a good one, preferably home-made, though the fresh stocks now bought in tubs in the supermarkets come a close second. Remember, though, that they are unseasoned.

FOR 4

4 eggs	1 tablespoon fine semolina
25g / 1oz grated Parmesan cheese	1.1 litre / 2 pints home-made chicken stock

Beat the eggs and, using a fork, whisk in the Parmesan and semolina. Pour in a teacupful of the stock and mix to a cream.

Bring the rest of the stock up to the boil. When small bubbles are rising quickly to the surface, lower the heat and pour in the egg and cheese mixture. Whisk for 2 or 3 minutes, without letting the water actually boil. When the mixture starts to form little flakes in the stock – a further minute or so – it is ready. Serve immediately, passing more Parmesan.

An Egg Sandwich

MAKES 1 ROUND

2 eggs, hard-boiled, but soft in the centre	butter
	salt
2 rounds of soft white sandwich loaf	freshly ground black pepper

Slice the eggs thinly, using one of those steel egg slicers if you have one. Butter the bread and lay the egg slices on one round. Sprinkle over the salt and pepper and place the second slice of bread on top. Cut in half diagonally.

A Better Egg Sandwich

MAKES 1 ROUND

2 eggs, hard-boiled, but soft in
    the centre
2 tablespoons home-made or
    good bought mayonnaise
2 rounds of brown bread

a bunch of watercress, washed
    and tough stalks discarded
salt
freshly ground black pepper
cayenne

Slice the eggs thinly. Spread the mayonnaise on the bread. Lay some small sprigs of watercress on one piece of the bread. Put the egg slices on top, season with salt, pepper and a little cayenne pepper. Place the second round of bread on top and cut in half.

Good things to team up with Eggs in a Sandwich

* Lettuce, the floppy variety

* Spinach, small tender leaves, left whole

* Grated Cheshire or Cheddar cheese

* Mango chutney

* Lime pickle

* Chopped black olives or tapenade

* Spring onions

* Cold Béarnaise sauce from a bottle

* Anchovy fillets, drained, rinsed and dried

3

Fish

*F*ish is the finest of all fast foods. The less time it cooks the better, the flesh having only to set rather than, like meat, to tenderise. Flat fish, such as sole and plaice, can be cooked whole or in fillets. They cook in minutes, either dusted with seasoned flour and laid in a pan of sizzling butter or brushed with oil and grilled. For a sublime supper serve with a salad of soft green leaves, or with green beans cooked for 4 or 5 minutes in boiling water.

Use your fishmonger. He is not there just for selling fish – part of his work is to prepare your fish for you. He will do all the horrid bits, ridding your chosen fish of the inedible, the uninteresting and downright disgusting. An extra three minutes in his shop can save a good ten at home. If you prefer to buy your fish from the supermarket, packed in neat cartons and wearing little sprigs of parsley, then do so. It is good fresh fish, but you are unlikely to be offered a great choice.

With this in mind I have stuck to a fairly catholic selection of fish here. This may seem unfair to the enterprising and passionate fishmongers who stock unusual fish and shellfish. But not really. Almost any fish you may choose can be cooked in the ways mentioned; for example, the cod recipes are perfectly suitable for hake, haddock, pollack or ling. If your fancy turns to a flat fish, then plaice or brill are covered by the sole recipes.

I have included several ideas for rather anonymous 'fish steaks'. There is a reason for this, which is that most cuts from the middle of common white fish cook similarly. The finished result will have a wonderfully different flavour, but the basic method remains the same. The choice is yours.

You know how to buy fish, but I will remind you. Go for bright vivid colours, sparkling eyes and a smell that is of the sea rather than fishy. Avoid, at all costs, any specimen that is dry, limp and sad-looking. If your fishmonger doesn't display his fish on ice, then go elsewhere, especially in summer. And remember, the biggest sin you can commit against a fish is to overcook it.

Shellfish are perhaps the highest order of fresh ingredients on the fast foodie's shopping list. I have deliberately included some and not others. Prawns are here because they cook in seconds and are relatively easy to find, while fresh crab is not because it takes an age to prepare (not to mention the need for a hammer and a set of pliers) and the tinned stuff tastes horrid. Scallops and oysters are covered because they are genuine fast feasts and mussels because they are such fun to cook and eat. (Accept nothing from your fish-monger that is not positively quivering with freshness.) Lobsters are missed out on the grounds that if they are to be really succulent they must be bought alive and kicking and cooked at home and most of us are too squeamish to kill one. And that includes me.

Cod with Parsley Sauce

Thick, lumpy parsley sauce was one of the many horrors that helped to put me off cod. Forget the flour, make a thinner sauce with the cooking juices from the fish, lots of vivid green parsley and a little cream. Sharpen the sauce with a squeeze of lemon juice, at the end, if you wish.

FOR 4 AS A MAIN DISH

a little butter

4 cod steaks, about 2.5cm /
 1 inch thick

225ml / 8fl oz fish or vegetable
 stock

a small bunch of fresh parsley

100ml / 4fl oz double cream

salt

freshly ground black pepper

squeeze of lemon juice
 (optional)

Rub the inside of a shallow baking dish with the butter. Put the cod steaks in the dish and pour over the stock. Bake for 8–10 minutes in a preheated hot oven at 220°C/425°F (gas mark 7). Chop the parsley. Pour the stock from the fish into a shallow pan and return the fish, covered by a plate, to the switched-off oven to keep warm.

Reduce the stock over high heat to about half of its original volume. Pour in the cream, tip in the parsley and leave to bubble over a high heat till slightly thickened, about 2 minutes.

Taste the sauce, adding salt and pepper and a squeeze of lemon juice if you want. Pour the sauce over and around the fish and serve.

Cod in Crumbs

750g / 1½ lb cod fillet, cut from
   the head end of the fish
flour
2 eggs, beaten

fresh breadcrumbs
groundnut or sunflower oil and
   butter
lime or lemon halves

Cut the fish into 4–5-cm (1½–2-inch) cubes. Roll them in flour, dip them in the beaten egg, then roll them in breadcrumbs.

Shallow-fry the fish in hot oil and butter till golden, turning carefully, for 10 minutes at the most. Serve with halves of lime or lemon and a few salad leaves.

Cod, Parsley and Warm Potato Salad

Cod, potatoes and parsley, the most basic of fish, vegetables and herbs, make a fine *ménage à trois*, this time as a warm salad. Two important points: don't overcook the potatoes, and mix the salad gently so as not to crush the juicy pieces of fish.

FOR 2 AS A MAIN COURSE

2 large or 4 medium potatoes
375g / 12oz cod fillet or steaks,
   2.5cm / 1 inch thick
6 tablespoons olive oil
2 tablespoons lemon juice

freshly ground black pepper
4 bushy stems of fresh parsley,
   chopped
1 medium Spanish onion, thinly
   sliced

Cut the potatoes into quarters or halves and cook in boiling salted water till tender to the point of a knife, about 10 minutes.

Meanwhile, put the fish in a small, shallow pan, cover it with water and poach gently until the flesh is opaque and firm, about 5–7 minutes. Turn off the heat.

Mix the olive oil and lemon juice with the black pepper in a large serving bowl. Drain the potatoes thoroughly. Slice them into pieces as thick as pound coins and put them in the serving bowl. The warm potatoes will soak up the dressing.

Drain the cod, peel off the skin and break the flesh into bite-sized chunks. Toss the dressed potatoes with the chopped parsley and onion, and gently mix in the pieces of cod. Serve warm.

Baked Cod with Butter Sauce

The chemistry of white fish, butter and wine is hard to beat, even when it is as simple as this. New potatoes, or the Waxy Potato, Anchovy and Parsley Salad on page 173, and a leafy salad afterwards would be the best accompaniments.

SERVES 2

50g / 2oz cold butter, plus 30g / a heavy ounce to finish

2 pieces of cod fillet, cut from the thick end, 3cm / 1½ inches thick

1 wineglass of dry white wine

4 large sprigs of fresh parsley, chopped (or 6 of tarragon, or 7–8 of chervil)

salt

freshly ground black pepper

Spread a little of the butter on the inside of a shallow baking dish. Place the cod fillets in the dish and pour over the wine. Dot the rest of the butter over the fish and bake in a preheated oven at 220°C/ 425°F (gas mark 7), until firm and opaque, about 10–15 minutes. Baste the fish once or twice with the juices.

Remove the fish from the oven, pour the liquid into a small shallow pan and return the fish to the switched-off oven. Reduce the cooking liquor over a high heat till it is one-third of its original quantity, about 8 tablespoons. Whisk in the remaining butter with the fresh herbs. Whisk hard, until the sauce has slightly thickened, about 1 minute. Taste and add salt and pepper if you wish.

Remove the fish from the oven, and lift on to plates with a fish slice. Spoon the sauce over the fish and serve.

Grilled Sole

The simplest treatment for the finest of fish.

Heat the grill. Lay the whole sole in the grill pan, bathe it with butter – no, not oil – butter. Place it under the grill and cook for 4 minutes per side, a minute less if you have lemon sole, basting twice with butter from the pan. Season on each side with a little salt and pepper from the mill before and after you turn the fish.

Lift carefully, using a fish slice or even two, from the pan to a large, warm plate. Spoon over the buttery cooking juices, and serve with half a lemon.

Pan-fried Sole

Ask your fishmonger to fillet a nice large fish, or buy prepacked fillets from the supermarket. Dust the fillets lightly with flour. You can season the flour with salt and pepper if you wish. Heat some butter to a depth of 5mm (¼ inch) in a frying pan till hot, but not so hot that it smokes or colours. Fry the fish for 4 minutes per side, a minute less on each side if you have lemon sole.

Remove the fillets to a warm plate. Throw some freshly chopped parsley into the pan and squeeze in the juice from half a lemon. Tip the butter over the fillets and eat while hot.

Skate with Black Butter

A quick classic.

FOR 2 AS A MAIN DISH

1 onion
salt
bay leaves
6 black peppercorns
2 medium skate wings, about
    450g / 1lb in weight

1 teaspoon capers, rinsed of
    their brine or salt
75g / 3oz butter
1 tablespoon red wine vinegar
a little chopped fresh parsley

Put 1 litre (1¾ pints) water on to boil in a saucepan. Slice the onion into very fine rings and toss them into the water with 1 teaspoon salt, a couple of bay leaves and the peppercorns. When the water comes to a boil, turn down to a simmer and leave to cook for 10 minutes.

Slide the skate wings into the simmering water. Cook gently for 10 minutes, a little longer if the fish is more than 2.5cm (1 inch) at its thickest part. Drain the wings, keeping the cooking liquid for stock, and put them on warm plates. Scatter over the capers.

Melt the butter in a small frying pan, let it foam and darken to a nutty brown. Add the vinegar to the pan, followed by the parsley, then immediately knap the whole lot over the fish.

Sautéed Halibut Steaks

Halibut is not essential for this dish. Use any white fish steak about 2.5 or 4cm (1 or 1½ inches) thick; cod, hake or haddock will be fine. As this dish is so quick, you have time to prepare a salad, say rocket leaves with a dribble of extra virgin oil and a grinding of black pepper.

FOR 2

flour

2 halibut steaks, about 2.5cm / 1 inch thick

juice of 1 lemon

oil for frying – olive would be good

lemon wedges, to serve

Put a thin layer of flour on to a plate. Dip the halibut steaks into the lemon juice, then into the flour. Don't forget the other side.

Fry the fish until firm and cooked right through, about 5 minutes on each side. Serve hot with large pieces of lemon.

Fish Steaks with Lemon, Coriander and Cream

A rather luxurious dish, its richness cut only slightly by the coriander and lemon. Fennel, either finely shredded in mild vinaigrette or stir-fried until just tender but still crisp, works well here.

2 fish steaks, cod or halibut, about 2.5cm / 1 inch thick	2 tablespoons fresh coriander leaves, loosely packed
100ml / 4fl oz double cream	salt
juice of ½ lemon	freshly ground black pepper

Place the fish steaks in a shallow baking dish. Mix the cream with the lemon juice and coriander leaves, and grind over a little salt and black pepper. Pour the lemon cream over the fish steaks and cook in a preheated oven at 200°C/400°F (gas mark 6), for 12 minutes. Serve with the fennel salad described above.

Fish Fillets with Parsley and Garlic

This bright-flavoured sauce is slightly adapted from a chicken recipe in *Cook's Garden* by Lynda Brown. I have tried the recipe with large pieces of cod and mackerel fillets, and both worked extremely well. I prefer not to thicken the sauce, so suggest you serve it in deep-rimmed plates to hold the juices.

FOR 4, WITH TINY STEAMED POTATOES

5 large sprigs of fresh parsley	3 tablespoons grain mustard
3 plump cloves of garlic, peeled	1 wineglass of dry white wine
4 steaks or large fillets of white fish, about 175g / 6oz each	3 tablespoons double cream
	1 teaspoon wine vinegar

Pull the leaves off the parsley, keeping the stems for stock. Finely chop the parsley leaves and the garlic together. Brush the fish fillets with the mustard and roll them in the parsley and garlic.

Lay the fillets in a gratin dish. Pour the wine around, but not over, them and cover with a butter paper, or piece of buttered foil. Bake in a preheated oven, 200°C/400°F (gas mark 6), till firm, about 10–12 minutes. Carefully remove the fish with a palette knife and keep warm, then boil the wine over a direct heat for 2 or 3 minutes till it has reduced by half. Pour in the cream and vinegar, boil for a minute or two then serve under, rather than over, the fish.

Baked Fish Steaks with Tomato and Breadcrumbs

I think this idea works best when the breadcrumbs are kept coarse, almost like diminutive croûtons. If you have some fish in the freezer and a bunch of fresh parsley this makes a quite reasonable emergency supper.

FOR 2, AS A MAIN DISH WITH SALAD

50g / 2oz butter

1 clove of garlic, chopped

1 × 225g / 8oz tin chopped plum tomatoes

salt

freshly ground black pepper

2 fish steaks, about 175g / 6oz each, and 2.5cm / 1 inch thick

2 tablespoons stale, coarse breadcrumbs

2 tablespoons chopped fresh parsley

Melt the butter in a frying pan. Add the garlic and cook for 2 or 3 minutes over a medium heat, until it has softened, taking care that it does not scorch. Stir in the chopped tomatoes and their juice and simmer for 5 or 6 minutes, until most of the liquid has evaporated.

Add salt and pepper. Put most of the tomato mixture in a gratin dish, lay the fish steaks on top and cover with the breadcrumbs. Bake in a preheated oven at 200°C/400°F (gas mark 6) for 10 minutes. Sprinkle with the parsley and serve.

Grilled Spiced Fish Steaks

A dish born while trying to re-create a similar dish I had eaten in India. If 'fish steaks' sound a little anonymous it is quite deliberate. Use whatever fish you have to hand; cod, tuna, swordfish, halibut are all fine, and frozen will do. Serve with a side dish of sliced sweet tomatoes.

1 slightly heaped tablespoon *garam masala*	300ml / ½ pint plain natural yoghurt
1 onion, roughly chopped	salt
3 large cloves of garlic	freshly ground black pepper
2.5cm (1 inch) knob of fresh root ginger, peeled and grated	4 fish steaks, about 225g / 8oz each, and 2.5cm (1 inch) thick
½ teaspoon chilli powder	2 tablespoons chopped fresh coriander leaves
juice of 1 lime or ½ lemon	

Put the *garam masala*, onion, garlic and ginger in the bowl of a food processor. Whizz. Add the chilli powder, lime or lemon juice and yoghurt and mix slowly, on a low setting or with a spoon or spatula. Add salt and pepper to taste.

Place the fish steaks in a shallow dish and smother them with the marinade. Set aside for as long as you can, but 20 minutes will do.

Heat the grill, transfer, the fish steaks on to the grill pan and cook for about 8 minutes, 10cm (4 inches) away from the heat. Pull a little of the fish away from the bone, which is the test for 'doneness'; if the fish resists it will need a couple of minutes longer. Eat hot with a sprinkling of coriander leaves.

Grilled Salmon

Salmon is a fish rich in oil. When cooked, it needs something piquant to offset this, particularly if grilled, but less so if poached. Lively partners include salty olives, sharp sorrel, tiny green-tinged tomatoes and peppery basil.

Your salmon steaks for grilling should be no more than 2.5cm (1 inch) thick. They need little lubrication, having enough of their own oil. Brush each steak with a small amount of oil, olive for preference, just enough to glisten but hardly enough to be seen. Set them under a very hot, and I mean very hot, grill. Set the grill pan about 10cm (4 inches) away from the heat.

Cook the steaks until the flesh is firm but springy. At 2.5cm (1 inch) thick this will take barely 4 minutes a side, but test them after 3. Transfer them to a warm plate. Don't forget to scoop up the pan juices.

Good things to serve with Grilled Salmon

Basil Butter

Cream 125g / 4oz butter in a bowl. This is easier if the butter is at room temperature first. Chop up a little shallot and stir it into the butter. The shallot is not essential, so no matter if you haven't one. Shred a small handful of basil leaves. Stir them into the butter with a pinch of salt and a good squeeze of lemon. Chill in the fridge until you need it. Drop a spoonful on to the hot salmon as you serve it.

Black Olive Butter

There are two ways to make a good olive butter. Either whizz a handful of stoned black olives, an anchovy fillet or two and a clove of garlic in the blender till smooth, then mix in about 50g or a couple of ounces of softened butter. Alternatively, if time or temper forbid even that, stir a spoonful of black olive paste from a jar into an equal amount of softened butter. Either way, serve a dollop of it, as chilled as you can get it, on the hot salmon as you serve.

Quick Cherry Tomato Sauce

Cut 200g / 7oz cherry tomatoes in half. Scoop out the seeds and discard them, or add to a vegetable stock later. This won't take as long as you think it will. Chop the tomato flesh and scoop it into a small bowl. Add 2 tablespoons fruity extra virgin olive oil and a splash of white wine vinegar. If you have any fresh herbs – tarragon, basil or coriander – now is the time to throw a tablespoon of the chopped leaves in too. Taste the purée, add salt and white pepper if you wish, then spoon over the salmon.

Sorrel Sauce

Sorrel, thanks to the marketing men, now comes in cellophane packs in the supermarkets. Its sharp lemon notes are just what is needed with the salmon. Melt some butter in a small frying pan and drop in a handful of washed sorrel leaves. Stew them in the butter for 4 or 5 minutes. Stir. They will have melted into the butter. You have a sauce.

Grilled Salmon with Watercress Cream Sauce

Watercress has a pleasing peppery bitterness, which works magically with oily-fleshed fish like salmon. A green salad, perhaps of iceberg lettuce with a mustard seed dressing, would go well with this.

FOR 4 AS A MAIN DISH

25g / 1oz butter

4 salmon steaks, about 100g / 4oz each

100ml / 4fl oz double cream

2 teaspoons lemon juice

2 bunches (approximately 100g / 4oz) of watercress leaves and tender stalks, chopped

Heat the grill. Set the grill rack 10cm (4 inches) from the heat. Place the butter in a rectangular dish large enough to hold the fish. Let it melt under the grill. Remove the dish from the heat, place the fish in the butter, turning to coat. Grill until firm and lightly golden on top, about 4 minutes. Turn them over, baste with the butter and grill for 4 minutes. Remove and test the fish; if it comes away from the bone easily it is done.

Pour the butter into a small pan and set over a high heat. Keep the fish warm. Stir in the cream, lemon juice and the chopped watercress. Let it bubble for 2 minutes. Taste it, you may like to add salt and pepper. Pour the sauce, scraping up any crusty bits from the dish, over the fish.

Salmon Steaks with Dill Butter

As an apprentice in a restaurant kitchen I prepared this dish almost daily. In those days I had to gut, clean and scale the fish, then cut it into steaks (everything, in fact, except actually go fishing for the thing). Nowadays, a prepacked salmon steak from the supermarket or a prepared piece of wild fish from the fishmonger is more my style. Beautifully moist in its foil wrapping, it is particularly suitable for those who prefer their fish without a rich sauce.

FOR 2

2 salmon steaks, about 2.5cm / 1 inch at their thickest part
2 tablespoons chopped fresh dill fronds
50g / 2oz softened butter
salt
freshly ground black pepper
4 tablespoons dry white wine

Lay each salmon steak on a piece of foil or baking parchment large enough to wrap up the fish. Mix together the herbs and butter and spread over the pieces of fish. Season with salt and pepper. Tip the wine over the fish and quickly close the foil to make a parcel. Bake in a preheated oven at 220°C/425°F (gas mark 7) for 12–15 minutes. Serve with boiled unpeeled potatoes and a green vegetable.

Baked Salmon with Soured Cream

Sharp creams such as *crème fraîche* or soured cream enhance and lift the flavour of salmon.

FOR 2 AS A MAIN DISH

2 salmon steaks, about 100g / 4oz each
1 small onion, very finely chopped
100ml / 4fl oz soured cream or *crème fraîche*
1 tablespoon lemon juice
2 tablespoons chopped fresh dill

Place the salmon steaks in a small baking dish. Mix together the remaining ingredients, retaining half of the dill. Spoon the sauce over the salmon steaks. Bake in a preheated oven at 220°C/425°F (gas mark 7) for 15–18 minutes. Scatter with the remaining herbs and serve with a cucumber salad or sautéed courgettes.

Pan-fried Salmon with Capers and Vinegar

Capers are the buds of the Mediterranean caper plant picked just before they burst into flower. Whether they come packed in salt from old-fashioned Italian delicatessens, or in jars of horrid brine from the supermarket, they need rinsing. An ideal accompaniment would be a mound of fresh spinach that has been cooked quickly in a pan with a little water and no butter.

FOR 2 AS A MAIN DISH

75g / 3oz butter

2 pieces of salmon fillet, about 150g / 5oz each

2 tablespoons capers, rinsed

1 tablespoon red or white wine vinegar

Melt half the butter in a frying pan over a medium heat. When the butter starts to froth, add the salmon pieces and fry until the fish is firm and gold-tinged, about 3 minutes on each side. Cook for 2 minutes longer if you like your fish cooked right through.

Remove the fish to a warm dish. Melt the remaining butter and add the capers. Pour in the vinegar and let it bubble away for a couple of minutes, scraping at any crusty bits on the bottom of the pan with a wooden spatula. Pour the sauce over the fish.

A Way with Raw Salmon

FOR 2 AS A SUMMER MAIN DISH

Chop 225g (8oz) salmon very finely. Do not reduce it to a pulp, though. Drop it into a bowl and pour over the juice from two limes. Chop a bunch of watercress, and stir it in with 2 tablespoons thick natural yoghurt. It is important that the watercress, and the salmon, are very, very fresh. Serve in little mounds with a cucumber salad.

Poached Salmon

Many people make a *court bouillon* in which to cook their piece of salmon; I am not sure that poaching it in a broth of wine, cloves, herbs and vegetables is altogether necessary. Water, with a little sea salt, is fine.

For two people you will need two pieces of salmon weighing about 175g / 6oz each. Bring enough water to cover the fish to the boil, salt it generously. Turn it down to a simmer. Shudder would be more accurate. Slide in the fish, and cook for 3 minutes. Press the salmon with your finger, it should be firm rather than squashy and should be opaque. If not, cook it for another minute and test again. Remove the fillets with a fish slice and drain, briefly, on a tea towel or kitchen paper. Place on warm plates and serve with tiny new potatoes and whatever takes your fancy.

Good things to serve with Poached Salmon

* Spoonfuls of thick natural plain yoghurt with chopped fresh tarragon and a splash of wine vinegar stirred in

* Black olive paste from a jar

* Parsley and lemon butter; stir a generous amount of chopped fresh parsley into softened butter and sharpen with a good squeeze of lemon juice

* A verdant mustardy sauce; throw a handful of chopped fresh parsley in the blender with a small onion, finely chopped, a teaspoonful chopped fresh tarragon, a garlic clove, 6 tablespoons olive oil, 2 tablespoons wine vinegar and a tablespoon grain mustard. Whizz

* Fennel, grated coarsely, then pan-fried in a little butter, and moistened with a glug from the Pernod bottle

Trout

To cook a trout to perfection you need nothing more than some butter, half a lemon, and 10 minutes.

For two trout, which depending on their size may feed one or two people, melt enough butter in a frying pan to come 1cm (½ inch) up the sides of the pan. Dust the cleaned fish with flour, though this is not essential, and when the butter has started to foam pop the trout in the pan. The heat should be moderate, the butter bubbling.

Cook for about 4 minutes on each side. You cannot see the flesh, so trust your judgement and remove the fishes when each side of the skin is deep shiny brown. Eat as it is, with lemon, or:

* Discard the cooking butter. Drop a new knob of butter, a generous one, in a pan and let it melt. It will foam. When the foam subsides, pour in the juice from the lemon. It will spit. When the butter has turned slightly brown, and smells rich and nutty, knap it over the trout and serve

* Add a large and juicy clove of garlic, flattened but not peeled, to the butter in the pan, cook it over a moderate heat for a minute or two till soft, making sure it does not burn. Its purpose is to scent the butter sauce subtly. Tip in a small carton of double cream and stir while it bubbles till thick, about 2–3 minutes. Throw in some chopped fresh parsley or chervil if you have some, then pour it over the fish

* Use that expensive jar of fancy mushrooms sitting on the shelf. Ceps, *shiitake*, chanterelle and all manner of exotic mushrooms are sold in jars in expensive food shops, where they sit on the shelves for months on end. If you have ever bought one, or have been given one, and don't know what to do with it, then let me tell you

Remove the trout from the pan. Add a clove or two of chopped garlic. The amount will depend on the size of the cloves. Cook them over a moderate heat until soft. Drain the bottle of mushrooms, discarding the brine. It is important to rinse the fungi well in a sieve under running water. Shake them dry. Tip the mushrooms into the butter, stir around for a couple of minutes till hot and buttery. Throw in a small handful of chopped bright green, fresh parsley. Taste, and add black pepper, and perhaps salt. Eat hot, with the trout

Trout in a Fresh Herb and Lime Crust

The fresh herbs and citrus juice here work together to lift the slightly dull flavour of farmed trout. Use lemons if you don't have limes, and any suitably delicate herbs.

FOR 2 AS A MAIN COURSE

4 large trout fillets, skin removed

3 limes

4 tablespoons mixed, chopped fresh herbs: parsley, tarragon, dill

2 tablespoons fresh breadcrumbs

salt

25g / 1oz butter

Check that all the bones have been removed from the fish by running your fingers over the flesh and remove any stubborn ones. Finely grate two of the limes and add their zest to the herbs and bread-crumbs. Add a little salt.

Melt the butter in a small pan and add the juice from the two grated limes. Put the herb mixture on a flat plate and press the fillets down firmly on one side. The herbs will stick to the fish. Place the fillets on a baking sheet and spoon over the lime butter.

Bake in a preheated oven at 200°C/400°F (gas mark 6) for 6 minutes. Serve with crisp green beans and the remaining lime cut in half.

Red Mullet

The red mullet is enjoying something of a renaissance. Beloved of the Romans, it has a sweet, rich flesh and is currently a favourite on restaurant plates, no doubt partly due to its beautiful pink colour. A saltwater fish, the red mullet is rarely more than 450g / 1lb in weight. You will find it in most fishmongers, and even in a few enterprising supermarkets.

When the fishmonger cleans the fish, ask him to leave intact the liver, which is a delectable little morsel, and should be left in during cooking. As mullet, at least the red one, is not a big fish, cook it whole, on the bone. Natural partners are olive oil, tomatoes, olives and fennel, all from the Mediterranean, though the fish is often caught during the summer months off the coast of Cornwall.

Red mullet has a high ratio of bone to flesh, so if you hate struggling with fish bones, ask your fishmonger to fillet the fish and reduce the cooking time by half.

Red Mullet with Fennel and Pernod

A wonderfully light dish for a summer evening, where the fish is perfumed with a fennel bulb and a glug of Pernod. A chilled rosé, perhaps one from Provence, and some olive bread would complete the picture.

FOR 2 AS A MAIN DISH

2 red mullet, cleaned, livers intact
salt
freshly ground black pepper
2 heads of fennel, about 100g /
  4oz each, trimmed

1 small onion, sliced
1 tablespoon olive oil
Pernod

Season the mullet inside and out with salt and pepper. Shred the fennel finely, and sweat it with the onion in the oil in a shallow pan until it starts to soften, about 5–7 minutes. Try not to let it colour, which will coarsen the flavour of the dish. Put the sweated mixture in a gratin dish to form a bed for the fish. Lay the fishes on the fennel, add a good glug from the Pernod bottle, or use Ricard if that is what you have. Bake in a preheated oven at 180°C/350°F (gas mark 4) for 20 minutes, until the fish is firm and tender.

Red Mullet with Tomatoes and Thyme

FOR 2 AS A MAIN DISH

2 red mullet, cleaned, livers intact	olive oil
salt	½ lemon
freshly ground black pepper	4 tomatoes
2 bay leaves	1 wineglass of dry white
2 sprigs of fresh thyme	wine

Rub the fish inside and out with salt and pepper. Put a bay leaf and a sprig of thyme inside each fish, then put them in a gratin dish. Dribble over a little olive oil, remembering this is a rich fish, and squeeze half a lemon over both fish and bake for 7 minutes (10 for a fish weighing over 375g / 12oz) in a preheated oven, 220°C/425°F (gas mark 7). Remove the fish from the oven, and add the tomatoes cut in half and the wine. Cook for a further 7 (10) minutes. Test the fish for 'doneness'; it should be firm to the touch, and a small piece should slide easily from the bone. Spoon the pan juices over the fish as you serve. Eat with a salad of thinly-sliced fennel dressed with oil and lemon juice.

Grilled Mackerel

Of all grilled fish, it is the mackerel that undergoes the most magical transformation. A small whole one takes barely 10 minutes to grill, its flesh becoming rich and sweet, taking on a smoky note from the skin as it chars. I find an earthy accompaniment, such as a plate of cracked wheat salad or skirlie, hot fried oatmeal (see page 189 or 195), better here than the more traditional sharp fruit sauces such as gooseberry.

FOR 1

1 mackerel, fine and plump, about 20cm (8 inches) long, cleaned
1 lemon, cut in half

Heat the grill, squeeze half the lemon over the fish and put it under the grill. What you are trying to do is to cook the skin to a golden crisp while keeping the flesh sweet and juicy. Cook under a high heat for about 4 minutes – 5 if the fish is very plump – per side. Serve, with more lemon juice, plus the juices that have escaped into the grill pan.

Fried Mackerel with Mustard and Coriander Seed Sauce

The coriander seeds add a fruity spiciness to the mackerel, the mustard a deep warmth. Eat the fish with a plate of bitter leaves and citrus fruits: watercress and orange, chicory and grapefruit, or rocket leaves with lime juice and black pepper.

FOR 2 AS A MAIN DISH

2 mackerel, cleaned, but not filleted by the fishmonger
flour
butter and oil
1 tablespoon coriander seeds

25g / 1oz butter
100ml / 4fl oz double cream
½ lemon
2 teaspoons mustard, Dijon or whatever

Dust the mackerel with flour. Heat a little oil and a knob of butter in a frying pan, no more than 5mm (¼ inch) depth. Fry the fish till it is cooked right through to the bone, about 5 minutes on each side. Remove the fish to warm plates, and keep warm.

Crush the seeds with a pestle and mortar, or in a small bowl with the end of a rolling pin. Pour off most of the fishy oil and melt the butter in the pan. Throw in the crushed coriander seeds. After a minute or maybe less they will fill the kitchen with a spicy, orangey aroma. Take care that they do not burn. When the spiced butter starts to foam lift the pan off the heat, pour in the cream and return to the heat. When it foams again, lift the pan up from the flame, swoosh the sauce round the pan and put it back down again.

Let the sauce bubble for a couple of minutes, then squeeze in the juice from the lemon. Stir in the mustard. Stop cooking now or you will lose the aroma of the mustard. Spoon the sauce around the fish and serve.

Mustard Mackerel

This quick and deliciously savoury way with mackerel is one of my favourite recipes. It takes barely 15 minutes from start to finish. Serve with a watercress and blood orange salad.

FOR 2

2 tablespoons grain mustard
juice of ½ lemon

1 tablespoon olive oil
4 mackerel fillets (2 mackerel)

Lightly oil a shallow ovenproof pan. Mix the mustard with the lemon juice and olive oil and spread it over the mackerel fillets. Cook in a preheated oven, 220°C/425°F (gas mark 7), until tender enough to cut with a fork, about 8–10 minutes.

Lift the sizzling fish from its pan, and serve with the afore-mentioned salad and a hunk of wholemeal bread.

Mackerel Teriyaki

I was inspired to cook this particularly savoury dish after a light lunch at Wakaba, the beautifully minimalist designer-Japanese restaurant in North London. The recipe is based on one in Joan and Peter Martin's *Japanese Cooking*. I have used the same idea, with differing degrees of success, using herring (jolly good) and salmon (less so). A few beansprouts and mushrooms, quickly stir-fried with garlic in oil over a high heat, make an interesting bed for the fish. Spoon a little of the fish marinade over the vegetables just as they finish cooking.

FOR 2 AS A MAIN DISH

4 mackerel fillets

2 tablespoons *mirin* (sweet rice wine) or pale, dry sherry

2 tablespoons *sake* (rice wine)

1 clove of garlic, finely chopped

3 tablespoons soy sauce, shoyu for preference

Lay the mackerel in a shallow dish. Mix together all the remaining ingredients in a small saucepan and bring to the boil. Pour over the hot marinade and leave for 15 minutes.

Heat the grill, lay the marinated fish fillets in the grill pan and cook for barely 5 minutes on each side. Brush with some of the marinade as they cook. The fish are done when they are coated with a shiny brown glaze.

Fish Finger Sandwich

A fish finger is a piece of fresh cod or haddock, frozen at sea, then coated in breadcrumbs. Most people seem to like them but will rarely admit to it. I suspect they think fish fingers are rather common. You may be interested to know that these useful freezer standbys were originally marketed as 'crispy cod-pieces'.

FOR EACH PERSON

2 fish fingers – a reputable brand

1 small baguette or ⅓ of a French stick

ready-made tartare sauce, tomato ketchup or mayonnaise

1 gherkin

lettuce, the floppy-leaved variety

½ lemon

Grill the fish fingers till crisp, turning once, taking care not to overcook them to dryness. Split the little baguette, spread with the lubricant of your choice, though I suggest the tartare sauce. Chop the gherkin and scatter over. Pile on a few small lettuce leaves, which you have rinsed and shaken dry. Lay the fish fingers on top of the lettuce, squirt with lemon juice and add the other half of the bread.

SHELLFISH

Mussels

Mussels, now sold in bags at supermarkets and fishmongers, make surprisingly fast food. Cleaning them need not be a tedious chore if you are cooking for no more than two or three. Choose small mussels, which have no barnacles to remove and are usually cleaner than larger ones. Soak them for a few minutes in cold water, scrupulously discarding any that float (miss any at your peril), and pull away their coarse beards with a little knife. A good rinse and they are ready to cook.

A mussel is cooked when its shell opens. This will take from 30 seconds to 4 minutes over a fierce flame. Obstinate mussels that refuse to open should be thrown away. One of the best seafood suppers imaginable can be made in just 10 minutes with a bag of mussels, some dry white wine, a clove of garlic and a few sprigs of fresh parsley. Add double cream and lemon juice and you have a warming meal for eating on cold winter nights.

More adventurous quick-cooks may want to test the 30-minute time limit on the recipes by removing the mussels from the shells, frying them till crisp, and stuffing them into rolls slathered with garlicky mayonnaise, see pages 76–7. Friends of the mussel, apart from white wine and garlic, are cider, tarragon and, perhaps surprisingly, bacon.

Allow a kilo (2½ lb) bag of mussels between 2 diners, and copious amounts of crusty white bread and chilled Muscadet.

Mussels with Cream and Herbs

Fill the sink with cold water. Tip the mussels from their bag and leave for a couple of minutes. Scoop up any mussels that are floating on the surface, or bobbing up and down questionably. Throw them out. Pluck each mussel from the water, and pull off its fibrous beard with the help of a small knife. Scrub them if they are dirty, but this is unlikely, and drop them into a bowl of clean cold water. Do not feed them with oats or whatever else you have been told about; mussels do not eat porridge.

FOR 2 AS A MAIN DISH, WITH PERHAPS A SALAD TO FOLLOW

2 wineglasses of dry white wine	a large knob of butter
1 fat clove of garlic, or 2 smaller ones, crushed	2 tablespoons chopped fresh herbs, parsley and tarragon or chervil
5 or 6 black peppercorns	
550g / 1lb 4oz scrubbed mussels	freshly ground black pepper
4 heaped tablespoons *fromage frais*	an optional squeeze of lemon juice

Bring the wine to a fierce boil in a deep saucepan – one to which you can find a lid. Throw in the garlic and the peppercorns. Tip in the washed mussels. Clap on the lid and cook the mussels till they start to open – about 4 minutes at the most. Shake the pan now and again. Scoop out the mussels with a draining spoon as they open and put them in a large bowl. Keep warm. Strain the cooking liquor back into the pan.

Boil until it is reduced by half, a matter of 2 minutes on a high heat, add the *fromage frais* and the butter and throw in the herbs. Check for seasoning; it may need pepper and lemon juice but salt is unlikely. Ladle into warm bowls and serve with the mussels and lots of bread, the crustier the better. Eat the mussels with your fingers, scooping up the sauce with the shells. You will need napkins, or at least paper towels.

Hot Mussels in Curry Cream

Mussels in jars suffer from the horrid liquid in which they are bottled. The offending liquid permeates the mussel and renders it useless for almost any recipe. Except, I think, this one.

½ teaspoon mild curry powder
150ml / ¼ pint single cream
a dozen mussels from a bottle,
  drained

1 teaspoon lemon juice
1 round of hot toast, lightly
  buttered

Stir the curry powder into the cream. You may need a little whisk to do this. Simmer till it is reduced by about half. Rinse the mussels thoroughly under running water. Tip them into the curry cream sauce for a minute or two to warm through. Sharpen the flavour with the lemon juice and serve on hot toast.

Other good things to do with Mussels

* Use cider, a dry one, instead of wine in the recipe on page 75

* Cut 4 rashers of bacon, smoked or unsmoked, it matters not, into small dice. Cook in a frying pan, with a little extra fat if necessary, until crisp and golden. Cook a bag of cleaned mussels with a little white wine and garlic, as in the recipe on page 75, but without the herbs. Keep the mussels warm. Add a wineglassful of white wine and the sieved cooking liquor from the mussels to the bacon and boil to reduce, then pour in a small carton of double cream. Bubble till thickened, then serve with the mussels, and plenty of bread

* If you have the time and patience (a good friend will also do), cook the mussels briefly with a little white wine, then quickly remove from the heat, and remove the mussels from their shells. This is easy, just push the fat little molluscs out with your thumb. The most important point here is not to overcook the mussels, which must be removed from the heat as soon as they open. Toss the mussels in flour, which you have seasoned with salt and pepper, and shallow-fry them in very hot groundnut oil till golden, plump and crisp, a minute or so. Eat them as they are, with lemon,

or stuff them into crisp rolls which you have spread with garlic mayonnaise. A feast

Scallops

Whether you buy them fresh or lift a bag from the freezer, scallops are expensive. They have a fine delicate flavour that can easily be spoilt by overcooking. The wobbly flesh with its beak of salmon-pink coral, needs only to set, which takes just a couple of minutes.

Scallops are a luxurious ingredient for the short of time. Their inherent richness allows you to get away with 450g / 1lb between three people. If their price really is a problem, but scallops it must be, then slice them thinly and toss them with waxy potatoes for a substantial salad. Buy them fresh if you can as they are often cheaper this way than frozen. Ask your fishmonger to clean them for you, but insist on keeping the shells, for which you will find untold uses, few of which will have anything to do with a scallop recipe. He will discard everything except the white nugget of flesh and the crescent-moon shaped coral.

Perfect partners for scallops include mundane storecupboard staples such as butter, breadcrumbs and lemons. Basil and garlic, and fresh coriander and cream, are welcome too, though scallops need little to make them memorable. If you come across the tiny, pink-shelled Queen scallops, pick some up; they are wonderful when steamed for 2 minutes (no longer) and served with melted butter and lemon.

Grilled Scallops with Garlic Butter

This is cheating, I suppose, but it smells and tastes too good to matter. It is my interpretation of a dish mentioned by Alan Davidson in his book *North Atlantic Seafood*, from an idea he picked up on the pier in Boston.

Brush a grill pan with butter, and be generous about it. Sprinkle lightly, and I mean lightly, with garlic powder. Put cleaned scallops on the buttered and seasoned pan and cook under a hot grill for 5–6 minutes, till firm and lightly golden. Serve with all their buttery juices.

Crumbed and Pan-fried Scallops with Parsley and Lemon

The rich person's answer to fish fingers. A lemon and garlic butter, flecked with parsley, is as near as we get to tomato ketchup. But a tomato salad, scattered with olive oil and black pepper, would make a quick accompaniment.

FOR 2, AS A MAIN DISH WITH A SALAD OR VEGETABLES

1 clove of garlic, crushed
finely grated zest of ½ lemon
3 tablespoons chopped flat-leaf
    fresh parsley
75g / 3oz butter, at room
    temperature
freshly ground black pepper

8 large juicy scallops, cleaned
1 egg, beaten
fresh breadcrumbs
butter and groundnut oil, for
    frying
2 handfuls of mixed salad
    leaves

Mix the garlic, lemon zest and parsley into the butter. Season with the black pepper. Dip the scallops in the beaten egg, then roll them in the breadcrumbs.

Heat enough oil and butter to measure one finger's depth in a shallow pan. When hot slide in the scallops and fry till the crumbs are golden and crisp, about 3 minutes on each side. Place the salad leaves on 2 plates and put the hot scallops on top. Throw the oil and butter out of the pan, add the lemon and parsley butter and warm for 30 seconds. Spoon over the scallops and serve.

Scallops and Potato Salad

Cut into thin slices, scallops marinate to perfection in minutes. Orange or lemon juice will alter their texture, sometimes almost jellylike, to firm tender morsels. Served with warm waxy potatoes they make a good main-course salad for a special occasion. The parsley, in this instance, plays an important part.

FOR 2 AS A MAIN-COURSE SALAD

6 large scallops, cleaned

6 tablespoons light oil, such as groundnut

2 tablespoons olive or nut oil (hazelnut for preference)

2 tablespoons each orange and lemon juice, or 4 lemon

salt

freshly ground black pepper

350g / 12oz waxy potatoes, such as Maris Peer or Pink Fir Apple

a small fistful of shelled hazelnuts

2 handfuls of assorted salad leaves

chopped fresh parsley, to garnish

Slice the scallops into large discs; you should get 4 from each scallop. Lay them in a shallow glass or china dish. Pour over them half the oils and citrus juice, seasoned with a little salt and pepper. Leave them in the fridge for at least 25 minutes.

Boil the potatoes, scrubbed but unskinned, till tender to the point of a knife, about 15 minutes. Toast the nuts under a preheated hot grill. Rub them with a cloth while still hot to remove some of their skins. Chop them coarsely. Drain the potatoes and slice into rounds 1cm / ½ inch thick. Toss them in the remaining citrus juice and oils. Taste and season. Remove the scallops from the marinade and place them, prettily if you wish, on 2 large plates. Spoon a pile of dressed potatoes in the centre and spoon their dressing over the lot. Scatter some chopped bright green parsley over the dish and serve.

Grilled Scallops with Coriander and Lime Butter

Peppery basil and fresh lime juice lift a fresh scallop to even greater heights, if that is possible. Use plenty of butter, sweet and unsalted; it is not the time for olive oil.

2 tablespoons chopped fresh coriander leaves	juice of 1 lime
75g / 3oz butter, at room temperature	10 large scallops, cleaned

Mix the coriander with the butter and the lime juice and use a third of it to spread over a grill pan. Put the scallops, a good 5cm / 2 inches apart, on the grill pan. Dot with the rest of the butter and cook under a medium-hot preheated grill for 4–5 minutes, till firm. Test regularly, as they easily overcook. Spoon over the buttery, herby juices from the pan and serve with a crisp *frisée* salad or bread, tiny new potatoes or Jerusalem artichokes.

Oysters

You cannot have a much faster meal than a plate of freshly-opened oysters. If you are a dab hand at opening them, then fine, go ahead; if not, then ask your fishmonger to do the honours. But remember that you will inevitably lose some of the precious juices in the back of the car on the way home.

You will need at least 6 oysters per person. This is not the time to practise the 'less is more' philosophy. Ignore everything you have been told (and certainly what I was told at Hotel School) about Tabasco sauce, horseradish or, God forbid, tomato ketchup and chilli concoctions.

You need lemon, and nothing more, to accompany your fine, and probably quite expensive, oysters. (They sometimes come down to about 40p each at my local fishmonger.) Eat them all by yourself, with some brown bread and butter, cut thin, and a glass or two of chilled dry white wine.

Oyster Po' Boys

Ask the fishmonger to shuck and clean the oysters for you. Persuade him to save the juices, which he will probably expect you to carry home in a plastic bag. The garlic mayonnaise here will raise a few purist eyebrows, but to my mind is far more suitable than the usual tartare.

FOR 1

6 oysters, shucked and cleaned, and their juice, the larger and fatter the better
1 small baguette, or 2 crusty rolls
1 egg, beaten
fine cornmeal or fresh breadcrumbs

50g / 2oz butter
1 tablespoon olive oil
good-quality garlic mayonnaise from a jar
a handful of salad leaves
¼ lemon

Strain the oyster liquid meticulously through a sieve to remove any grit and shell. Split the bread in two lengthways, scrape out enough dough to make a hollow, warming the bread slightly in the oven if you like. Put the egg in a shallow bowl and the cornmeal or bread-crumbs on a deep plate.

Melt the butter with the oil in a shallow pan – an omelette pan is fine – then drop the oysters into the egg, and next the breadcrumbs. When the butter is sizzling, slide in the oysters. They need 1 minute per side, no more.

Slather mayonnaise into the bottom of the hollow bread. Be gener-ous in the extreme. Cover with a layer of salad. Fish the oysters from the hot butter with a draining spoon and slide them on top of the leaves. Pour half of the butter out of the pan, tip in the oyster juice and bring quickly to the boil. Squeeze lemon juice over the oysters, then pour the bubbling buttery juices from the pan over the bread. Put on the top half of the bread, press gently and eat immediately with a bottle of very cold beer.

Three more good things to do with Oysters

* Grill them: put the opened oysters, in their half-shells, in a grill pan on top of a thick layer of baking beans or salt to stop them rolling over and spilling their juice. Pour enough double cream into the shells to come to the top, grind over a little pepper and sprinkle with finely-grated Parmesan cheese. Place under a pre-heated hot grill until the edges of the oyster curl, about 2 or 3 minutes

* Sauté them: dredge the opened oysters, freed of the shells, in seasoned flour. (You might like to add the merest touch of paprika with the salt and pepper.) Fry them in hot, sizzling butter for 2 minutes till golden. (Any longer and you might as well not bother.) Serve them as a snack with hunks of crisp baguette and lots of lemon. They are, incidentally, quite sublime in a crisp roll with lashings of garlic mayonnaise

* Bake them: set the oysters in their half-shells in lots of salt in an ovenproof dish. Place a knob of butter, the size of a half walnut, on each oyster and sprinkle over a tablespoon fresh white bread-crumbs. Bake them in a very hot oven, 220°C/425°F (gas mark 7), for 4 or 5 minutes till the butter and juices are bubbling

Prawns

Most prawns offered for sale in this country are frozen. Even when fresh they are almost certain to have been cooked. No doubt this is because they spoil within hours unless they are cooked or frozen (and even then they should not hang around). More than anything with prawns it is a case of you get what you pay for. Fifteen cm / six-inch tiger prawns will cost you six times as much as the diminutive pale pink frozen lumps packed into 450g / 1lb bags, but are probably worth it, though I can think of more than a few uses for the latter. It may be worth remembering that despite the fact they are rich they are hardly filling and will need bolstering with something substantial if they are to be truly satisfying. A warm potato salad or some such starchy offering usually works well.

Grilled Prawns

You will need about 700g / 1½lb large fresh uncooked prawns for 4 people. If you are lucky enough to have a supply of these then you will know that they are best cooked simply. Flashing under a hot grill is, I think, far superior to all the fancy sauces and preparations that abound elsewhere. I often cook them whole, as the prawn tends to stay juicier that way.

Lay the prawns flat on a grill pan and cook under a preheated very hot grill till pink, sizzling and opaque, about 3–4 minutes. Eat while hot, peeling back the shells with your fingers and dipping the prawns in melted butter mixed with a generous amount of coarse salt and ground black pepper.

A dozen ways to cheer up a bag of Frozen Prawns

Prawns lose a great deal of flavour during freezing but more often than not that is what we have to hand when time is short.

* Marinate the defrosted prawns in plenty of lemon juice for at least 20 minutes, an hour will perk them up even more

* Leave the prawns in a mixture of olive oil, crushed garlic, salt and pepper for 25 minutes before cooking them under a preheated hot grill

* Sprinkle the prawns with Pernod just before you serve them. Pernod-laced prawns are particularly good tossed with a little olive oil and lemon juice, finely-shredded bulb fennel and thinly-sliced mushrooms

* Serve them dressed with thick natural yoghurt and very finely-chopped watercress and tarragon

* Soak them in a marinade of groundnut oil, finely-grated fresh root ginger, lime juice and garlic. Drain and toss them briefly in a hot frying pan

* Scramble them with eggs and chopped fresh coriander leaves

* Marinate defrosted prawns in lemon juice, a little ground turmeric and crushed garlic. Toss them in a hot pan, or egg and breadcrumb them and deep-fry till golden, about 3–4 minutes

* Serve defrosted prawns with a warm dressing of crisply-fried bacon and its cooking fat and balls of chilled melon. Scatter with fresh chives

* Marinate the prawns in a mustardy vinaigrette (5 parts olive oil, 2 parts white wine vinegar, generously seasoned with smooth French mustard, crushed garlic and salt). After half an hour stir them into good-quality mayonnaise with a drop of Tabasco sauce. Serve them with bitter salad leaves and lemon

* Cook a chopped onion in butter for about 5–7 minutes, till soft and golden, stir in a teaspoonful mild curry powder, fry for 1 minute, then slowly pour in enough water to make a thick sauce. Simmer for 10–12 minutes, until it has thickened. Stir in 4 tablespoons chopped tomatoes (these can be tinned and drained) and 2 hand-fuls of prawns. Simmer for a further 5 minutes, taste and correct the seasoning with salt and pepper. Serve very hot, on toast or with some cooked plain rice

* Sandwich the prawns, well seasoned with salt and freshly ground black pepper, between pieces of hot toast spread with butter, mango chutney and rashers of crisp, hot bacon

* Get out the Pernod bottle again. This time cook the prawns in a little butter in a frying pan for 2 minutes. Add a good slug of

Pernod. Stir. Lift out the prawns with a slotted spoon and pour in a small pot of double cream. Let it bubble for 1 minute, then return the prawns to the pan. Taste and correct the seasoning. Serve while bubbling with cooked plain rice or on toast

SMOKED FISH

When buying smoked fish choose the ones with the moistest flesh. Fishmongers who smoke their own are often the best source, as well as mail-order smokers from the Highlands. The workaday supermarket frequently stocks the vacuum-packed variety whose apparent juiciness is actually oil brushed on before packing.

All manner of fish are smoked: trout, kippers (which are, in fact, herrings before they are 'kippered') and, of course, salmon. But I would rather have a lightly smoked mackerel any day than some of the bright orange shiny salmon I have eaten recently.

Look out also for smoked fish that are supple and pale in colour; a kipper as stiff as a board and as brown as a coffin will be far from the juicy and subtly smoky supper you are probably hoping for. Mackerel should be silvery-blue when smoked; the visually tempting golden ones have probably been dyed with Tartrazine, which was banned from use in soft drinks and children's food years ago.

A smoked trout or mackerel is a fine supper with little more than some bread and salad, perhaps tomato and onion, or a green salad with mustardy dressing. Kippers likewise. But a piece of lightly-smoked haddock cooked in milk can be soothing after a busy day, especially when it shares a plate with a pile of smooth, mashed potatoes. Smoked salmon can sometimes fit the bill too, but only when there is plenty of it and it is cut in thick enough slices.

Grilled Kippers

To keep kippers moist I use the 'jugging' method that Jane Grigson mentions in her book *Good Things*, and then grill them for a shorter time than usual.

Put the whole kippers, 1 for each person, head down, into a large jug and pour over enough boiling water to cover them. Leave them for 2 minutes, then remove and discard the water.

Place the kippers on the grill pan and cook – under a preheated grill – for 2 minutes on each side. Serve with a little butter and lots of brown bread.

Kipper and Cucumber Pâté

I use the word pâté loosely here, it is actually more of a paste.

SERVES 2

1 pair of kippers
½ small cucumber (about 100g / 4oz)
squeeze of lemon juice
1 spring onion, trimmed and finely chopped
freshly ground black pepper

Put the kippers in a large bowl. Pour over boiling water and leave for 3–4 minutes. Lift out the kippers, drain and throw away the water.

Remove all the bones from the kippers, dropping the flesh into a bowl. Grate the unpeeled cucumber into a small bowl, squeeze it to remove some of the water, and stir it into the kipper, mashing thoroughly with a fork.

Add a squeeze or two of lemon juice and the chopped spring onion. Season with the pepper, and chill if you have time. Serve with wholemeal bread or a salad of mustard and cress.

Grilled Breadcrumbed Kippers

With a small bowl of salad, perhaps watercress and tomato, this makes an elegant supper for two.

4 kipper fillets
1 tablespoon olive oil

6 tablespoons fresh
   breadcrumbs
lemon, to serve

Brush the kipper fillets with the oil. Spread the breadcrumbs on a plate and gently press the kipper fillets into them.

Place the breadcrumbed fillets on a grill pan and cook under a preheated grill for 7 minutes on each side. Serve with brown bread and butter and lemon.

Hot Kipper Toasts

FOR 2 AS A SNACK

2 slices of hot brown toast
butter
Worcestershire sauce
2 kipper fillets, cooked and
   mashed

a cupful of grated mature
   cheese
2 tablespoons double cream

Spread the hot toast quite generously with butter and shake over a few drops of Worcestershire sauce.

Stir the kipper fillets with the cheese and the cream. Add more cream if necessary. Spoon on to the buttered toast and flash under a preheated hot grill till bubbling.

Smoked Haddock Grilled in Milk

FOR 2 AS A MAIN DISH WITH MASHED POTATOES

butter
2 large, plump smoked baddock fillets
200ml / 7fl oz milk

Heat the grill. Butter a dish that will withstand the heat from the grill. Lay the fillets of smoked haddock on the buttered dish. Place it in the grill pan, and pour in enough milk to barely cover the fish. It should just lap the edges of the haddock. Dot over a little butter.

Grill, under a medium heat, until the fish is firm and a flake will come out easily when pulled, about 6–7 minutes.

Smoked Haddock with Cream

Cream and smoked fish make a smashing combination. Think of smoked salmon and soured cream, or smoked trout and horseradish cream. A light lunch or supper dish this, with perhaps a couple of large tomatoes, grilled whole in their skins, at the side.

FOR 2

350g / 12oz smoked haddock	freshly ground black pepper
butter	4 tablespoons fresh
175ml / 6fl oz double cream	breadcrumbs

Poach the haddock for 5 minutes, just covered with barely simmering water. Drain, remove the skin, and flake the fish, removing any fine bones. Place the flaked fish in a buttered ovenproof dish. Pour over the cream, season with black pepper and scatter over the bread-crumbs. Bake in a preheated oven, 200°C/400°F (gas mark 6), for 20 minutes or so, till bubbling.

Smoked Salmon

There is only one way to eat the best smoked salmon and that is in generous slices with brown bread and butter.

Serve it with a little lemon if you like, but ignore those who say the salmon should be carved thinly; it is at its most glorious only when served in slices as thick as ten-pence coins, and not, I repeat not, drowned in lemon juice.

Smoked Salmon Offcuts

These can be useful for the snacker, and are often sold cheaply in delicatessens and supermarkets. Take care, though, that they are fresh; too often they are hard and of little use to anyone other than the cat.

When they are good – that is, a soft orangey-pink colour and moist but not shiny – then take advantage of their cheapness and throw them into salads and plates of creamy pasta, or best of all, into soft and runny scrambled eggs.

FOR 1

2 knobs of butter, each the size of a walnut
2 large eggs, beaten with a fork
salt
freshly ground black pepper
4 tablespoons shredded smoked salmon trimmings

Melt a knob of the butter in a small solid saucepan. When the butter starts to foam, add the eggs all at once with the salt and pepper. Stir the egg with a wooden spoon, making sure to get right into the edges of the pan, otherwise the egg will stick.

While there is still a goodly amount of liquid egg remaining, take the pan off the heat, stir in the second knob of butter and the smoked salmon and serve immediately.

Smoked Salmon with Warm Pasta

Heat does nothing for smoked salmon, but gentle warming with hot pasta and cold, sharp *fromage frais* seems to bring out the flavour.

FOR 2 AS A MAIN DISH

dried shell or tubular pasta for two
1 tablespoon olive oil
leaves from 2 sprigs of fresh tarragon, chopped
100g / 4oz smoked salmon
225g / 8oz *fromage frais*
salt
freshly ground black pepper

Put the pasta on to cook in plenty of boiling salted water, until it is tender but still *al dente*.

Place the oil in a warmed large serving bowl. Toss the chopped tarragon in the oil. Cut the smoked salmon into wide ribbons.

Remove the pasta from the heat and drain. Tip it into the serving bowl with the olive oil. Add the shredded smoked salmon and stir in the *fromage frais*. Season lightly with salt and pepper.

Smoked Salmon Pâté

You can make a quick pâté with salmon offcuts by mixing equal quantities of smoked salmon pieces and curd cheese in the food processor, squeezing in a generous amount of lemon juice and seasoning with freshly ground black pepper. Allow 50g / 2oz salmon and cheese per person. Serve with fingers of hot brown toast.

Smoked Mackerel, Hot Potatoes and Bitter Leaves

Radicchio, the deep red and white chicory, the fashionable rocket or just plain watercress are all good leaves to use in this substantial warm salad. I think the mustard in the dressing quite important.

FOR 4

450g / 1lb new potatoes, scrubbed

2 heads of radicchio, about the size of tennis balls

225g / 8oz smoked mackerel, skinned and filleted

a wineglassful of salad dressing, preferably one made with a milder olive oil and a good dollop of seed mustard

Boil the potatoes until tender, about 15–20 minutes. Peel the leaves of the radicchio away from each other, wash them if you think it important (I do not) and shred them into manageable-sized pieces.

Break the mackerel into large chunks, though probably no larger than you would like to put into your mouth, and put it into the dressing.

Drain the potatoes and cut each one in half so that the dressing can soak into the flesh. Warm the dressing and mackerel in a shallow pan over a gentle heat, don't let it boil, then add the potatoes while they are still warm. Throw in the radicchio leaves and move everything gently around the pan for about 2 minutes, without breaking up the fish or the potatoes. Divide between 4 warm plates and eat with hunks of wholemeal bread.

CANNED FISH

A tin of sardines has saved my life many times when I've come home without having shopped or in need of something savoury and comforting and very, very fast. Sardines tin almost better than anything. They are, in fact, one of the few foods that actually improve in the can. Posh sardine shippers even declare vintages, like those in wine.

I have no doubt that French sardines, canned in fruity golden oil, have the best flavour. They also rarely crumble when you lift them from their oil. The more popular, and a darned sight cheaper, Portuguese numbers are a different 'k of f' altogether. But they are not to be despised just because they are cheap and the oil is less than interesting; they can still provide a perfectly decent supper when grilled or jazzed up with a little mustard. The French ones are good enough to eat alone for supper with hunks of bread and perhaps a glass of cider.

Tuna, smoked oysters and mussels can be useful storecupboard hoards too. First, they must be rid of their packing liquid, which is almost invariably horrid. Drain tuna gently of its brine, but put mussels and oysters in a sieve and rinse under running water. They will need a bit of help if they are to be really good to eat, such as a dressing of some sort, and perhaps a little lemon juice or mustard.

Anchovies on Bread

A very good picnic snack, this open sandwich tastes better eaten outdoors – but then doesn't almost everything? It is worth remembering that something like this stands or falls by the crustiness of the bread and the flavour of the tomato.

2 slices from a fresh brown or white loaf	1 × 50g / 2oz tin anchovy fillets, drained of their oil
your best olive oil	2 tomatoes
wine vinegar	16 black olives, stoned
freshly ground black pepper	

Place the slices of bread flat on the bread board. Drizzle over a little olive oil and a few drops of vinegar; the bread should be juicy rather than drenched.

Season with a little black pepper. Divide the anchovy fillets among the bread, laying a few on each slice. Slice the tomatoes, lay them on the bread and scatter over the olives.

Anchoïade

A classic garlicky, fishy paste made in minutes from storecupboard ingredients. If you have a few capers and some black olives scatter them over the toasts as they emerge from the grill.

FOR 2

1 × 50g / 2oz tin anchovy fillets, drained of their oil	2 tablespoons olive oil
2 cloves of garlic, chopped	1 teaspoon white wine vinegar
	10 thin slices of French bread

Rinse the anchovies, pat them dry and pound them in a mortar or bowl with the end of a rolling pin till reduced to a thick paste. Blend in the garlic. Add the oil, gradually, pounding all the time. Stir in the vinegar.

Toast the bread lightly on one side. Spread the *anchoïade* on the untoasted side and place under a preheated hot grill for 2 or 3 minutes. Serve immediately.

See also Scrambled Eggs, page 31.

Anchovy Mayonnaise

Mash 4 rinsed and dried anchovies with the blade of a knife; it will take a matter of seconds. Stir them into 250ml / 9fl oz (a large breakfast cup) home-made or good-quality bought mayonnaise. Add a hefty squeeze of lemon juice and a grinding of pepper, white if you have it.

Use it as an instant dressing for vegetables that have been cooked briefly in boiling salted water, such as green beans, broccoli or tiny new potatoes.

Anchovy Idea

Fry rounds of white bread in olive oil till crisp. Lay 3 rinsed and dried anchovy fillets on each one and put on hot plates. Spoon a dollop of thick, cold natural yoghurt on top and serve.

Sardine and Smoked Oyster Savoury

Another snack made almost entirely with things from the store-cupboard.

FOR 2

1 × 100g / 3½ oz tin smoked oysters
1 × 100g / 4oz tin sardines in olive oil, drained

large knob of butter
lemon juice
cayenne pepper
2 rounds of wholemeal toast

Drain the smoked oysters of their nasty oil. Rinse, pat dry and put them in a small bowl. Roughly flake the sardines. Add a large knob of butter, a drop of lemon juice and a generous pinch of cayenne pepper. Spread the mixture on toast and cook under a preheated hot grill till bubbling, a couple of minutes.

Sardine Butter

Drain the oil from a tin of sardines and tip the sardines into a small bowl. Mash them, using a fork, with an equal quantity of butter, preferably at room temperature. Squeeze in a little lemon juice and season with salt and freshly ground black pepper.

Good things to do with Sardine Butter

* Spread the sardine butter on hot toast

* Spoon it into a split baked potato

* Spread the butter on toast and scatter over a handful of grated Cheddar cheese

* Stir a double portion of it into a dish of cooked, drained pasta for two

* Eat in a sandwich, spread generously, with slices of peeled cucumber dressed with lemon juice, white pepper and chopped fresh tarragon

Sardine Sandwiches

* Mash up a large tin of drained sardines and add a teaspoon lemon juice. Chop half a small cucumber very finely and add to the sardines

* Make a sardine butter by mashing a large tin of drained sardines with a heaped tablespoon butter. Add some chopped fresh parsley if you have some. Use this mixture to spread on the bread, preferably granary, and fill the sandwiches with watercress and thin slices of tomato

* Mash the contents of a large tin of sardines, drained, with a fork. Mix it with roughly an equal quantity of soured cream and spread it on dark bread

* Sardine paste sandwiches are terribly good. Mash a large tin of drained sardines, removing any large bones, to a paste. Add a drop of anchovy paste if you have some and 25g / 1oz butter. Squeeze in the juice of ½ lemon and add a finely-chopped spring onion. Stir the mixture well and spread it on crusty French bread

Sardines with Butter Sauce

An idea inspired by Ambrose Heath, one of the most prolific cookery writers of the 1940s and 1950s. He produced practical little books with titles such as *Good Food from Tinned Food* and *What's Left in the Larder*.

FOR 2

2 rounds of bread cut into
  fingers
75g / 3oz butter
2 × 100g / 4oz tins sardines in
  olive oil

2 egg yolks
½ teaspoon English mustard
1 teaspoon tarragon vinegar
salt
freshly ground black pepper

Fry the fingers of bread in 50g / 2oz of the butter until golden. Drain the sardines and place them on the fingers of fried bread in an ovenproof dish.

Place them in a preheated hot oven, 220°C/425°F (gas mark 6), and while they are heating through, mix together the egg yolks, mustard, remaining butter, and vinegar. Add a little salt and pepper and heat through in a small saucepan until the mixture starts to thicken. Coat the sardines with the sauce and serve hot.

Mustard Sardines

A storecupboard snack if ever there was one.

FOR 1 AS A SNACK

1 × 100g / 4oz tin sardines in olive oil
2 tablespoons grain mustard
lemon wedges, to serve

Drain the sardines of their oil, pat them dry with a paper towel and put them in a shallow heatproof dish. Brush them with the mustard and cook them under a preheated grill for 1–2 minutes, until they sizzle. Serve them with lemon wedges, and thick pieces of brown bread, and eat them while they are still very hot.

Grilled Curried Sardines with Mango Chutney

I know this sounds distinctly dodgy but it is an interesting way of approaching yet another can of sardines. I first came across the idea in Goa, where of course, they used fresh fish.

FOR 2 AS A SNACK

1 × 100g / 4oz tin sardines in olive oil
1 teaspoon curry powder

1 tablespoon lemon juice
mango chutney

Carefully lift the sardines from the tin with the help of a flexible knife. Discard the oil. Slide the fishes on to a grill pan, preferably lined with tin foil to cut down on the washing up.

Stir the curry powder into the lemon juice. Spoon it all over the sardines then flash them under a preheated hot grill until they start to sizzle, barely 1 minute. If you overcook them they will taste horrid. Serve them with brown bread and a dollop of mango chutney.

Herring Roes on Toast

Nancy Shaw's slim volume, *Food for the Greedy*, has given me many ideas in hungry moments. This is my version of her lovely dish, to which I always add some chopped fresh parsley if I have some, but only if it is very fresh and green and has lots of flavour.

50g / 2oz butter

1 × 100g / 4oz tin herring roes, drained

salt

freshly ground black pepper

50ml / 2fl oz double cream

1 tablespoon chopped fresh parsley

4 slices of hot buttered toast

Melt the butter in a small saucepan. Put in the herring roes and stir them round with the salt and pepper, mashing them against the side of the pan, for 3 or 4 minutes.

Stir in the double cream and the parsley and spoon the lot over the hot buttered toast. Serve immediately.

Pasta with Tuna, Capers and Cream

Use whichever pasta you happen to have around for this. Serve freshly grated Parmesan cheese separately.

FOR 4

100g / 4oz dried shell or tubular pasta

2 cloves of garlic, finely chopped

a small handful of fresh parsley, chopped

1 tablespoon capers, rinsed

6 tablespoons double cream

1 × 200g / 7oz tin line-caught tuna, drained

salt

freshly ground black pepper

Cook the pasta in boiling salted water until it is tender but still has some bite to it.

Put all the remaining ingredients in a serving bowl and mash roughly with a fork. Drain the pasta and tip it into the other ingredients. Stir it round and serve.

Tinned Salmon Bake

Tinned bears little resemblance to fresh. That said, it has its uses. It is quite good here, baked with tomato juice and breadcrumbs.

FOR 2 AS A MAIN DISH

1 × 375g / 13oz tin salmon, drained, or cooked flaked salmon
½ lemon
whites of 4 spring onions, trimmed and finely chopped
salt
freshly ground black pepper
8 tablespoons tomato juice from a can or bottle
4 tablespoons coarse fresh breadcrumbs
25g / 1oz cold butter, cut into tiny dice

Put the salmon into a small gratin dish. Flake the salmon a little with a fork, don't mash it. Squeeze over the lemon juice and stir in the spring onions and salt and pepper. Spoon over the tomato juice.

Mix the breadcrumbs and the butter and scatter over the salmon. Bake in a preheated oven, 200°C/400°F (gas mark 6), for 25 minutes. It is ready when the crumbs are golden brown and the fish is bubbling.

Salade Niçoise

Salade Niçoise is one of those wretched foods that never seems to taste quite the same as it does in the South of France, when eaten at lunchtime on the beach. I think this has more to do with sea air than the ingredients, though it may be true to say that the tomatoes will have had more sunshine, and that makes a great deal of difference. Some green beans, blanched for a couple of minutes in boiling water, then cooled under running water and drained, make a rather good addition to this substantial snack.

a handful of leaves from the heart
   of a crisp lettuce
6 ripe tomatoes
3 hard-boiled eggs, cut into
   quarters
450g / 1lb line-caught tinned tuna,
   drained and roughly flaked

6 anchovy fillets, drained of
   their oil
16 black olives

FOR THE DRESSING:

4 tablespoons virgin olive oil
1 tablespoon wine vinegar
1 clove of garlic, crushed
2 tablespoons chopped fresh
   parsley

1 teaspoon capers, rinsed
salt
freshly ground black pepper

Divide the lettuce leaves between 4 bowls. Cut the tomatoes into quarters and add them to the lettuce. Add the eggs and the roughly-flaked tuna. Mix together the dressing ingredients and pour over the salad, tossing the ingredients gently in the dressing. Lay the anchovy fillets over the top of each salad and scatter over the olives.

Tinned Tuna for Supper

Tuna from a tin can make a fine supper. Open a small tin and remove the fish to a bowl. Scatter over a few capers, rinsed of their nasty vinegar, and a couple of chopped anchovies if you have them. Stir. Pile the fish on to lumps of crisp French bread to which you have generously applied some thick bought or home-made mayonnaise.

Tuna with Haricot Beans, Tomato and Chilli

There are times when recipes like this, made entirely from store-cupboard items, are a godsend. It is quite good as it stands but will benefit from any fresh herbs you may have around, especially parsley or oregano. It is particularly useful as a sauce for pasta and can also be topped with cheese and baked till melted and golden.

ENOUGH FOR 4 AS A MAIN DISH

2 tablespoons olive oil
1 medium onion, sliced
2 large cloves of garlic
1 medium-hot fresh chilli pepper, halved, seeds removed and finely chopped
1 medium tin, weighing about 400g / 14oz, plum tomatoes, chopped
1 medium tin, weighing about 400g / 14oz, haricot beans, drained and well rinsed
225g / 8oz tinned line-caught tuna, drained and coarsely flaked
2 tablespoons chopped fresh herbs, parsley and oregano
salt
freshly ground black pepper

Heat the oil in a saucepan. Add the onion and let it soften over a medium heat, about 5 minutes.

Add the garlic and the chilli and stir it into the onion. Cook for a further 5 minutes, or until the onion is quite translucent and the chilli is soft. Tip in the tomatoes and their juice, haricot beans, tuna and herbs. Cook until the beans are heated through. Season generously with black pepper and salt. Serve hot.

Tuna Sandwich

I love this sandwich. Even in the depths of winter it can remind me of summer. The ingredients are based on the classic *Pan Bagna*, or bathed bread, where the bread is stuffed with a *salade niçoise* mixture and then pressed by a weight so that the olive oil dressing soaks into the bread. We don't have time for all that, so here is a speeded-up version, and hardly the worse for it.

FOR 2 AS A RATHER SUBSTANTIAL SNACK

a round flat loaf or French baguette

100ml / 4fl oz virgin olive oil

4 tablespoons wine vinegar

salt

freshly ground black pepper

1 clove of garlic, crushed

2 large tomatoes, thinly sliced

1 medium sweet onion, thinly sliced

1 red pepper, cored, seeded and cut into strips

12 anchovy fillets, washed and patted dry

12 black olives, stoned

1 small tin line-caught tuna, drained and roughly crumbled

Slice the loaf in half horizontally. Sprinkle the oil, vinegar, salt, pepper and garlic on the cut sides.

Arrange the tomatoes, onion, pepper, anchovies, olives and tuna on one half of the loaf. Place the other half on top. Wrap the bread well in clingfilm and press gently but firmly with your hands. This will spread the dressing through the bread. Unwrap and enjoy.

A Piquant Sauce for Tinned Tuna

FOR 2 AS A MAIN DISH

2 tablespoons smooth French mustard

300ml / ½ pint olive oil

4 tablespoons wine or tarragon vinegar

2 tablespoons finely-chopped fresh parsley

2 tablespoons finely-chopped fresh chives

2 tablespoons finely-chopped fresh tarragon or chervil

1 small pickled gherkin, finely chopped

4 tablespoons double cream

½ small cucumber, cut into small dice

½ head small iceberg lettuce

1 large tin line-caught tuna, drained and coarsely flaked

Whizz the first 8 ingredients in a food processor or blender for a few seconds. Stir in the diced cucumber. On a large plate make a bed of the lettuce and tip the tuna in the centre. Cover with the sauce.

4

Pasta

*T*he British have finally embraced pasta. Its soft comforting form fits in with our love of bland, warming food, like porridge, bread sauce and rice pudding. Pasta's cheapness and convenience appeals to our rumoured disapproval of spending money or time on food.

Good-quality dried pasta made with durum wheat flour cooks in about 9–11 minutes. Fresh pasta cooks in 2 or 3, depending on its thickness. The best sauces will cook in the time it takes the pasta to cook. What could be better news to those who long for sustaining food – fast? It is worth remembering that different shapes take different times to cook. Noodles are about the quickest while some of the complicated shapes, especially those made from wholemeal flour, can take up to 20 minutes.

You need lots of water to cook pasta. And a generous amount of salt. Allow 4.5 litres / 8 pints water per 450g / 1lb pasta and ½ teaspoon salt per 1.1 litres / 2 pints.

Cook the pasta in a covered pan to bring it back to the boil quickly. Pasta is cooked when it is al dente, that is, tender but with a bite to it. The only real way to tell is to test it; the pasta should be firm to the bite without any taste of flour. Ignore those who tell you to put oil in the water to stop the pasta sticking together. It certainly works, but it also stops any sauce sticking to it as well.

I eat pasta several times a week. Rarely spaghetti, which I am convinced is the Italians' idea of a practical joke, or those little butterflies, farfalle, *which go floppy at the tips by the time the knot in the middle is cooked. I find the most useful shapes are those that have good sauce-holding properties.* Conchiglie *holds sauces well in its shell shape as does the nib-shaped* penne.

Wholewheat noodles are deeply satisfying. Matched with earthy ingredients, like parsley, spicy sausage, garlic, mustard or mushrooms, it takes on a robustness that I find pleasing during cold weather. In summer I need little excuse to make fresh pesto with basil leaves and pine nuts; simple it may be, but what can beat lightly-cooked fettuccine *with warm pesto sauce? Cold pasta is rarely good. I prefer to toss warm noodles in cold sauces, such as an impromptu one of cottage cheese and any fresh herbs, perhaps marjoram, that I have to hand.*

* Many delicatessens keep a supply of home-made sauces and pastes. Black olive paste, subtle and addictive artichoke paste, and tomato and garlic rich *Napoletana* sauce can be brought home with a bundle of fresh pasta. You have a meal in 5 minutes

* Parmesan cheese is the accepted accompaniment for most pastas. Forget the ready-grated stuff in packets. You might as well scatter sawdust instead. Go for a block and grate it as you need it. If you are desperate for time or a decent grater, then ask the grocer to do it for you in his machine. Really fresh Parmesan and a little butter is all you need to make good pasta sing

* Commercial soft cheeses, the ones sold in pleated foil packages and which reek of garlic, make a wonderfully fragrant sauce when cut into chunks and thrown into hot pasta

* A great favourite of mine are the stuffed pastas sold in delis and made on the premises: pumpkin, available in the autumn and winter, and Ricotta and spinach are the best buys. The meat filling of *tortelloni* can sometimes resemble cat food. Butter, softened rather than melted, is a straightforward lubricant, while grated cheese can be added for those who like it rich

Pasta with Yoghurt and Herbs

A dish for summer eating with a sauce that can be made in the time it takes to cook the pasta. Use as few or as many herbs as you like, and alter the combination to suit what you have. Fresh chervil, parsley and tarragon are good together, as are parsley and basil or mint and watercress.

Tip a pot of thick Greek-style yoghurt into a heatproof bowl. Place the bowl over a pan of simmering water. Stir in a loosely-filled teacupful of chopped fresh herbs. Season with 4 or 5 twists of the peppermill and heat until the yoghurt is just warmed through.

Cook enough pasta for two in boiling salted water till *al dente*. Any shape of pasta will do. Drain and return it to the pan, off the heat. Stir in the warm yoghurt and herb sauce, scooping out the dish with a rubber spatula.

Pasta with Whole Garlic, Goat's Cheese and Thyme

When garlic is cooked whole, the cloves lightly crushed, at a low temperature for a long time, it takes on a deep, sweet flavour. Its fragrance is warm and soft and makes this a dish truly for all the senses.

You will need fresh thyme too; no, not dried, fresh. A little cellophane packet from the supermarket will be enough. The garlic takes about 25 minutes to cook, so don't attempt it if you have only 10.

FOR 2 AS A MAIN DISH

a large head of garlic, the cloves
   plump and pink
50ml / 2fl oz extra virgin olive oil
   about 6 healthy sprigs of thyme

175g / 6oz dried pasta
175g / 6oz crumbly white
   goat's cheese

Separate the garlic cloves. Crush each one lightly by pressing down hard with the flat of a knife blade or the heel of your hand, which will loosen the skins. Pop the cloves out of their papery skins.

Pour the oil into a small pan and add the garlic. Cook over a gentle heat for 20–25 minutes, until the cloves are tender, golden and sweet. They must not burn or they will turn horribly bitter.

Strip the thyme leaves from their branches and add them to the garlic, 15 minutes after it has started cooking. Cook the pasta in boiling salted water until it is *al dente*, drain and toss gently with the olive oil, garlic cloves and thyme. Crumble the goat's cheese and stir in.

Pasta with Grilled Tomatoes and Onions

Grilling the tomatoes and onions gives the sauce a wonderful, cara-melised flavour. But there is nothing subtle about this dish. It is one I value on cold autumn evenings when I am in search of sweet robust flavours and something that will stand up to a bottle of cheap red wine.

SERVES 2

5 large tomatoes, very ripe
1 tablespoon fresh thyme
   leaves, chopped
salt
freshly ground black pepper
olive oil
275g / 10oz dried pasta

2 medium onions, sliced into
   rounds, about 5mm / ¼ inch
   thick
2 cloves of garlic, very finely
   chopped
Parmesan cheese, to serve

Slice the tomatoes in half and scoop out the seeds. Put them, skin side up, in an ovenproof dish in a grill pan and scatter them with half the thyme and a little black pepper and drizzle them with olive oil. Set under a preheated hot grill and cook until the skins blacken and smell sweet – about 4–6 minutes.

Cook the pasta in boiling salted water until it is *al dente*. Remove the tomatoes from the ovenproof dish and place the onion slices, drizzled with olive oil and the rest of the thyme, under the grill. Turn them once as they cook. They should be soft and browned at the edges – about 6–7 minutes. Chop the tomatoes roughly, charred skins and all, and throw them in a pan with the grilled onions, their oil and the garlic. The easiest way to chop the tomatoes is to use a knife and fork or to whizz them briefly in the blender. Add the garlic and simmer for 2 minutes.

Season with salt and some more black pepper. Drain the pasta and stir in the tomato, onion and oil. Be generous with the Parmesan.

Fusilli *with Olives, Anchovies and Capers*

A storecupboard supper with a Mediterranean flavour that is as good cold as it is hot. If you don't have any corkscrew-shaped *fusilli*, then quill-like *penne* or almost any tubular pasta is just as good.

FOR 2

50g / 2oz stoned black olives
4 anchovy fillets, rinsed and dried
1 tablespoon capers, rinsed
3 tablespoons olive oil

2 sun-dried tomatoes packed in oil, finely sliced
450g / 1lb fresh or 100g / 4oz dried pasta
freshly-grated Parmesan cheese

Chop the olives and anchovies, but not to a purée, then add the capers. Warm the oil in a shallow pan and stir in all the ingredients except the pasta and Parmesan. Let the ingredients warm through gently, but do not let them bubble (if the capers become too hot they tend to overpower everything else).

Cook the pasta in boiling salted water until it is *al dente*. Drain and tip into a warm serving bowl. Pour over the heated olive sauce. Stir gently and serve. Pass the Parmesan.

Wholewheat Pasta with Sausages, Mustard and Caramelised Onions

A marvellously robust dish to come home to on a winter's night. Any wholewheat (or any other for that matter) pasta is fine, though *fettuccine* is my favourite. It is very good with a glass of beer.

FOR 2

175g / 6oz fresh spicy sausage
3 tablespoons olive oil
2 large onions, cut into thin rings
225g / 8oz wholewheat pasta
150ml / ¼ pint chicken or vegetable stock

2 tablespoons chopped fresh parsley
1 tablespoon grain mustard
salt
freshly ground black pepper

Slice the sausage into thick rounds. Fry it in the oil for 4 minutes, then add the onion rings. Continue cooking, covered, until the onions start to soften, adding a drop more oil if necessary.

Bring a large pan of water to the boil, add a little salt and throw in the pasta. Cook until it is firm but tender.

After about 15–20 minutes, when the onions are golden and have caramelised and are ever-so-slightly burned at the edges, add the stock. Bring to the boil, scrape up the good things stuck to the pan with a wooden spatula and stir in the chopped parsley and the grain mustard. Add the cooked, drained pasta and season with salt and pepper. Serve hot.

Cold Pasta with Tomatoes and Spring Onions

The sharp vinaigrette and cherry tomatoes, of the fork-dodging variety, lift cold leftover pasta into a bright-tasting, quickly-put-together snack. Be generous with the herbs – basil is not essential but the parsley certainly is. No matter if your leftover pasta has a little of last night's sauce clinging to it, just put it in a colander and rinse it under lots of cold running water.

450g / 1lb leftover cooked pasta
6 spring onions, trimmed and
  chopped
350g / 12oz cherry tomatoes
2 tablespoons wine vinegar

4 tablespoons olive oil
salt
freshly ground black pepper
fresh parsley and basil

Rinse the pasta in cold running water to separate the pieces and remove any remaining sauce.

Chop the spring onions and place them in a serving dish with the cherry tomatoes. Mix together the wine vinegar, olive oil and salt and pepper with a fork and pour over the tomatoes and onions.

Drain the pasta thoroughly and tip into the serving dish. Chop as much parsley and shred as many basil leaves as you can spare and add to the pasta. Toss together the ingredients and eat cold.

Noodles with Butter and Green Peppercorns

For this you will need a small jar of those soft green Madagascan peppercorns that you can buy in smart delicatessens. Incidentally, the brine they are stored in takes up enough of their flavour to render it a spicy addition to salad dressings and sauces. Just remember to go easy on the salt. Serve as an accompaniment to grilled poultry or meat.

FOR 4 AS AN ACCOMPANIMENT
225g / 8oz thin noodles
50g / 2oz butter
2 tablespoons bottled green peppercorns

Cook the noodles in boiling salted water until firm but tender. This will probably take 2 or 3 minutes once the water has returned to the boil.

Soften the butter in a small pan over a medium heat until it has almost melted. Chop the peppercorns roughly and add to the butter.

You can leave them whole, but they are the devil to get on to your fork.

Drain the noodles and add to the butter, tossing them so that the noodles are coated in butter and peppercorns.

Fried Noodles with Beanshoots and Broccoli

I like the contrasting textures of the soft noodles and crisp broccoli in this dish. Sometimes I use sugar-snap peas, or even asparagus instead.

FOR 2

100g / 4oz Chinese or Japanese noodles

4 tablespoons vegetable oil

1 medium onion, diced

a small knob of fresh root ginger, peeled and chopped

4 cloves of garlic, crushed

175g / 6oz broccoli, broken into large florets

2 handfuls of beanshoots, about 150g / 5oz

4 spring onions, trimmed and sliced

3 tablespoons dark soy sauce, plus more at table

Cook the noodles for about 2 or 3 minutes in boiling salted water until they are just tender. Drain and toss them in half the vegetable oil. In the remaining oil, fry the onion, ginger and garlic for about 2–3 minutes, until they start to soften. Add the broccoli and stir-fry for a couple of minutes, then tip in the noodles. Toss in the beanshoots and stir-fry, keeping the ingredients in the pan moving, for 3 minutes. Add the spring onions, soy sauce and salt and pepper and stir-fry for another minute. Serve hot.

A Spicy Sauce in which to Toss Noodles

I once shared a kitchen briefly with a young Chinese cook. When it was discovered that he was working illegally he disappeared into thin air. His legacy was this instant and exceptionally garlicky sauce, for which I never had the chance to thank him.

FOR 4 AS A MAIN DISH
4 tablespoons sesame paste
5 tablespoons light soy sauce
2 tablespoons dry sherry
1 tablespoon wine vinegar
1½ tablespoons sesame oil

4 cloves of garlic, finely chopped
hot noodles for 4, cooked and drained

Put all the ingredients except the noodles in a food processor or blender with 4 tablespoons water. Whizz. Pour into a pan and bring slowly to the boil. Pour into a large serving bowl. Add the drained noodles and toss. Serve with a crisp salad, perhaps beanshoot, pepper and banana dressed with lots of lemon juice.

Blue Cheese Pasta

Any dried pasta is suitable for this dish. I use a soft blue cheese, such as Gorgonzola, Dolcelatte, or that rather delicious hybrid with layers of Dolcelatte and Mascarpone found in delis nowadays.

FOR 2
225g / 8oz dried pasta
175g / 6oz soft blue cheese, such as Gorgonzola

50g / 2oz butter, cut into small pieces
freshly ground black pepper

Cook the pasta in boiling salted water until it is *al dente*. Meanwhile, mash together the cheese and butter in a large warm serving bowl.

When the pasta is cooked, drain it and toss with the cheese and butter in the bowl. Give the pasta one or two grinds of the peppermill and serve.

Fettuccine *with Cream and Parmesan*

FOR 2

275g / 10oz *fettuccine*
225ml / 8fl oz double cream
50g / 2oz butter

75g / 3oz freshly-grated
  Parmesan cheese
freshly ground black pepper

Cook the *fettuccine* in boiling salted water until it is *al dente*.

Pour the cream into a saucepan, add the butter and bring slowly to the boil. Reduce the heat and leave the sauce to simmer gently for 2 minutes. Stir in the Parmesan and several grinds of black pepper. Pour over the *fettuccine* and toss the pasta in the sauce.

Pappardelle *with Olive Paste and Gruyère*

Pappardelle is my favourite of the flat noodles. It is wider than *fettuccine* or *tagliatelle*, and sadly more difficult to find. You can, of course, use any ribbon pasta for this, and any cheese.

FOR 2 AS A MAIN DISH

225g / 8oz dried *pappardelle*
1 tablespoon olive oil
4 tablespoons black olive paste

1 tablespoon pine nuts
75g / 3oz cheese, grated on the
  fine side of the grater

Cook the *pappardelle* for 6 minutes in boiling salted water. Drain. Pour the oil into a medium gratin dish and add the drained noodles. Toss the noodles in the olive oil and the olive paste. Cover with the pine nuts and the grated cheese. Bake in a preheated oven, 200°C/ 400°F (gas mark 6), for 15–20 minutes, until the cheese has turned crispy, the dish is singing and the pasta on top has turned slightly crisp with the underneath moist and fragrant.

Dolcelatte Gnocchi

I think *gnocchi* from a vacuum pack is rather good. It isn't as light as home-made, but on a cold winter's night I am often thankful for a plate of rib-sticking creamy, cheesy dumplings. Buy the pasta and the cheese from the deli and serve with a refreshing salad, such as watercress and grapefruit.

FOR 2, GENEROUSLY, AS A MAIN DISH

1 × 450g / 1 lb packet of
   vacuum-packed *gnocchi*
200g / 7oz Dolcelatte cheese

150ml / ¼ pint double cream
salt
freshly ground black pepper

Cook the *gnocchi* in boiling salted water. It is done when the dumplings rise to the surface. Scoop them out with a draining spoon and put them into a shallow gratin dish.

   Cut the cheese into chunks and add, with the cream, to the *gnocchi*. Season with black pepper. Bake in a preheated oven, 200°C/400°F (gas mark 6), for 15 minutes, or until bubbling.

Wholewheat Spaghetti with Anchovy and Garlic

I love wholewheat pasta, it is so comforting, earthy and rich. I use it with other robust ingredients it will stand up to such as the anchovies, garlic and parsley here.

FOR 4

4 anchovy fillets, rinsed and
   dried
275g / 10oz wholewheat
   spaghetti
75ml / 3fl oz olive oil

3 cloves of garlic, chopped
6 large sprigs of fresh flat-leaf
   parsley, chopped
freshly ground black pepper

Chop the anchovies finely. Place the pasta into a large pan of boiling salted water and cook until firm but tender. Pour the oil into a saucepan, add the garlic and heat very gently for about 1 or 2 minutes, until the garlic sizzles. If the garlic becomes black and burned the dish will be ruined. When the garlic starts to turn golden and has softened, add the anchovies and the parsley. Immediately remove the pan from the heat, drain the pasta and add it to the anchovy and parsley mixture. Season with a little black pepper, toss thoroughly and serve hot.

Spaghetti with Herbs and Toasted Crumbs

I often snip tender herbs, such as chervil and tarragon, over a bowl of cooked pasta. I include toasted breadcrumbs if there is some bread that needs using.

FOR 4

2 large handfuls of fresh breadcrumbs
3 tablespoons olive oil
1 loosely-packed teacup of snipped fresh herbs: parsley, chervil, tarragon, and basil

4 spring onions, trimmed and chopped, or 2 small shallots, chopped
225g / 8oz dried spaghetti
freshly ground black pepper

In a shallow pan fry the crumbs in 1 tablespoon of the olive oil until golden and crisp, stirring regularly so that they do not burn. Put to one side.

In a warm serving bowl, place the chopped herbs, the spring onions or shallots and the remaining olive oil.

Cook the pasta in boiling salted water until it is *al dente*, then drain it and mix it with the herbs and olive oil. Mix well and grind some black pepper, quite coarsely, over the pasta. Scatter over the breadcrumbs and serve warm.

Pasta with Hot Butter and Herbs

A lovely buttery sauce for pasta. Most fresh herbs work well, including dill, flat-leaf parsley, tarragon and chervil. If you fancy coriander pasta you will only need 1 tablespoonful.

FOR 2

225g / 8oz dried pasta	2 tablespoons fresh herbs
225g / 8oz unsalted butter	2 tablespoons chopped parsley
1 small onion, finely chopped	juice of ½ lemon

Cook the pasta in boiling salted water. Melt the butter in a saucepan. Add the onion and your chosen fresh herbs, but not the parsley, and cook over a gentle heat for about 5–7 minutes, until the onion has softened. When the pasta is tender but still firm, drain and tip it into a large warm serving dish. Throw the parsley into the butter sauce, squeeze in the lemon juice and pour over the cooked pasta.

EVEN FASTER PASTA

These sauces, although that is too grand a word for them, are instant additions for pasta that you have brought home from the deli. Fresh pasta cooked for 3 or 4 minutes and a spoonful or two from the list below is literally a meal in minutes.

Crème d'olive, Black Olive Paste
Kalamata olives from Greece are very finely chopped and mixed with olive oil to make a savoury paste. It is available from supermarkets and delicatessens. Warm it gently in a small pan and toss it with cooked, drained pasta.

Carciofini sott'olio, Artichokes in Oil
Of all the good things that come in jars, baby globe artichokes must be among my favourites. So tiny and tender that they can be eaten

whole, choke and all. Preserved in olive oil, they are often sold loose in Italian delis. Cut each one in half and add them to hot spinach or egg pasta.

Some delicatessens carry jars of artichoke paste. A wonderful addition to the storecupboard, this soft green paste has a gently addictive flavour. Stir it straight from the jar into cooked pasta. Throw in an olive or two if you have some.

Frozen Spinach

Although I find frozen spinach useful, I avoid buying it in blocks. Those dark green bricks take ages to thaw, and if you try to speed up the process, by leaving it in a saucepan over a low heat, the outside overcooks while the middle remains frozen. Far better are the bags of loose frozen leaves.

Defrost them in seconds in a shallow pan over a gentle heat. Add a chopped anchovy fillet or two and some thick natural yoghurt and warm, without boiling, for a couple of minutes. Stir in the drained pasta.

Pomodori Secchi, Sun-dried Tomatoes in Oil

Tomatoes that have been dried in the sun, usually in Italy, have a deep, concentrated tomato flavour, with salty and smoky overtones. They come in three forms: dried, bottled in olive oil, and as a purée or cream. Whichever way you buy them, they are far from cheap, but to my mind worth every penny.

Those with little time will find the oil-preserved ones a better bet than the loose, slightly cheaper dried ones. A couple of oil-packed tomatoes, thinly sliced, will brighten up a bowl of wholewheat macaroni like nothing else. Don't throw the oil away. It is full of flavour. Drizzle some over the pasta as you toss it, throwing in a few fresh basil leaves if you have some.

Creamed dried-tomato is an expensive little delicacy. Made from crushed dried tomatoes and olive oil, it needs nothing more than a pan of steaming *al dente* tubular pasta to show its worth.

Cottage Cheese

Don't heat cottage cheese for pasta. Cold, straight from the fridge, it makes a nice contrast to ribbons of hot pasta. Add a handful of chopped fresh herbs or a blob of crunchy grain mustard. The one with tarragon in it is good.

Olive Oil

I often lubricate pasta with nothing more than a glug or two from a bottle of olive oil. But if supper is going to be that simple, then both the pasta and the oil must be very, very good. Wide ribbons of, say, *pappardelle*, from a good pasta-maker and thick, deep green, extra virgin olive oil, preferably estate-bottled at that, is the minimum.

Nut Oils

The deep flavour of walnut and hazelnut oil is achieved by pressing the nuts after they have been roasted. Pour any nut oil over hot pasta and toss gently to release the wonderful rich fragrance as the pasta warms the oil. Scatter over a handful of nuts, preferably toasted quickly first.

Sesame Oil

A bowl of hot noodles, a drop or two of toasted sesame oil and a pinch of dried chilli flakes make a supper hard to beat.

Butter, Fridge-cold

I find paper-thin slices of butter, cold and hard from the fridge, rather fine with hot pasta ribbons. To be really good the butter must be extremely fresh, very sweet and *unsalted*.

Butter, Melted and Nut Brown

By melted I mean softened. Leave unsalted butter in a warm place, such as at the back of the cooker, for a few minutes and it will become soft but not liquid.

Best of all, I think, is to cook butter until the solids in it start to turn brown. This gives the butter a fragrant nutty quality. Slowly melt the butter in a heavy-based pan over a low heat. Foam will rise to the surface. Skim this off with a spoon. Pour the golden liquid off the white milky sediment. Discard the sediment and return the liquid to the pan. Heat gently until it turns a light golden brown. When it smells nutty and sweet pour it over the cooked pasta.

Chilli Paste

A hot and spicy paste from southern Italy. Most commercial chilli purées also have garlic, tomatoes and red peppers added to them. Try stirring chilli paste into a pot of double cream, a spoonful at a time, and keep tasting, then warming it over a low heat before tossing it with steaming noodles.

Bottled Pimientos

Turn the grill on full. Drain the peppers of their bottling juice and lay them flat on a chopping board. Slice them into long thin strips. Put on the grill pan and drizzle over the merest amount of olive oil. When they start to sizzle and have caught appetisingly at the edges, lending a wonderful sweetness, tip them, with their juices, into a bowl of cooked pasta. Add a little more olive oil, and a few shredded fresh basil leaves. Toss in a handful of black olives if you have them. Sublime.

5

Vegetables and *Salads*

*O*f all my food shopping, it is poking around the vegetable stalls that I enjoy most. My diet contains a vast amount of vegetables, and there is almost none I do not enjoy. Although, for the record, I am not very fond of yams, mangetout peas or cooked carrots.

Crisp white fennel, huge flat field mushrooms and rude green asparagus I find hard to resist, knowing that they need little or no time in which to cook in order to taste wonderful. Fat purple aubergines and bright red peppers need only olive oil and heat to change miraculously from the bland and hard to the sweet and tender. Potatoes too, fascinate me, with their earthy smell and comforting, homely quality.

The vegetable and salads chapter of this book is particularly large, though far from comprehensive. Peppers are grilled, aubergines are fried and avocados come dressed with bacon and seedy mustard. Potatoes are sautéed with olive oil, mashed with butter and herbs or served, nutty and new, with spoonfuls of crème fraîche. Given all the quick ways of preparing the vegetable family it is not difficult to eat the recommended 400g / 14oz per day in order to keep us healthy.

There is probably more choice in our greengrocers and supermarkets than ever before. The major chains work hard at bringing us year-round summer vegetables and up to a point I am grateful to them, but what can match the excitement of finding the first British asparagus or the first peas of the season, and rushing them home for a quick feast? But it is difficult to resist the year-round runner beans and lush spinach imported from hotter climates, though their flavour rarely reaches the heights of freshly-picked local produce. And, what beats grabbing a clutch of greens from the grocers on the way home for an instant stir-fry supper?

There has been much talk about organically-grown vegetables lately, that is, vegetables produced without the excessive use of chemicals. I am lucky enough to have a reasonably good supply of organically-grown vegetables locally, and London now has a thriving organic market, but supplies elsewhere are hardly abundant. Even so, there is usually a fair selection at the chain stores and farm shops, though the message is proving more difficult to get through to the high street greengrocers. When vegetable shopping, the organic section is my first stop, though short supply inevitably means a further rummage through the rest of the display.

I find the best way to store salad stuffs and green vegetables is in damp newspaper in the fridge, not necessarily in the euphemistically-named 'salad crisper'. A little and often seems the best way to buy if freshness is your aim, and I am sure that it is. Generally speaking, the softer the leaf then the shorter time it will stay in peak condition. Lambs' lettuce or mâche and baby spinach leaves are notoriously difficult to store. My favourite leaf, rocket or roquette, with its pungent aromatic bitterness is all fine and dandy when I know I can devour it straight away, but there is much to be said for having a crunchy cut-and-come-again iceberg lettuce in the fridge too.

AUBERGINES

The aubergine is more evident nowadays in British cooking. This is no doubt due to our embracing of the food, if sadly not the way of life, of the Mediterranean. No longer do I have to trek to Indian or Cypriot shops for the versatile vegetable; it is here in the high street, in all its shining purple glory.

I think of the aubergine as the beefsteak of the vegetable world. Sliced and brushed with oil it grills aromatically, and tastes even better. For all its connections with Middle Eastern cookery, *imam bayildi* – stuffed aubergines – and mousaka, it is actually from Asia proper, the fat purple-black variety being just one of many. The reason for its American name, eggplant, was obvious once I had seen the white, almost oval varieties now imported.

I am not convinced of the need to put aubergines through the ritual salting that many cooks say is obligatory to rid them of bitterness. It is rare I come across a bitter one. Perhaps it is necessary with the enormous examples, which, like monster marrows, I never buy.

Aubergines are heavy drinkers. Allow a generous amount of oil, which must be of the best quality, when you are grilling them. They will soak up extra virgin olive oil greedily, and store it in their tender flesh, so that they taste even better.

Grilled Aubergine with Chick Pea Purée and Harissa

FOR 2 AS A LIGHT LUNCH OR SUPPER WITH SALAD

1 × 400g / 14oz tin chick peas, drained

a sprig of fresh thyme, plus 1 tablespoon chopped leaves

225g / 8oz / 1 large diced, peeled potatoes

3 large cloves of garlic, halved

salt

1 large aubergine, weighing about 275g / 10oz

150ml / ¼ pint virgin olive oil

50g / 2oz butter

2 tablespoons natural plain yoghurt

harissa sauce

1 lemon

Tip the chick peas into a pan and cover them with water or vegetable stock. Throw in the thyme sprig and bring to the boil. Add the diced potato and 2 of the garlic cloves. Salt and simmer for 15 minutes.

Meanwhile, slice the aubergine into 12 rounds about 1cm / ½ inch thick. Chop the 2 remaining garlic cloves and add to the oil with the thyme leaves. Brush the aubergine with the thyme and garlic oil and cook under or over a preheated hot grill for 7–8 minutes, brushing with more oil as necessary and turning once. They are ready when tender and golden brown. Remove the thyme sprig from the chick peas, drain them and mash with a potato masher. Stir in the butter and yoghurt. Season with salt.

Put 6 of the hot grilled aubergine slices on a warm serving dish, place a generous spoonful of chick pea purée on each. Spread the remaining slices with a thin layer of *harissa*, then place on top of the others to form 6 aubergine and chick pea sandwiches. Serve 3 to each person, with an extra dollop of chick pea purée in the centre. Cut the lemon in half and squeeze the juice over as you eat.

Grilled Aubergine with Lemon, Basil and Cracked Coriander

Whole coriander seed, lightly crushed as you need it, is quite different from the ready-ground spice. Release the ribbed spice's subtle orange scent by cracking the seeds with the end of a rolling pin in a small bowl, or by grinding briefly with a pestle and mortar. The idea is to crack the spice, rather than to pulverise it. It is rare to come across an aubergine dish without garlic, but this recipe brings out the full flavour of the aubergine.

1 large aubergine, weighing
about 225g / 8oz
extra virgin olive oil, about
60ml / 2½fl oz
½ teaspoon coriander seeds,
lightly crushed

2 teaspoons lemon juice
1 tablespoon shredded fresh
basil leaves
salt

Slice the aubergine lengthways about 5mm / ¼ inch thick. You will get roughly 6 slices. Brush each slice generously with olive oil. Scatter over half the cracked coriander seeds and cook under a preheated grill, turning once. They will need approximately 6 minutes on the first side and 4 on the second. Scatter over the remaining coriander seeds as you turn the aubergines. The object is to get the outside crisp while keeping the inside meltingly tender and slightly charred at the edges.

Mix the lemon juice and basil with a little salt, drizzle over the aubergines and serve warm.

Pesto Aubergines

This is my approximation of a dish cooked by Simon Hopkinson at his London restaurant, Bibendum. Set in the magnificent Michelin Building, it is one of my favourite places for lunch with food that I would describe as a professional version of Mother's cooking.

FOR 2 AS A MAIN DISH

2 large aubergines, not too
plump, weighing about 225g /
8 oz
3 cloves of garlic, peeled
2 handfuls of fresh basil leaves,
about 10g / ½ oz

2 tablespoons pine nuts
2 tablespoons freshly-grated
Parmesan cheese
4 tablespoons olive oil, plus
about 100ml / 4fl oz for
frying

Cut the aubergines in half lengthways. Cut slits into the aubergine flesh in a lattice fashion, without piercing the skin. This will allow the aubergine to cook right through quite quickly. Heat a finger's depth of olive oil in a shallow pan, slide in the aubergines, skin side up, and cook till golden and tender, about 10 minutes. Turn the aubergines over and cook for 2 minutes more.

Meanwhile, whizz the garlic, basil, pine nuts, Parmesan and 4 tablespoons of olive oil in the food processor or blender.

Lift out the aubergines. Put them flesh side up in a grill pan. Spread with the pesto and cook under a fairly hot preheated grill until the pesto just starts to bubble. Overcooking will turn it bitter. Serve with a lightly-dressed salad of lamb's lettuce or spinach.

AVOCADOS

The less you do to an avocado the better. Ignore anyone who tells you that it tastes good when puréed and set with gelatine into a dinky little mousse. Avocados demand gentle treatment; perhaps a dash of lemon juice, some crisp bacon or a dribble of olive, or better still walnut, oil, or at a push grilled with a covering of nutty English cheese.

There are several varieties of this pear-shaped fruit. My favourite is the small Hass avocado, recognisable by its dark knobbly skin, hence its other name, the alligator pear. I find its greeny-yellow flesh has the richest flavour. I also find it the easiest to peel.

To test an avocado for ripeness squeeze the stalk end very gently; if it yields slightly then it is ready. It is unusual to find an avocado ripe, and still in good condition, in the shops. I buy them unripe and put them in a brown paper bag to ripen. Once sliced they should be eaten as soon as possible, though a squeeze of lemon or lime will hold off the inevitable discoloration for an hour or two.

Sprouted Salad with Avocado Dressing

FOR 2 AS A SNACK

1 ripe avocado

225g / 8oz thick natural plain yoghurt

freshly ground black pepper

100g / 4oz sprouted mung beans

50g / 2oz sprouted wheat seeds

225g / 8oz Caerphilly or white Wensleydale cheese

a bunch of watercress

Mash the peeled avocado with a fork in a small bowl until it is smooth. Stir in the yoghurt, then grind over a little black pepper and mix thoroughly. In a salad bowl toss together the beans and seeds. Crumble the cheese into rough pieces and add to the beans. Spoon over the avocado dressing and fold in gently.

Wash the watercress, cutting off any coarse stems. Scatter the watercress on 2 plates and spoon the cheese and sprouted salad on top. Serve with wholemeal bread.

Avocado Sandwich

Avocados are rich and filling and make a much more satisfying snack than you might imagine. This is the sort of sandwich I make for myself at lunchtime when I am working at home. I usually use wholemeal bread, though on the occasion when there was some walnut bread in the house this particular sandwich scaled new heights.

FOR 1 AS A SNACK

2 slices of wholemeal bread
1 ripe avocado, preferably Hass
1 tablespoon wine vinegar
2 tablespoons olive oil or 1 each
  olive and nut oil

salt
1 small onion, sliced into thin
  rings

Toast the bread. Cut the avocado in half, peel it and remove the stone. Cut the flesh into thick slices. Mix the wine vinegar with the oil or oils and add the salt.

Place the slices of avocado on the bread and add the onion rings. Spoon over the dressing.

Avocado with Warm Bacon Vinaigrette

Small, hard-skinned Hass avocados are perfect for this. The bacon is not essential to the dish, but I find its affinity with avocado quite irresistible.

2 rashers of streaky bacon

2 tomatoes, skinned if you have
time, and diced

3 tablespoons red wine vinegar

50ml / 2fl oz olive oil

2 tablespoons Dijon mustard

2 ripe avocados, preferably Hass

Cut the rashers into 2.5-cm (1-inch) pieces and fry till crisp in a shallow pan. Throw in the tomatoes, the vinegar and the olive oil. Stir in the mustard and leave to bubble for 1 minute.

Halve, stone and peel the avocados, place two halves on each plate and slice into thick wedges. Pour over the bubbling dressing and serve hot.

Guacamole

This is a basic *guacamole*. Try adding chopped spring onions, fresh coriander leaves, a skinned chopped tomato, and a crushed clove of garlic. I often eat it with bread rather than the traditional tortilla chips, but it is also good when scooped up in generous quantities by hot and crisp pitta.

MAKES 300ML (½ PINT)

2 large ripe avocados

½ small onion, very finely diced

1 or 2 small fresh green chilli
peppers, very finely chopped

juice of 1 lime

salt

Halve the avocados, remove the stones and peel away the skins. In a bowl, mash the green flesh with a fork. Stir in the onion, chillies and lime juice and season with a little salt.

Another Guacamole

Great debate exists over whether this avocado dip should be smooth and creamy or roughly diced. I think they are both excellent. I use this one if my avocado is on the firm side. It is particularly good with sweet red onions.

FOR 2

1 ripe avocado
2 medium tomatoes
1 clove of garlic, minced
2 fresh chilli peppers, seeds removed, finely diced

juice of ½ lemon
1 tablespoon olive oil
1 tablespoon chopped fresh coriander salt
freshly ground black pepper

Halve and stone the avocado and peel away the skin. Place the avocado on a board and chop it into small dice, then scrape it into a bowl.

Put the tomatoes in boiling water, count to 20, remove them and peel away the skins. (Depending on the ripeness of the tomatoes it may take another go.) Cut in half, remove the seeds with your fingers, then dice the flesh and add to the bowl.

Mix in the garlic, chillies, lemon juice and olive oil and season with the coriander, salt and pepper. Chill for a few minutes, longer if you can, for the flavours to amalgamate.

BEANS AND PEAS

I could not have had a more convincing introduction to green beans. As a child I was sent to pick runner beans from the local farm. Weaving my way in and out of the lush leaves and scarlet flowers is probably my happiest memory, together with the smell of the broken raw beans. Boiled when truly fresh till they lose their opaqueness, and eaten hot and crisp without their usual smothering of butter, is my favourite way with the runner bean.

Broad beans stir some sort of passion in most people, with the majority firmly shunning them. Perhaps those who dislike them so positively have never eaten them peeled of their papery skins. I have great affection for their flavour, smell and their fat fur-lined pods. I like them every way, but never fail to enjoy the flat foetus-shaped pulse with piquant goat's cheese or peeled and beaten to a buttery mush. Great things can come of their pairing with ham. I find the thin Kenya green bean a poor man's runner bean, but millions would disagree.

I prefer peas before they meet hot water or the freezer. Try them freshly shelled with sharp sheep's cheese (try them on the same fork as Harbourne or Beenleigh Blue cheese), tossed with a green salad, or cooked in olive oil and stirred through with warm green lentils. Sugar-snaps, the peas where the pod and peas are both edible can be fun, but nothing can persuade me to eat mangetout. Like the miniature Thai sweetcorns with which they too often share a plate, they have no flavour. I have a theory that they are popular only because they are as convenient as frozen peas and as sweet as sugar.

Green Beans, Poached Eggs and Fancy Leaves

Perhaps my dislike of the dark green French bean, sometimes called the Kenya bean, comes from working in restaurants in the late 1970s, when it was *the* ubiquitous vegetable, and having to top and tail hundreds of the things each night. That said, I do still pick up a pack of them occasionally for a crisp addition to a plate of salad.

Cook some green beans, topped and tailed, in boiling water for 3 or 4 minutes. Fish one out to see if it is ready: it should be bright green and very crisp but must be cooked through. If not, leave them for another minute or two. Drain into a colander and rinse under the tap for a few seconds, not to cool them but just to arrest their cooking.

Toss a few handfuls of fancy salad leaves, one of those mixed bags from the supermarket will do, in a little olive oil and lemon juice. Divide on to individual plates. Place a handful of the crisp, blanched green beans over them and top with a nice, soft, poached egg.

Broad Beans with Ham

This is fast food, but should you have some time on your hands then I suggest that removing the papery skins from the broad beans is time well spent. A dish to eat with a bottle of beer.

FOR 2 AS A MAIN DISH

450g / 1lb shelled broad beans, fresh or frozen	**100g / 4oz bacon, diced**
	salt
1 tablespoon olive oil	**freshly ground black pepper**

Drop the beans into a pan of boiling salted water and blanch for no more than 3 minutes if frozen, 10 if fresh.

Warm the olive oil in a frying pan and fry the diced bacon until it starts to crisp at the edges. Drain the broad beans and add them to the bacon with a light grinding of pepper. Stir well and then cover with a lid. Taste the beans with some of the bacon to see if you need to add salt; you probably will not. Cook for 5 minutes until the beans are absolutely tender.

Broad Beans and Goat's Cheese

Broad beans and goat's cheese are an extraordinarily good combination. It was Claudia Roden who first brought them to my attention in her book, *The Food of Italy*. Ms Roden adds the shelled beans to chopped onion fried in olive oil, then simmers the two with water until very tender, drains them and serves with cheese warmed under the grill.

I have also cooked the beans in boiling water till tender, drained and placed them in a shallow gratin dish. Then I covered them thoroughly with slices of cheese cut from a goat's log and popped them under the grill until the cheese had just melted. Eaten with crisp French bread it made a delightful lunch.

Very soft goat's cheese can be stirred into a bowl of freshly-cooked and still hot broad beans as a side dish for a plate of thinly-sliced ham, such as Italian Parma, Spanish *serrano* or Cumbrian Air Dried.

Possibly best of all is a simple lunch dish for eating outside in the early summer sunshine. Catch the beans when they are very young and tender. Place them on the table, in their furry pods, alongside a small whole goat's cheese in perfect condition. Let everybody shell their own beans, eating them as they go, with slices from the cheese washed down with a bottle of cold, dry white wine.

Good ways to cook Green Beans

* Green beans may be boiled or steamed and tossed with hot new potatoes, butter and lots of chopped fresh parsley. A fine accompaniment to a plate of cold roast beef or a grilled sole

* If your green beans are past their best, try cooking them in vegetable stock spiked with fresh chillies. Top and tail the beans. Cook a chopped spring onion in vegetable oil till it wilts, then add the beans, and a chopped small chilli pepper. Pour in enough vegetable

stock, from powder or cube if necessary, just to cover the beans. Simmer uncovered for 6 or 7 minutes, then drain and serve

* Green beans make a good substitute for the yard-long beans found in Oriental greengrocers. If you have a few basic Chinese ingredients in the house you can knock up this savoury salad very quickly

For 450g / 1lb beans, rinse a tablespoon Chinese black beans thoroughly, then pat dry. Chop them roughly with a large knife, then fry in 2 tablespoons bland-tasting oil such as groundnut or vegetable for about a minute. Add a small knob of peeled fresh root ginger, grated or finely shredded, and stir-fry for a further minute, taking care not to burn the beans. Remove from the heat and stir well with a tablespoon vegetable oil, a tablespoon vinegar (wine or rice if you have it) and half a tablespoon sesame oil. Blanch the beans, topped and tailed, in boiling salted water, then drain and dress with the black bean and ginger dressing. Enough for 4 as a side dish.

Peas with Fettuccine, Basil and Pumpkin Seeds

Pumpkin seeds are not essential here; sunflower seeds or pine nuts are just as good. I have a jar of pumpkin seeds in the kitchen which I constantly pick at, and they often get added to food that will benefit from something nutty and crunchy, such as pasta. Use mint instead of the basil if you like, and use another shaped pasta if you have no *fettuccine*. Be resourceful.

FOR 2 AS A MAIN DISH

50g / 2oz pumpkin seeds
fresh *fettuccine* for two
225g / 8oz shelled peas, fresh or frozen
4 tablespoons olive oil

1 clove of garlic, crushed
8–10 fresh basil leaves, torn to shreds
salt
freshly ground black pepper

Scatter the pumpkin seeds on a baking sheet and cook under a preheated hot grill until lightly brown and fragrant. Cook the pasta, uncovered, in boiling salted water, till tender.

Put the peas and oil in a small pan, add the garlic and the basil, season with a little salt and pepper, and cook over a gentle heat for 10 minutes, or 7 if using frozen.

Drain the pasta and toss in a large bowl with the hot peas and their olive oil, and the toasted pumpkin seeds.

Peas Cooked in Butter with Fresh Garlic

New season's garlic, which is fresh and mild with a soft fragrance, is perfect with peas. Use older cloves if that is what you have, but the dish loses some of its subtlety.

FOR 4 AS AN ACCOMPANIMENT

3 cloves of garlic, the fresher the better
75g / 3 oz butter
450g / 1 lb shelled peas, fresh or frozen

a small bunch of fresh parsley, chopped
6 tablespoons vegetable stock or water
salt

Peel the garlic and slice each clove very thinly. Melt the butter in a medium saucepan and tip in the garlic. Cook over a gentle heat until the garlic has perfumed the butter, about 5–7 minutes. On no account should the garlic colour.

Add the peas, a drop or two of water and the parsley. Pour in the stock or water, add a little salt, and cover with a lid. Simmer fresh peas for 15 minutes and frozen for 6 or 7. Serve alongside grilled fish or meat, with rice or pasta, or best of all, with mashed potato to soak up the buttery, garlicky juices.

Artichoke Hearts and Peas

A hot vegetable dish for serving as an accompaniment or perhaps as a starter. A fresh herb, such as tarragon, basil or mint, would be an interesting addition, but it is quite good as it is.

FOR 4 AS A SIDE DISH OR STARTER

2 tablespoons olive oil
100g / 4oz button mushrooms, the smaller the better
225g / 8oz shelled peas, fresh or frozen
juice of 1 lemon
salt
freshly ground black pepper
8 artichoke hearts, tinned or bottled, drained

Put the oil into a medium-sized saucepan and warm slowly over a moderate heat. Add the mushrooms, the peas and the lemon juice. Simmer for 10 minutes (6 or 7 if the peas are frozen) with a little salt and some freshly ground pepper, covered with a lid.

Cut the artichokes into quarters. Add them to the pan and cook for 3 or 4 minutes, until the artichokes are cooked through.

Warm Pea and Lentil Salad

The marvellous thing about this light warm salad is the sharp contrast of flavour and texture; the nutty lentils with the fresh green peas, the earthy pulses and the sharpness of the lime. Small lentils, such as the French *de Puy*, need no soaking and cook surprisingly quickly.

FOR 4 AS AN ACCOMPANIMENT, OR 2 AS A LIGHT LUNCH WITH CHEESE AND FRUIT TO FOLLOW

175g / 6oz lentils, green or brown
175g / 6oz shelled peas, fresh or frozen
4 tablespoons olive or sunflower oil
4 fresh chives, snipped into short lengths
juice of 1 lime or lemon
salt
freshly ground black pepper

Wash the lentils in a sieve under running water. There is no need to soak them. Place them in a saucepan, cover with water, add a little salt and bring to the boil. Turn the heat down to simmer and cook for 12 minutes. They should be cooked through but still have bite to them.

Tip the peas into a small saucepan with the oil and chives. Cook over a gentle heat for 8–12 minutes, or 5–6 if you are using frozen peas.

Drain the lentils and place them in a serving dish, tip over the hot peas together with their cooking juices. Squeeze the lime or lemon juice over the peas and lentils, grind over a little pepper and salt and serve hot.

Peas with Olive Oil and Mint

Gentle cooking, in olive oil rather than water, with salt, fresh mint and an onion gives a much more interesting result than just throwing peas into a pan of water. Use them as an accompaniment or toss with cooked pasta.

FOR 2 AS AN ACCOMPANIMENT

4 tablespoons olive oil
225g / 8 oz shelled peas, fresh
   or frozen

1 small onion, sliced into
   paper-thin rings
2 springs of fresh mint
salt

Pour the oil into a medium saucepan, tip in the peas, the finely-sliced onion and the mint. Add the salt and 1 tablespoon water and cover with a lid. Bring to the boil, then turn down the heat and simmer over a gentle heat for 10 minutes if the peas are fresh, or 6 or 7 if frozen. Shake the pan occasionally, then serve.

GREENS

The Cabbage Family

Once the most dreaded word in a child's vocabulary, 'greens' has a new hopeful ring to it. Perhaps this will have the side effect of inducing more of us to eat them up. Cabbage has been beneficially linked to reducing risk of cancer. Broccoli is particularly well blessed with minerals and vitamins. Spinach is a splendid source of iron, though best assimilated when eaten with a partner rich in vitamin C, such as a squeeze of orange.

Brussels sprouts, cabbage, broccoli and cauliflower are all brassicas, a group of vegetables linked by their colour and strident, sometimes coarse, flavour. Textures vary from the glass-like hard white cabbage to tough and frilly kale, colours from mauve-green Drumhead cabbage to the soft pastels of the bizarre Romanesco, which resembles a fairy-tale castle.

Hard, round white cabbages provide a welcome crunch in winter salads. Shred them finely and match them with something fruity, like huge juicy raisins, black grapes or slices of tangerine or grapefruit. They keep for several days in the bottom of the fridge, but like any vegetable, will leach vitamins and minerals during storage. Avoid buying any with a yellow tinge, which indicates age and bitterness.

Pork, in the form of bacon or sausage, is a happy match with all of the cabbage family. A stir-fry of shredded dark green Savoy cabbage with garlic and smoked bacon is frugal and comforting. Anchovies work well with both broccoli and spring greens, especially when chopped into a garlicky dressing. Mustard, either in a creamy binding for shredded Brussels sprouts or whisked into a vinaigrette dressing for coleslaw, has an affinity with both the greens and their porky partners.

Spinach

Interest in leafy green vegetables such as spinach has blossomed since we learned how to cook it (briefly), and Popeye with his pipe and muscles was exposed as the antithesis of the modern man. Spinach needs virtually no water at all. Wash the leaves, even if you have bought them ready-washed, but do not shake them dry. Drop them into a pan, slam on the lid and cook over a medium heat till they wilt. They will be ready in 2 or 3 minutes, maybe less if the leaves are young. Boil the tenderest spinach leaves in water and you will end up with slime.

Many dislike the effect spinach has on the teeth, as if a layer of it has dissolved on your enamel; you can limit this by cooking large leaves as above, then draining and tossing them in butter or oil. When buying spinach check the leaves carefully for any sign of sliminess, as they rot easily. Avoid very large leaves, which are inclined to be tough. Tiny gentle-flavoured leaves are perfect for a salad.

Orientals

If you have ready access to Oriental greens such as tiny-leaved Chinese water spinach, yellow-blossomed flowering cabbage and stubby crisp-stalked *pak choi* use them in much the same way as spinach. They are tender and need brief cooking only, especially the mildly hot, floppy-leaved mustard cabbage. The crisp and refreshing pale green and white Chinese leaves store well, and can be sliced in much the same way as an iceberg lettuce for stuffing pittas and sandwiches.

White Cabbage with Orange and Sesame

An idea inspired by the late food writer, Jeremy Round.

FOR 4 AS AN ACCOMPANIMENT

3 tablespoons vegetable oil

900g / 2lb crisp white cabbage, finely shredded as if for coleslaw

freshly-grated nutmeg

finely-grated zest of 1 orange

1 tablespoon sesame oil

Heat the vegetable oil in a large saucepan until it starts to simmer. Tip in the cabbage and cook in the hot oil, stirring and tossing to move it around the pan, for 4 or 5 minutes, until it has started to turn golden in parts but is still crunchy.

Grate a little nutmeg over the cabbage, then stir in the orange zest. Tip into a warm serving dish and drizzle over the oil.

Rumbledethumps

The name of this Scottish way with mashed potatoes and cabbage was what first tempted me to try this traditional dish, which is known as Colcannon in Ireland. In her book, *Scottish Cookery*, Catherine Brown tells us that the name is derived from rumble, meaning to mix, and thump, to bash together. Whatever, this is good food of the first order.

FOR 4 AS A PRINCIPAL DISH

450g / 1lb green cabbage	salt
50g / 2oz butter	freshly ground black pepper
1 medium onion, finely chopped	extra butter
450g / 1lb cooked potatoes, mashed	

Wash the cabbage and shred it finely. Throw it in a pan with a little water and cook it, covered, for a couple of minutes till tender.

Melt the butter in a large saucepan and cook the onion until soft, about 5–7 minutes. Add the cooked mashed potatoes, the cabbage, drained of any water, salt and pepper and mix well. Put into a warm serving dish and stir in a few knobs of extra butter. Eat hot.

Cabbage with Black Beans

Arriving home one cold February evening I scanned the previous week's papers for something interesting to cook. Michael Bateman, who writes the cookery column in the *Independent on Sunday*, had given a recipe for spinach with black-eyed beans. Rummaging in the fridge I failed to come up with the required spinach, but did find half a small dark green cabbage. Here is my version of his good idea.

FOR 1 AS A COMFORTING, SOLITARY SUPPER

50g / 2oz black-eyed beans
4 tablespoons olive oil
1 bay leaf (optional)
1 small onion, quite finely
  shredded

200g / 7oz dark cabbage, such
  as Savoy, shredded
salt
freshly ground black pepper

Throw the beans in a pot with water to cover, a tablespoon of the oil and a bay leaf if you have one. Salt and cook the beans at a steady boil for half an hour. If you cannot wait that long, open a tin of black-eyed beans, drain and rinse them well. Heat them up in a spoonful of the olive oil.

Cook the onion slowly for about 10–15 minutes in the remaining oil; it should caramelise slightly. Throw in the cabbage, cook for a minute or two, then drain the beans and add them to the cabbage and onion. Season with a little salt and pepper.

Bubble and Squeak

This dish, where cabbage greens are mashed with potatoes then fried, is not fast food. But if it is made with yesterday's leftover cooked potatoes and cabbage, then it is. I have eaten this delightfully buttery and frugal food made from freshly-prepared ingredients but, more often, made from leftovers. They both taste just as good.

The potatoes, whether mashed or not, have probably hardened. You will need to soften them, and you might as well do it in butter. Melt plenty of butter in a pan over a low to medium heat, say about 50g / 2oz to a small pudding basin full of potato. Add the potato and let it warm in the butter. Mash it, and not too finely, with a potato masher or fork. Chop the cooked cabbage into pieces roughly 2.5cm

(1 inch) square. There should be, I think, always more cabbage than potato, but in any case at least an equal amount.

Stir the cabbage, which can also be kale or even spinach, into the potato. Season it well with plenty of salt and pepper. Melt enough butter, or better still, dripping, to cover the bottom of a frying pan. Pile in the cabbage mixture and squash it down flat with a palette knife. Turn the heat to low and cook until the bottom has crisped and browned in the butter. If you wish, turn the whole thing over in the pan to brown the other side. I often don't bother, and instead just tip it out on to a warm serving plate.

Traditionally, Bubble and Squeak was served as an accompaniment to sliced cold beef. I think it deserves to be eaten as a main dish in its own right. It is, I concede, improved immeasurably by being surrounded with a pool of hot gravy.

Stir-fried Cabbage

FOR 2 AS A PRINCIPAL DISH

450g / 1lb green cabbage
2 tablespoons oil, vegetable or peanut

2 cloves of garlic, finely sliced
½ teaspoon salt

Remove any tough stalks from the cabbage. Roll the cabbage leaves into tight rolls, then shred them finely with a large knife.

Heat a large frying pan or wok over a high heat until very hot, pour in the oil and the garlic. Fry, stirring constantly for no longer than 30 seconds. Add the salt and the shredded cabbage and cook, stirring and tossing the cabbage in the hot oil, for 3 minutes until the cabbage is wilted but still crisp and with a bright colour. Tip on to a warm serving dish.

Savoy Cabbage and Bacon

Cabbage and smoked meat are a wonderful combination and, of course, all cabbages, spring greens and sprout tops will work here too. The carrots are a sweet addition and not essential, but their bright colour adds a bit of life to this otherwise dark dish. I will happily eat this as a main dish, though it makes a good side dish too. Make sure to drizzle any bacon fat and cooking juices from the pan over the cabbage as you serve it. If there is more than one of you eating, then you'll need a very large pan or a wok.

FOR 1 AS A MAIN DISH OR 2 AS AN ACCOMPANIMENT

2 cloves of garlic, peeled
2 medium carrots, scrubbed
100g / 4oz smoked fatty bacon, rashers or in the piece
1 teaspoon caraway seeds

450g / 1lb Savoy cabbage leaves, washed
salt
freshly ground black pepper

Slice the garlic finely and cut the carrots into matchstick-size strips. Cut the bacon into dice about 1cm / ½ inch square. Shred the cabbage leaves finely with a large knife.

Cook the bacon in a large frying pan until it starts to brown. Add the garlic, carrots and cabbage to the bacon and toss the vegetables in the bacon fat over a medium heat. Cook until the carrots are tender but still have some crunch to them, about 5 minutes. Sprinkle over a few caraway seeds, about a teaspoonful, then season with salt and pepper.

Recycled Greens

Many a mini feast has been made from the pathetic leftovers lurking in the fridge. Next time you open the fridge door to be greeted by little more than some leftover greens and a cup of juices from yesterday's roast, consider this:

* Heat up the juices in a wide pan, adding a few glugs of wine or some stock or water if they are very concentrated. As they come to the boil, stir in a teaspoon arrowroot mixed with a tablespoon water. When the mixture starts to thicken put in the leftover greens, roughly chopped, and toss them in the meat juices. Eat as soon as the greens are warmed through. Soak up any of the juices that remain on your plate with bread

* Shred half a small, tight cabbage. Chop an apple, without bothering to peel it, into rough cubes, discarding the core. Melt some butter in a shallow pan, put in the shredded cabbage and chopped apples, some salt and freshly ground pepper and cook over a medium heat, covered with a lid, until the cabbage has softened. (About 10 or 12 minutes depending on how finely you shredded the cabbage.) When the cabbage is tender but still crisp, stir in a small tub of thick yoghurt, the Greek sort, or some soured cream. Grind over a little nutmeg if you have some around, then serve with proper pork sausages or, better still, black pudding

Spring Greens and Anchovies on Garlic Toast

FOR 2 AS A HEARTY SNACK

450g / 1lb spring greens or purple sprouting broccoli
100ml / 4fl oz extra virgin olive oil
2 plump cloves of garlic, thinly sliced

12 anchovy fillets, rinsed and patted dry
salt
freshly ground black pepper

FOR THE TOAST:

4 slices from a crusty, chewy white loaf
1 clove of garlic

Remove and discard any tough stalks from the greens and then cook for 2 minutes in a large pot of boiling salted water. Drain.

Pour half the olive oil into a large frying pan and, over a medium heat, cook the thin slices of garlic and 4 of the anchovy fillets for 2 minutes. Add the greens and some salt and pepper. Be enthusiastic with the pepper.

Toss the greens around in the oil until they are warmed through. Meanwhile, toast the bread, under the grill or preferably in the oven if it is on. Cut the garlic clove in half and rub the toast with the cut side.

Put the toast, which should now really be called *bruschetta*, on plates and divide the spring greens and anchovies over them. Dribble over the remaining olive oil and add the rest of the anchovy fillets.

Spinach with Blue Cheese and Pasta

Any soft blue-veined cheese will be right for this. There is little point in using a great cheese, such as Gorgonzola or Irish Cashel Blue, unless you have some to use up. A Dolcelatte or blue Brie is quite adequate. I like to follow this rich and almost instant dish with a plate of salad leaves to mop up the cheesy sauce, lamb's lettuce if I happen to have some, or just some floppy-leaved lettuce.

ENOUGH FOR 2 AS A MAIN DISH WITH SALAD TO FOLLOW

275g / 10oz fresh pasta, any curled or ribbon shape

2 double handfuls of spinach leaves, washed and torn up

300ml / ½ pint single cream

175g / 6oz soft, blue cheese, cut into cubes

salt

freshly ground black pepper

Cook the pasta, uncovered, in salted, boiling water till *al dente*. Put the spinach, still wet from washing, in a pan over a medium heat. Cover with a lid, and cook till it starts to wilt, a matter of 2 minutes or so. Add the blue cheese and the cream. Cook over a gentle heat until the cheese melts into the cream. Taste it and then season accordingly, remembering that some blue cheeses are a little salty.

When the cheese has melted and the spinach is still bright green, drain the pasta and fold it into the sauce. Eat hot.

Other ways to cook Spinach

* Spinach can be hot and ready to eat in 2 minutes. Dunk the leaves into deep cold water. Lift out the spinach and, without shaking off any water, drop it into a large pan set over a medium heat. Cook, covered with a lid, for a couple of minutes, shaking the pan now and again. The wrinkly, deep green leaves will cook in their own steam. Pour over some smart olive oil, and perhaps a hefty squeeze of lemon juice, or smother with butter

* Spinach salad is one of the most satisfying leaf-based salads I know. The young and tender pale green leaves are fine enough eaten whole, thin stalks included. The larger, older ones should not be dismissed, and should be just torn or shredded finely

Try a simple dressing of natural plain yoghurt beaten with a crushed garlic clove and a fairly generous addition of salt and freshly ground pepper. Lemon juice and walnut oil is a splendid dressing too, particularly if you can throw in a handful of shelled walnuts, toasted under the grill till fragrant, and a few halved black grapes.

Bacon, diced and cooked in its own fat till crisp, can be zapped over a bowl of shredded dark-leaved spinach. Turn it into a complete meal by tossing with haricot or black-eyed beans, either freshly cooked, or canned ones which have been warmed through in the bacon fat.

Brussels Sprouts

Brussels sprouts have never grabbed me. I find their flavour coarse and difficult to marry with other ingredients. Retrieved from boiling water 1 minute too soon and they are hard as bullets, 1 minute too late and they are little balls of pungent yellow slush. They also smell disgusting.

But Brussels sprouts *can* be good. The trick is to keep them well away from boiling water. Try them stir-fried with bacon or in a salad with a mustard dressing. I have also enjoyed them shredded finely and deep-fried – sprinkled with salt and a little sugar, they distinctly resemble the so-called seaweed of Chinese restaurant fame.

Choose the smallest sprouts you can find, preferably no bigger than large marbles. Real whoppers are most likely to be bitter. Romanticism it may be, but I really cannot look at a sprout until the first frosts have appeared – year-round Brussels I can live without.

Brussels Sprouts in a Creamy Mustard Dressing

Small sprouts, when they are nutty and new, can be shredded and dressed with a mixture of nut oil and lemon juice. Or you can turn them into a more substantial affair with some soured cream spiked with mustard. They then make a nice lunch with a lump of Stilton or very mature Cheddar and a glass of apple juice or cider.

FOR 4 AS A SIDE SALAD
Choose 225g / 8oz young, tight little sprouts. Shred them with a large sharp knife, or push them through the food processor armed with the shredding disc.

Make a mustardy, creamy dressing by stirring together 1 tablespoon white wine vinegar, a good pinch of salt, 2 tablespoons Dijon mustard and 4 heaped tablespoons soured cream in a bowl. With a fork or a small whisk, beat in at least 3 tablespoons oil. This can be olive or a mixture of olive and a nut oil. Toss the shredded sprouts in the dressing and serve.

Brussels Sprouts and Bacon

This is the best way of cooking sprouts I know of.

FOR 2, OR 4 AS A SIDE DISH WITH SAUSAGES OR FRIED EGGS
Heat 2 tablespoons dripping or butter in a large, shallow pan. When it is warm add 75g / 3oz bacon (pancetta, the Italian streaky bacon has a deeper flavour than most), cut into small dice.

Shred 450g / 1lb Brussels sprouts. This can be done in minutes with a sharp knife or in seconds with the slicing disc of the food processor.

When the bacon has crisped throw in the shredded sprouts. Salt and pepper them. Fry the shredded sprouts till slightly golden in parts, about 3 or 4 minutes.

The sprouts are ready to eat when they have turned slightly golden brown here and there and are thoroughly coated with the bacon juices and dripping or butter. Eat with a glass or two of cold beer.

Broccoli with Bagna Cauda

Anchovies, those salty little fillets, and olive oil, a light and fruity one, seem to have an affinity with broccoli. A simple lunch can be made from little more than a tin of anchovies, a head of garlic and some olive oil, simmered and served as a hot dipping sauce for broccoli. *Bagna Cauda* (hot bath), for that is what it is called, is a classic sauce from Piedmont, and as old as the hills. I tend to blanch the broccoli in boiling water, though many would eat it raw. Don't forget some crusty bread and a bottle of red wine, as rough as you like.

FOR 4 AS A LIGHT LUNCH

75g / 3oz butter
8 cloves of garlic, crushed
12 anchovy fillets, rinsed and
  dried

250ml / 8fl oz olive oil
450g / 1lb broccoli

Melt the butter in a small saucepan. Add the garlic and cook over a gentle heat for 2–3 minutes. It must not brown and turn bitter. Add the anchovies, which will virtually dissolve with a bit of stirring. Pour in the olive oil, slowly, stirring all the time. Simmer, not boil, for 10 minutes. Blanch the broccoli in boiling water for a couple of minutes; keep it crisp. Serve the sauce hot, in a bowl, stirring it up with the drained sprigs of broccoli each time you dip them in. Soak up the remaining sauce with hunks of bread.

Good ways to cook Broccoli

* Cook stalks and florets of broccoli in boiling salted water till tender but crisp, about 3 or 4 minutes. Drain and put on a serving dish. Drizzle with extra virgin olive oil while still warm. Serve with wedges of lemon to squeeze over and hot garlic bread

* Cook broccoli florets and stalks in boiling water till tender. They will be ready in 3 or 4 minutes, maybe even less. At any rate, they must be removed while they are still bright and crisp. Quickly cool the broccoli in a colander held under the cold tap for a few minutes. Set a bowl of garlic mayonnaise from a jar in the centre of a large plate. Surround the bowl with the blanched broccoli and leave in the middle of the table for everyone to help themselves

* Steam or boil some broccoli till tender, about 3 or 4 minutes. Keep it crisp and brilliant green. Heat a couple of tablespoons best olive oil in a shallow pan. Cut a few bottled or tinned red pimientos into long strips, toss them gently in the warm oil, with some sliced cloves of garlic, if you like. When they are warm and the garlic pale gold, add the broccoli and some salt and freshly ground pepper. Tip on to plates and scatter over a few rinsed capers – remember, though, what bullies they can be, and that many people don't like them anyway. Eat while warm with crusty bread

MUSHROOMS

Mushrooms are perfect for the cook in a hurry. They cook quickly, especially when quartered or sliced, and have a satisfying meatiness about them.

There is virtually nothing I enjoy more than large flat mushrooms, brushed with olive oil and a squeeze of lemon, then grilled and served with the juices that have collected in the grill pan. I find those huge flat mushrooms, the most mature of all cultivated fungi, as juicy and tender as a piece of steak. I am convinced that the flavour improves after a few days in a brown paper bag in the bottom of the fridge. The more earthy, woodsy or, well, mushroomy, they smell and the blacker the gills then the deeper the flavour.

Open cup mushrooms are probably the most common. Although they are often sliced for cooking and salads, I invariably cut them into quarters so they appear as juicy nuggets. Immature white button mushrooms have little of the sweet earthiness of the larger fungi. They are best tossed with a squeeze of lemon and some chopped fresh parsley and eaten raw. They have the ability to absorb other flavours, such as garlic or herbs, in the way that beancurd does.

I never peel mushrooms, believing that there is much flavour in the skin. If they are covered in little lumps of growing medium, then I wipe it off with a wet thumb. I do not, as some cooks insist, wash mushrooms. Even the freshest fungi soaks up water like a sponge.

Supermarkets have tried offering us all sorts, including the savoury *shiitake* and the soft grey oyster mushroom. They all have a place in the quick cook's repertoire; either in stir-fries, omelettes or risotto. Each has its own characteristic smell and flavour and makes a change from the workaday little brown cups. Mushrooms will all keep for a few days in the fridge. I find the fancier the fungi the faster it rots, so if I have treated myself to a punnet of something unusual then I eat it that day.

Grilled Mushrooms

Two ways to grill large flat mushrooms, the first with olive oil and garlic, the second with purely butter and lemon.

FOR 4

450g / 1lb large flat mushrooms
6 tablespoons olive oil
1 clove of garlic, chopped
1 tablespoon chopped fresh
   parsley

salt
freshly ground black pepper

Wipe the mushrooms and cut any soil from their stalks. Pull out the stalks and cut them in half. Place the caps and stalks on an oiled grill pan and brush with some of the oil. Scatter over the garlic and parsley and season with the salt and pepper. Cook under a hot grill for 5 or 6 minutes, occasionally spooning over a little more oil. Turn the caps and stalks over and grill for a further 3 or 4 minutes. Serve hot.

FOR 2

6 large flat mushrooms
75g / 3oz butter
salt

freshly ground black pepper
½ lemon

Wipe the mushrooms and brush away any soil. Place the mushrooms on a grill pan. Put large lumps of butter all over the mushrooms and season each one with salt and pepper and a good squeeze of lemon. Cook under a preheated grill for 10 minutes, spooning the butter and juices over them from time to time.

Mushrooms on Toast

Resisting the temptation to slice large flat mushrooms, I serve them whole, in all their glory, astride a piece of thick toast to soak up their juices.

2 very large flat mushrooms	**freshly ground black pepper**
butter, softened	**2 thick slices of white bread**
salt	

Brush the mushrooms generously with butter and grill or sauté them till soft and cooked all the way through, about 5–7 minutes. You can test this by removing the stalk and piercing the flesh with the point of a knife; if the juices run out, it is cooked.

Toast the slices of bread on both sides and top each with a mushroom, spooning over the buttery juices.

Mushroom Crostini

A somewhat elegant version of mushrooms on toast where the mushrooms are softened in garlic butter, then piled on to slices of French bread. Be generous with the parsley and pepper.

FOR 3

50g / 2oz butter	**salt**
1 clove of garlic, lightly crushed	**freshly ground black pepper**
450g / 1lb mushrooms, sliced	**12 slices of French bread, 5mm**
2 tablespoons chopped fresh	**(¼ inch) thick**
parsley	

Melt the butter in a small pan. Add the crushed garlic and cook gently until the butter smells sweet and garlicky. Remove the garlic clove before it turns dark brown and bitter, turn up the heat and toss in the mushrooms.

Cook for 4 or 5 minutes, stirring occasionally if the mushrooms stick to the pan, until they soften and soak up the garlic butter. Stir in the parsley and add a little salt and 2 or 3 twists from the peppermill.

While the mushrooms are cooking, toast the slices of bread. Spoon the mushrooms over the toasted bread and eat while hot.

Grilled Herbed Field Mushrooms

FOR 2 AS A STARTER OR LIGHT SUPPER WITH SALAD,
BREAD AND WINE

6 large field mushrooms
a small fistful of parsley and
  mint, chopped
salt

freshly ground black pepper
4 cloves of garlic, finely sliced
1 wineglass of olive oil

Twist out the stalks from the mushrooms and chop them finely. Wipe the mushrooms and lay them, gill side up, in a baking dish. Mix together the herbs and seasonings and stir in the chopped stalks.

Press the thin slices of garlic here and there into the mushroom caps. Scatter over the herb mixture and then pour the olive oil over the lot. Leave for 10 minutes while you heat the grill.

Grill the mushrooms, spooning over the cooking juices, until they are cooked right through, about 5–7 minutes.

Mushrooms with Potatoes and Garlic

If I have some, I use new potatoes, though nothing as good as Jersey ones, for this, but large potatoes cut into small chunks work just as well. I serve it either as an accompaniment or as a substantial *salade tiède* on a pile of salad leaves.

FOR 2 AS A MAIN COURSE SALAD, 4 AS AN ACCOMPANIMENT

450g / 1lb very small potatoes
2 tablespoons dripping
2 rashers of bacon, diced
350g / 12oz mushrooms,
  quartered

2 fat cloves of garlic, crushed
2 tablespoons chopped fresh
  parsley
salt
freshly ground black pepper

Scrub the potatoes and cut them in half. Heat the dripping in a frying pan, then fry the bacon till crisp. Tip in the potatoes and stir well. Cover and cook for 10 minutes on a gentle heat. Add the mushrooms, garlic, and 1 tablespoon of the parsley. Season with the salt and pepper, then cook for 15 minutes, covered, or until the potatoes are tender to the point of a knife. When it is ready, pour in 3 tablespoons boiling water, bring to the boil and scrape up any crusty sediment in the pan. Boil for 1 minute, toss in the remaining spoonful of parsley and serve hot or warm.

Stir-fried Mushrooms

I once went to a series of Chinese cookery demonstrations. Lots of good things came out of it, including the stir-fried courgette recipe on which this dish is based. If your local supermarket or greengrocer stocks the meaty East Asian *shiitake* mushroom variety, use them here; if not, use button or open cup ones instead.

FOR 2 AS A MAIN DISH WITH RICE OR NOODLES

150ml / ¼ pint vegetable oil
450g / 1lb small mushrooms
2 cloves of garlic, chopped and crushed with 1 teaspoon salt

1 tablespoon soy sauce
2 tablespoons oyster sauce
2 tablespoons dry sherry
1 teaspoon sugar

Heat the oil in a frying pan or wok. Drop a tiny mushroom into it; when it starts to sizzle the oil is hot enough. Toss in the mushrooms and move them around with a draining spoon for 2 minutes.

Drain away the hot oil. Sprinkle the garlic salt over the mushrooms, turn over a few times, then add the soy and oyster sauces, sherry and sugar. Reduce the heat and leave the mushrooms to cook for 2 minutes.

Buttered Mushrooms

My interpretation of an idea from Eliza Acton.

FOR 2 AS A SNACK OR LIGHT SUPPER

100g / 4oz butter
225g / 8oz mushrooms, wiped
salt

cayenne pepper
ground mace

Melt the butter in a pan, tip in the mushrooms and cook over a gentle heat, shaking from time to time, until the mushrooms soften and give up some of their juices. Add a little salt and a fine sprinkling of both cayenne and mace. Serve hot with bread or, better still, some reheated mashed potato.

Mushroom Beignets

Antonio Carluccio's delicious little Wild Mushroom Beignets are for those lucky enough to know where to gather chanterelles, boletuses and horns of plenty. For those who make this recipe a good way is to use a mixed bag. Make sure the mushrooms are dry so that they do not exude too much water.

FOR 4

4 eggs
200g / 7oz flour
150ml / ¼ pint milk
salt
freshly ground black pepper
1 small onion, very finely
   chopped

800g / 1¾lb mixed wild
   mushrooms, cut into
   strips
plenty of groundnut or
   sunflower oil for frying

Beat the eggs in a bowl, then stir in the flour and the milk, followed by salt and pepper to taste, to form a thick batter. Now add the mushrooms and onion and mix together. Pour about 1cm / ½ inch of oil into a frying pan and bring to frying temperature. Carefully add the mixture, a tablespoon at a time. Fry the beignets gently until brown and crispy on one side, turn, and cook the other side. Serve hot.

Pan-fried Mushrooms with Onion and Cream

A quick and creamy dish to be served on toast or with a little boiled brown rice.

FOR 2 WITH RICE OR ON TOAST

Peel a small onion, or a couple of shallots, and chop finely. Put into a frying pan with a tablespoon vegetable oil and a large knob of butter and fry gently over a medium heat until the onion starts to turn golden.

Cut 450g / 1lb wiped mushrooms, plump white cups if possible, into quarters. Turn up the heat and add the mushrooms to the pan. When the mushrooms have absorbed most of the butter and oil, turn down the heat and season with salt and a few turns of the peppermill. Cook the mushrooms for 3 minutes, shaking the pan from time to time.

Pour in a small carton of double cream and simmer for another couple of minutes before serving.

Mushrooms à la Crème

Another idea for those who like a little cream with their fungi, this time peppered with basil.

Cook 450g / 1lb little mushrooms with a crushed garlic clove in 2 tablespoons olive oil until they have absorbed most of the oil, about 7–10 minutes. Season with a shake or two of salt, add the leaves of a healthy branch of fresh basil, torn into small pieces, and stir in 300ml / ½ pint single cream. Cook over a gentle flame for a couple of minutes, then serve very hot, with toast.

Funghi Ripieni

The Italian way of stuffing large mushroom caps with their chopped stalks and breadcrumbs is repeated here with the addition of anchovies and olives.

FOR 4

12 large mushrooms, wiped
1 onion, chopped
1 clove of garlic, crushed
olive oil
3 anchovy fillets, drained and chopped
1 tablespoon chopped green olives

2 tablespoons chopped fresh parsley
salt
freshly ground black pepper
6 tablespoons soft fresh breadcrumbs
1 egg, beaten

Remove the mushroom stalks and chop. Cook the onion and garlic in 2 tablespoons olive oil until the onion softens, then add the chopped mushroom stalks. Cook over a gentle heat for 5 minutes, and then add the chopped anchovies and the olives. Cook for 2 minutes more and stir in the parsley. Season to taste. Mix with half the breadcrumbs and bind the mixture with the beaten egg.

Fill the mushrooms with the anchovy and olive stuffing and place them in a lightly oiled ovenproof dish. Scatter over the rest of the breadcrumbs and a little olive oil, cover with foil and bake in a preheated oven, 200°C/400°F (gas mark 6), for 10–15 minutes. Remove the foil and bake for a further 5 minutes to crisp the stuffing.

Mushroom Rolls

Hollowed-out rolls, crisped in the oven and filled with a creamed mushroom mixture, are the idea of Elizabeth Raffald and appear in her 1782 edition of *The Experienced English Housekeeper*. The lemon juice is an important addition, averting the mixture from being too cloying.

4 rolls, white or brown	250ml / 8fl oz double cream
50g / 2oz butter	a good squeeze of lemon juice
1 small onion, chopped	salt
275g / 10oz mushrooms, sliced	freshly ground black pepper

Slice the tops from each of the rolls with a bread knife and hollow out half the bread. Melt the butter in a small pan and brush a little of it inside the rolls and on the cut side of the lids. Put them in a preheated oven, 200°C/400°F (gas mark 6), for about 7–10 minutes until crisp.

Meanwhile, fry the onion in the rest of the butter in the pan for about 5 minutes until soft, then add the mushrooms and cook for 4–5 minutes, until they start to soften. Pour in the cream and allow to bubble for a couple of minutes; the mixture will start to thicken. Season with the lemon juice and the salt and pepper.

Remove the rolls from the oven and spoon in the creamed mushroom filling. Cover with the lids and serve immediately.

Mushroom Soup

The simplest of mushroom soup recipes, this comforting autumnal dish is based on Mrs C. F. Leyel and Miss Olga Hartley's *The Gentle Art of Cookery* (1925). You can use it as a base to which you can add a glass of white wine, some chopped fresh parsley or a grating of coriander. Serve with chunks of bread for dunking.

FOR 6

50g / 2oz butter	250ml / 8fl oz double cream
225g / 8oz mushrooms, minced	250ml / 8fl oz milk
1 small onion, finely chopped	freshly grated nutmeg
1 clove of garlic, chopped	salt
2 tablespoons flour	freshly ground black pepper
900ml / 1½ pints chicken or	
vegetable stock	

Melt the butter in a saucepan and sweat the mushrooms, onion and garlic. When the onion becomes translucent, stir in the flour and cook for 2 minutes to cook out thoroughly the raw taste of the flour, which would show in a soup of this sort. Pour in the stock and simmer gently for 10 minutes.

Tip the soup into a food processor or blender, and whizz with the cream and milk and a grating of nutmeg until fairly smooth. Correct the seasoning and eat with crusty bread.

Dried Mushroom Broth

There have been times when I have had little more in the storecupboard than half a packet of those expensive dried mushrooms bought for a special occasion then carefully stored and forgotten. They make a richly scented and satisfying broth when cooked with some stock and a drop or two of sherry.

FOR 4

25g / 1oz dried ceps or other dried mushrooms

1.1 litres / 2 pints vegetable or chicken stock

bay leaf, thyme, parsley and rosemary

3 tablespoons sherry, or better still, Madeira

salt

freshly ground black pepper

Rinse the mushrooms and place in a bowl. Warm the stock and pour over the mushrooms. Leave the mushrooms for 10 minutes to reconstitute and then pour the stock and mushrooms into a saucepan, making sure that none of the grit lurking at the bottom of the bowl gets in.

Simmer the broth with the herbs for 25 minutes. Strain the broth and discard the mushrooms. Tip in the sherry or Madeira, season carefully, and serve steaming hot.

Suggestions

* In her book *The Cook's Garden*, Lynda Brown fills mushroom caps with a purée of cooked parsnips and covers that with thin shavings of Cheddar or Gruyère. Brushed with olive oil and baked for 20 minutes in a hot oven they make an earthy-tasting snack

* Edouard de Pomiane cooks tinned ceps by first adding 3 shallots and a clove of minced garlic to some olive oil in a frying pan. He heats them for 6–7 minutes and sprinkles them with salt, pepper and chopped fresh parsley

* Margaret Costa's Club Mushroom Breakfast:
  4 bacon rashers, 225g / 8oz mushrooms, 225g / 8oz soft roes, about 25g / 1oz butter, 4 slices of toast, salt and pepper. Fry the bacon and mushrooms in one pan. Fry the roes in the butter in another. When all are cooked, cover the slices of toast with bacon, then the roes and, lastly, pile on the mushrooms. Season well

* Garlic purée, either home-made or from a bottle (check, though, that it contains no sugar), makes a good accompaniment for grilled or baked mushrooms

PEPPERS

This indigestible vegetable has become a great favourite of mine since I discovered that it has rather more magic when roasted or grilled than it does sliced raw and tossed into a salad. The sweetness of a grilled pepper, skinned and anointed with rich sherry or balsamic vinegar, is a delicacy to remind of sunny summer lunches in the garden. The following recipes work with red or yellow varieties; somehow the hard green pepper fails to exude the same rich juices when heated.

Grilled Red Peppers and Black Olive Conchiglie

Conchiglie is shell-shaped pasta. I use it more than any other because its clever shape so neatly holds a good dollop of sauce, cream or olive oil. You could, of course, blanch the peppers in boiling water instead of grilling them, but you would be missing the sweet smoky juices released by grilling.

FOR 2 AS A MAIN COURSE

2 large red peppers, halved, cored and seeds and stalk removed
6 tablespoons virgin olive oil
2 cloves of garlic, peeled
100g / 4oz dried pasta

4 tablespoons black olive paste
salt
freshly ground black pepper
3 tablespoons grated Parmesan cheese

Put the halved peppers in the grill pan, skin side up, and pour over 4 tablespoons of the oil. Throw in the garlic cloves. Cook under a preheated grill till the skins blister and char, about 7–8 minutes.

Cook the pasta, uncovered, in a pan of boiling salted water till *al dente*, about 11 minutes. Drain. Stir in the olive paste.

Place the peppers carefully in an ovenproof dish. Pile the olive pasta into the grilled pepper shells. Pour the cooking juices with the grilled garlic into the food processor or blender with the remaining oil. Whizz. Taste the garlic dressing, then add salt and pepper. Pour the dressing over the pasta and peppers, scatter with Parmesan cheese and place under a preheated grill till it turns golden and crisp.

Grilled Peppers with Balsamic Vinegar and Basil

There is an exciting mixture of flavours here. The whole point of grilling the peppers is to release their sweet, smoky juices and exploit them in the warm dressing with the deep sweet-sour richness of balsamic vinegar. The resulting sweetness is then balanced by the basil and lemon.

FOR 2

2 medium red peppers
1 aubergine, weighing about 225g / 8oz
1 medium onion, peeled
4 bushy sprigs of fresh thyme
2 plump cloves of garlic, crushed
175ml / 6fl oz extra virgin olive oil
salt
freshly ground black pepper
2 large plum tomatoes, halved and cut into thick slices
1 tablespoon balsamic vinegar
juice ½ lemon
a small handful of fresh basil leaves, shredded

Cut the peppers in half through the stalk, then pull out and discard anything that isn't red. Put the halves in a grill pan, on the base rather than the wire mesh, with their cut sides down. Halve the aubergine lengthways, cut each half into 5mm / ¼ inch thick slices and put in a bowl.

Cut the onion horizontally in slices no thicker than pound coins. Separate the rings and add them to the aubergine. Strip the leaves from the thyme branches, add to the onion and aubergine with the garlic and pour over the olive oil. Grind over a little black pepper and salt, then toss together the vegetables and thyme with a spoon making sure they are all covered with oil.

Scatter them over the rest of the grill pan and cook under a preheated grill, about 7.5–10cm / 3–4 inches from the heat. When the pepper skins start to blacken, turn them over. Stir the aubergine mixture around as it starts to brown. After 15 minutes' cooking, add the tomatoes. Continue grilling until the aubergines and onion are tender, and the peppers have lightly charred skins and soft, but far from collapsing, flesh – about a further 10–12 minutes.

Remove the pan from the grill and carefully spoon out the pan juices into the bowl in which you mixed the vegetables. Whisk in the balsamic vinegar, lemon juice and shredded basil with a fork. Taste for seasoning; you may need a bit more salt and pepper. Place the peppers on warm plates and stuff with the grilled vegetables. Spoon over the warm dressing and eat straight away. Eat with crusty bread to mop up the juices.

POTATOES

Potatoes are one of our most loved foods. Almost everyone I have met seems to have a soft spot for them cooked in one way or another; fluffy baked potatoes oozing with butter, diminutive nutty new ones for dipping into soured cream or thick fingers of chips, eaten from newspaper.

As a crop the potato produces more food per acre than almost anything else. As a food it is cheap and plentiful and immensely satisfying. I am always happy to come home to a baked potato smothered in butter or a warm salad of waxy new potatoes with onion, wine vinegar and lots of fresh parsley.

The potato is far more nutritious than is often imagined. It is high in complex carbohydrate and fibre and is an important source of vitamin C and several minerals. When steamed, boiled or baked it is low in calories, only becoming a worry to people who care about such things when it is fried. I rarely peel potatoes, so saving fibre, vitamins and time. Most of the vitamins are stored just underneath the skin. New potatoes may have flaky skins that need nothing more than a gentle wipe, larger 'old' potatoes usually need a good scrub.

There are ways to cook potatoes for the short-of-time. Tiny potatoes, from Jersey or Cyprus, can be as good as a feast when piled high and steaming and served with a bowl of thick *crème fraîche*. New potatoes can be used as a substantial addition to a salad of rocket or spinach and Taleggio or Cantal cheeses.

Cubes of potato can be pan-fried with butter and garlic for an accompaniment to grilled chicken or fish. Or they can be made into chips for a chip butty. Baked potatoes take a good hour to cook, but I still think of them as fast food. I find their ability to look after themselves while baking a boon. I wipe a couple of large potatoes, dump them in the oven, then forget about them till 10 minutes before they should be ready when I make a filling.

To say I have a deep affection for mashed potato is something of an understatement. It is almost an addiction. Gloriously buttery mash fits into this book not just because it can be on the table within 20 minutes or so, but because it comes under the heading of comfort food along with porridge and risotto.

It is important to find the right potato for the job. A firm waxy-fleshed variety is perfect for a salad but will turn to glue if puréed for mash. Similarly, a floury variety for baking will crumble to nothing if you try to toss it in a vinaigrette dressing. It is sad to relate that there are hundreds of different varieties of potato and yet only four or five in the shops. Fancy varieties such as the long and knobbly Pink Fir Apple or the pale yellow-fleshed Charlotte are ideal for salads and can be found in some supermarkets. What I would like to see more of are varieties of maincrop potatoes, clearly marked, rather than the anonymous piles of potatoes at the greengrocers.

The Baked Potato

A plump baked potato with a crisp skin must be on everyone's list of comfort food. On a cold, rainy night the smell of a potato baking must be one of the most appetising of all. Baked potatoes fit into this collection of fast food recipes because of the absurdly small amount of work you need to do to them to make a meal. They take a good hour to cook, but it is an unattended hour, leaving you free to do other things. There is hardly a meal on earth that is less hassle than a baked potato and salad.

The best potatoes for baking are the big floury ones. I have had some success with smaller ones but they lack the majesty of a real whopper. King Edward are very fine, if there are none around try the common Maris Piper. I am not convinced that the red-skinned Desirée crisp up well, though some people swear by them.

I have exploded many baked potatoes in my time. Sometimes I have opened the oven door to find that just the skins remain, while the flesh has pebble-dashed the inside of my oven. The best way to avoid such potato bombs is to push a metal skewer straight through the middle. This will also cut down the cooking time as the heat travels along the skewer. Failing that, you can prick them all over with a fork to let out the steam.

The potato is done when the skewer pulls out easily and the skin is crisp. The best way to achieve perfection is by ensuring the potatoes are dry and the oven is set to at least 200°C/400°F (gas mark 6). A large potato will take about an hour. When it is cooked cut a cross in the centre and push hard with the fingertips of both hands. The quicker the steam leaves the potato the better the chance of the flesh turning to a lovely fluffy pile.

* Some of the potatoes sold in plastic bags or clingfilm are very dull. Take a look at the organic offerings. Although they take longer to scrub, as they are usually caked in soil, your hard work may be rewarded by a better flavour

* I have a notion that cold, sweet, unsalted butter hard from the fridge is nicer than soft room-temperature stuff on a baked potato, but it may, of course, just be my imagination

* A delicious result can be obtained by slicing the potatoes through the horizon, scoring the flesh in lattice fashion, then baking as normal. This method also cuts the cooking time by a third

* When the potato is cooked, try slicing off a 'lid' and scooping out the flesh. Mash it with butter or natural plain yoghurt and anything else you fancy, then stuff it all back into the potato shell. Sit the lid on top if you must

* Sweet potatoes are good too. Bake them in the usual way, putting them on a tray to catch the drips of caramelising sugar that leak from the sweet orange flesh. They need little in the way of adornment; butter and freshly ground black pepper are the most flattering, I think

Good things to top a Baked Potato

* Cold butter straight from the fridge

* *Fromage frais*

* Garlic cream cheese, such as Boursin

* Grated Cheddar or Gruyère cheese with chopped fresh flat-leaf parsley and walnuts

* A spoonful of tapenade

* Garlic mayonnaise

* Crushed goat's cheese and shredded baby spinach leaves

* Chicken or duck livers, sautéed in butter and sprinkled with balsamic vinegar

* Thinly-sliced Mozzarella and chopped fresh oregano

* Bottled roast peppers, grilled till sweet and slightly charred, then chopped and drizzled with warm extra virgin olive oil and black pepper

* Eat the flesh from the potato then pile a leafy, garlicky salad into the hollow skins

* Mash the flesh with pesto sauce from a bottle and scatter over a little grated Parmesan cheese; toast under the grill till hot

* Sliced avocado and toasted flaked almonds

* Sliced onions, sautéed in butter till sweet and golden

* Streaky bacon cooked till crisp then crumbled with toasted pumpkin seeds and melted butter

Mash

I love mashed potatoes above anything else edible. I am not sure that you get any brownie points for admitting you are happier eating a plate of mashed potatoes than some blue-eyed boy-wonder's latest gastronomic creation. But mashed potatoes are my comfort food, one that I turn to when I feel the world is against me.

I mash them with butter or with cream and olive oil in the modern French manner, depending on my mood. Sometimes I melt grated cheese into them. Occasionally I leave some of them to go cold, then fry them for breakfast in butter till crisp and very hot. Comfort food indeed.

ENOUGH FOR 2, AS A SIDE DISH

450g / 1lb potatoes, peeled,
    King Edward or Maris Piper
4 tablespoons double cream

2 tablespoons olive oil
salt
freshly ground black pepper

Cut the potatoes into even-sized pieces. Simmer them in salted water until they are tender, about 20 minutes, drain well and mash with a potato masher. Do not attempt to use the food processor, you will end up with glue. Warm the cream in a small pan, then stir into the mash. Beat in the olive oil, then taste and season with salt and pepper if you want.

Aligot

The most comforting, and to my mind the most delicious, supper of all. This cheesy potato purée will alter in texture as well as flavour depending on which cheese you use. In the Auvergne, where this recipe originates, mild Cantal cheese is used, though any good melting variety will do.

I mention Cheddar in the recipe, but I have had beautifully stringy results with other cheeses, particularly Gruyère and Taleggio. Use the heaviest-bottomed saucepan you have for this. The thick base will prevent the mixture from burning and keep it warm while you eat it from the pot.

SERVES 4

900g / 2lb medium floury potatoes, such as King Edward

50g / 2oz butter

4 tablespoons creamy milk or half cream and milk

1 clove of garlic, crushed

350g / 12oz good melting cheese, Cheddar, Gruyère or similar

salt

freshly ground black pepper

Put the potatoes in cold water and bring them to the boil. Add salt and simmer till tender to the point of a knife, about 20 minutes, depending on the nature of the potatoes. Drain and pull away the skins, then discard them. Mash the potatoes with the butter using a masher, or a food processor if you can be bothered with the washing up.

Return the pan to the heat and beat in the milk and garlic with a wooden spoon. Add the cheese, beating with a wooden spoon all the time, lifting the mixture up from the base of the pan. Taste and season with salt and pepper. The *aligot* will lighten and the cheese will melt into long strands. The mixture is ready when it is shiny and comes away from the sides of the pan. Put the pan on the table and eat the *aligot* from it with forks.

Grilled Potatoes

I cook these potatoes quite often, sometimes tossing them with chopped fresh thyme leaves before grilling. I have also eaten them for supper, lubricated with yoghurt, say 225g / 8oz, which I have stirred briefly into 2 crushed cloves of garlic, 2 teaspoons grated fresh root ginger and ½ teaspoon cayenne pepper, fried till fragrant in a little olive oil. I stir in a tablespoon chopped coriander leaves just before the sauce meets the potatoes.

2 medium potatoes, such as
  Maris Piper or King Edward
salt

2 tablespoons walnut or
  groundnut oil
2 small cloves of garlic, crushed
  and mixed with the oil

Slice the potatoes 5mm / ¼ inch thick lengthways. There will be about 4 slices per potato. Put the slices into cold water and bring them to the boil. Add salt and turn the heat down to simmer until they are tender to the point of a knife. This will take about 4 minutes.

Drain thoroughly, cut lattice slashes into the surface of each potato slice, and pour over the oil and garlic.

Cook under a preheated grill till crisp and golden, about 10 minutes, then turn and cook for a further 5. Grind salt over the crisp potatoes and eat while still hot.

* For a light supper, lay soft blue cheese such as Gorgonzola over the potatoes while they are hot and return to the grill till just melted. Eat with green salad

Walnut Oil and New Potato Sauté

Patricia Wells is the restaurant critic for *L'Express*, the French news-weekly. She once told me of a dish in her book *Bistro Cooking* where she cooked sliced potatoes in walnut oil. I tried and enjoyed her recipe and have since found it works well with new potatoes, which avoids the peeling and slicing involved with larger potatoes. Her book, a collection of recipes from the chic bistros in Paris, has since become something of a good friend.

FOR 4 AS AN ACCOMPANIMENT

75ml / 3fl oz walnut oil
4 cloves of garlic, unpeeled,
  crushed flat
450g / 1lb new potatoes, wiped
  clean

salt
freshly ground black pepper
2 tablespoons chopped fresh
  parsley

Warm the oil with the crushed garlic cloves in a shallow pan until it is hot, but not smoking. Add the potatoes and sauté them over a gentle medium heat for about 15–20 minutes. Shake the pan from time to time. They are cooked when brown on all sides and tender to the point of a knife.

Season with salt and pepper. Sprinkle the parsley over as you toss them from the pan into a serving dish.

* I have often made supper by tipping the hot potatoes out on to a plate of mixed salad leaves. The sort you buy in a bag from the supermarket, called *Salade Mesclun* in posh shops and French markets. Bread, thin and crisp-crusted baguettes, is good here too

Potatoes with Onions and Olive Oil

I often make this dish with leftover cooked potatoes. Floury potatoes, such as King Edward, will fall apart slightly as you toss them in the olive oil, and somehow the dish is better for it.

FOR 4 AS AN ACCOMPANIMENT

1 kg / 2lb 3oz floury potatoes

4 medium onions, roughly chopped

2 large cloves of garlic, finely chopped

100ml / 4fl oz olive oil

a small bunch of fresh parsley, roughly chopped

salt

freshly ground black pepper

Boil the potatoes in their skins. They are cooked when the point of a knife goes into them easily – about 20 minutes. Drain and cut them up roughly into bite-sized pieces. Keep warm.

In a shallow pan fry the onions with the garlic in the olive oil for about 5–7 minutes, until soft and shiny. Throw in the parsley and add the salt and pepper. Toss the potatoes in the onions and oil and, when bubbling, serve.

Quick Potato Ideas

Fried Potatoes with Garlic and Salt

Peel 2 huge potatoes, or 4 large ones. Dice them into 1-cm / ½-inch cubes. Toss them in a shallow pan with a finger's depth of hot olive oil. Throw in 6 cloves of garlic, flattened with a knife but not peeled. Fry over a medium heat for about 12–15 minutes, till golden, shaking the pan from time to time. Drain on kitchen paper, ditch the garlic, and salt the potato cubes liberally.

New Potatoes, Thyme, Garlic and Cream

Put 450g / 1lb new potatoes on to boil. Meanwhile, crush 3 or 4 sprigs of fresh thyme in your hand, just enough to bruise the leaves, and drop them into 175ml / 6fl oz double cream in a small, shallow pan. Add 3 plump cloves of garlic, flattened but not peeled, and bring to the boil. Simmer for 7–12 minutes, until reduced by one-third. The potatoes should be cooked by now. Drain them, break each one in half and drop into the scented cream. Serve with something grilled, like a red mullet or a chop.

Jersey Feast

In early spring you may spot in smart greengrocers tiny little new potatoes in wooden crates. They are the first Jersey Royals, as opposed to the more pedestrian Jersey Whites. They are recognisable by their flaky skins and kidney shapes. You will be asked to part with a king's ransom for them, but they are worth it. Bring them home, carefully wipe off the sand without tearing the papery skins, and put them into boiling salted water. Cook them till tender, about 10–15 minutes, then drain them and toss with a frugal amount of unsalted butter and a handful of chopped fresh parsley. For the first of the season I am not sure they need any other accompaniment than a glass of wine.

The Chip Butty

I love chip butties. But there are rules.

* The bread should be white and thick sliced. The 'plastic' type is more suitable than real 'baker's bread' because it absorbs the melting butter more readily

* The chips should be fried in dripping, not oil, and sprinkled with salt and malt – yes, I said malt – vinegar

* The sandwich should drip with butter

Good eaten when slightly drunk, and the perfect antidote to the char-grilled-with-balsamic-vinegar-and-shaved-Parmesan school of cookery. And so frightfully common.

Waxy Potato, Anchovy and Parsley Salad

I have a great fondness for potato salads, especially when eaten warm. The best potatoes for salad are the ones that have a waxy, rather than floury texture. Particularly suitable are early season Maris Peer and *Belle de Fontenay*. The fickleness of food fashion means that the Pink Fir Apple, an old English variety, has had its 15 minutes of fame. Buy it if you can find it; its buttery, yellow flesh is just the right texture for this salad. Tossing the salad while warm encourages the potatoes to absorb the savoury dressing.

FOR 2

12 medium waxy potatoes, wiped clean

5 anchovy fillets, rinsed and patted dry

2 teaspoons red wine vinegar

2 tablespoons extra virgin olive oil

2 tablespoons not too finely chopped fresh parsley

coarsely ground black pepper

Boil the potatoes in salted water till tender to the point of a knife, about 15–20 minutes. Mash the anchovies with a knife blade and scrape the fishy gunge into a small salad bowl. Mix the vinegar, oil and parsley in the anchovy bowl and grind in a little black pepper.

Drain and slice the potatoes thickly. Toss them in the anchovy parsley dressing and eat while still warm.

Warm New Potato Salad with Melted Taleggio and Rocket

Taleggio is just one of the mild-mannered cheeses that could work well with the pungent flavour of the rocket. Brie or a mildly-flavoured Cantal are possibilities.

FOR 2 AS A SUBSTANTIAL SNACK OR LIGHT SUPPER

450g / 1 lb new potatoes, wiped clean	1 tablespoon extra virgin olive oil
2 handfuls of rocket, washed and shaken dry	200g / 7oz mild, semi-soft cheese

Cook the potatoes in boiling salted water until tender to the point of a knife, about 12 minutes.

Toss the leaves in the olive oil and dump on two ovenproof plates. Drain the potatoes and slice each one in half. Scatter them over the salad leaves. Slice the cheese thinly over the potatoes. Set the plate under a preheated grill and cook till the cheese starts to ooze, about 1 minute. Eat immediately.

* No rocket? Try radicchio and Roquefort, or watercress and Gruyère

SALAD ACCOMPANIMENTS AND DRESSINGS

In French and Italian street markets there is always at least one stall with a huge basket of assorted salad leaves: rocket, *frisée*, radicchio, batavia and lamb's lettuce; sometimes a handful of chervil thrown in for good measure. I think of it as just about the most perfect of all salads, a lightly-dressed mixture of baby leaves, just right for accompanying a snack or for mopping up the juices of a main dish.

In Britain, only the most enterprising of greengrocers and stall holders offer us a box of similar leaves. A good second best are the cellophane bags of mixed salad on offer in the chain stores. I regularly buy one that contains tiny oak leaf lettuce leaves, watercress, rocket, *frisée* and batavia, all picked when very young. Salad leaves bought in this way work out to be surprisingly economical in comparison to buying five or six salad ingredients. Cooking for one or two, I find I cannot use up several different lettuces in mixed-leaf salads quick enough to prevent them turning the salad drawer into a swamp.

Dressings

The leaves require only a light dressing if their individual flavours are not to be lost. A delicately seasoned vinaigrette, with just the faintest waft of garlic, is just the job:

½ garlic clove, make it a small one	1 tablespoon lemon juice
a little pinch of salt	6 tablespoons light and fruity extra virgin olive oil

Crush the garlic with the salt using the flat blade of a large knife, grinding it to a fragrant, beige cream. Scrape it into a small bowl and whisk in the lemon juice, either using a fork or a small whisk. Whisk in the olive oil. The result need not be homogenous, though many people like it to be.

If the salad is to accompany something light and crisp, such as grilled fish fillets or vegetable fritters then something rich and herby may fit the bill:

1 tablespoon white wine vinegar, a tarragon-flavoured one if you like	2 tablespoons sharp, thick cream, such as *crème fraîche*, soured cream or *fromage frais*
1 shallot, very finely chopped	1 tablespoon chopped fresh parsley, and another of chopped tarragon or chervil
a good pinch of salt	
2 tablespoons extra virgin olive oil	

Mix the vinegar with the shallot and salt. Whisk in the oil and the cream, gently mixing till amalgamated. Stir in the fresh herbs.

Some of the bolder flavoured leaves such as the bitter red and white chicories, piquant rocket and lemony sorrel respond better to an assertive but richly-flavoured dressing. A drop or two from a bottle of balsamic vinegar, as precious as frankincense, will add a deep warmth to the other, more pedestrian ingredients.

1 tablespoon red wine vinegar	2 tablespoons hazelnut or walnut oil
2 teaspoons balsamic vinegar	2 tablespoons groundnut oil
a small pinch of salt	
freshly ground black pepper	

Mix the vinegars with the salt and pepper. Whisk in both the oils and check the seasoning.

Many chain stores now have a selection of more complicated salads prepared at a central depot and delivered daily. I must say that I am not impressed with the ones I have tried; they seem to suffer from their exposure to the air, protected only by transparent 'sneeze screens', as well as from a surfeit of tinned sweetcorn. Some of the ready-made salads stocked by upmarket grocers have a less 'manufactured' feel to them, and though expensive can be convenient. Possibilities are *tabbouleh*, aubergine 'caviar', grated carrot salad and artichokes marinated in oil and lemon. Beware the coleslaw.

TOMATOES

Fresh Tomatoes

What are we to do about tomatoes? For the majority of the year they are flabby and tasteless, the result of supermarkets' desire for uniformity rather than flavour. Yet in high summer and autumn they can be superb: fragrant, firm and flavoursome.

Tomatoes need sunshine. Relentless scorching sun that burns their leaves to a crisp and concentrates the fruits' flavour. I have crept into fields in Italy and France and eaten the odd one straight from the vine, the tomato-eaters' version of scrumping apples. At the first twist of the fruit from the stalk the difference is clear: they are at once spicily fragrant, with a deep, rich taste. They have a tartness to them.

A tomato needs to fight for its flavour. When the fruit has a tough time, sharing fields with other crops and exposed to the vicious sun, the flavour sings out loud. The fruits' magic is lost when it is pampered under plastic and fed on fertiliser.

My answer is to look for knarled, odd-shaped fruit that occasionally appear in the supermarkets, or to go for the egg-shaped plum tomatoes. If you have a choice, buy the ones with their stalks still intact, which to my mind taste better. Generally speaking the less perfect-looking the fruit the better the flavour. Beware too of those whoppers called beef tomatoes, which can be as disappointing as the small ones, only more so. A tomato's flavour is richest when freshly picked. It can be kept for a few days on the windowsill; refrigeration seems to dull the flavour.

Tinned Tomatoes

Some people are very sniffy about tinned plum tomatoes. I think they are life-savers in the winter when they will add much more flavour to a vegetable stew or sauce than fresh ones. I always try to have a couple of tins in the kitchen, Italian brands by preference. I chop them up before adding them to a dish as they have an amazing resilience if tipped in straight from the can. Their copious canning juices are a bonus, but can be a nuisance if you try to chop the fruit on a board. I tend to attack them with a small sharp knife while still in the can, which is bad news for the knife blade (metal against metal) but saves losing all those valuable juices.

Tomatoes with Garlic

I love to eat late-summer tomatoes when they are slightly warm, straight from the vine on my windowsill. This is an occasional treat, though, and for the most part I buy them from my local health food shop, which has a good supply of small organically-grown ones all summer long.

I am not convinced that a tomato salad needs vinegar in the dressing. A good tomato has enough natural acidity, and really only needs a drizzle of olive oil to make a fine salad. This is the time to use some of that bottle of terribly expensive extra virgin olive oil.

FOR 2

2 large tomatoes, ripe but firm	salt
1 clove of new season's garlic –	fresh basil
mild, fresh and sweet	extra virgin olive oil

Slice the tomatoes in half, without bothering to peel them. Score lines across the cut sides in a criss-cross pattern with a sharp knife. Peel the garlic and slice it very thinly – as thin as paper. Stick the slices of garlic into the cuts, and sprinkle with salt. Tear the basil into small pieces and scatter over the tomatoes. Drizzle over a little olive oil and eat immediately, preferably out of doors, in the sunshine.

Grilled Tomatoes

A piquant accompaniment to grilled meat or fish, I often eat these alone for lunch with just some very crusty white bread to mop up the buttery juices.

4 medium ripe tomatoes per
  person
salt

freshly ground black pepper
butter

Grill the tomatoes whole until the skins blacken slightly. Peel back the skins, which will be very hot, halfway down the fruits and squash the flesh slightly with a fork. Grind a little salt and black pepper over them and add a small knob of softened butter to each one. Serve hot.

Pomodori Fritti

In her book *The Tuscan Year*, Elizabeth Romer describes her life during a year spent in a secret Tuscan valley. Her account is spiced with recipes from her cook, Silvana. This idea is hers.

4 large, slightly underripe tomatoes
fine cornmeal
olive oil for frying

Cut the tomatoes into thick slices. Scatter the cornmeal on a plate then roll the tomato pieces in it.

Heat one finger's depth of olive oil in a shallow pan. Fry the tomatoes in it until golden and crisp. They will crackle and spit. Drain on kitchen paper and serve hot. Eat with a mozzarella salad scattered with basil leaves.

Deep-fried Tomato and Pesto Sandwich

Prepare the tomatoes as for *Pomodori Fritti*, then sandwich between halves of a crusty baguette spread with mayonnaise into which you have stirred a little pesto sauce from the jar.

* These fried tomatoes make a fine accompaniment to any plainly-grilled fish or meat or, especially, any of the aubergine dishes in this book

Tomato and Anchovy Toast

One of my very favourite snacks, I sometimes add a few fresh basil leaves torn into shreds or a scattering of oregano if there is some around.

FOR 2

1 small onion, very finely chopped
1 tablespoon wine vinegar
4 tablespoons olive oil
salt
freshly ground black pepper
4 tomatoes
2 thick slices of crusty bread
1 clove of garlic, peeled
6 anchovy fillets

Put the chopped onion in a bowl with the vinegar. Stir in half of the olive oil. Season and set aside.

Slice the tomatoes into thick pieces. Sprinkle over a little salt and pepper and grill them under a preheated hot grill. Toast the bread on both sides until golden, cut the garlic in half and rub the cut side over the crisp toast. Pour over the remaining olive oil.

Place the grilled tomato slices on the rounds of toast, crush them slightly with a fork and put the anchovy fillets on top. Drizzle over the onion dressing and eat while hot.

Tomato and Basil Sandwich

This is the most basic of cheese and tomato sandwiches. Add to it what you will: watercress, spring onions, cucumber, alfalfa sprouts or garlic mayonnaise. I always use white bread – somehow brown bread with tomatoes is not the same.

MAKES 2 SANDWICHES

100g / 4oz mature Cheddar cheese

2 ripe tomatoes

salt

freshly ground black pepper

8 or so fresh basil leaves, torn into thin shreds

6 tablespoons mayonnaise – home-made or bought

4 thick slices of crusty white bread

1 medium sweet onion, sliced thinly

Slice the cheese, though not too thinly. Wipe the tomatoes and slice them thickly. Grind over some salt and pepper and scatter over the basil leaves.

Spread the mayonnaise on the bread. Put the cheese and the tomato on two of the slices of bread. Place the onion rings over the tomatoes and cover with the remaining slices of bread.

Cherry Tomato and Watercress Salad

I like the acidity of bright orange-red cherry tomatoes, such as Gardener's Delight. If I can resist the temptation to eat them whole walking back from the shops they make a piquant addition to a leafy salad. Try them with young spinach leaves or watercress or those floppy, slightly furry, leaves of lamb's lettuce.

FOR 2

12 cherry tomatoes

2 handfuls of watercress, washed and tough stalks removed

50ml / 2oz virgin olive oil

salt

freshly ground black pepper

Cut the tomatoes in half; this is not strictly necessary, but they tend to have an annoying fork-dodging quality to them if you do not. Place them in a china bowl, strew over the watercress and drizzle over the olive oil. Add salt and pepper, toss gently and eat with white crusty bread – one of those Italian loaves such as the holey *ciabatta* would be good.

Tomatoes Fried with Butter and Sugar

I know the sugar sounds odd, but it really is worth trying.

FOR 2 AS AN ACCOMPANIMENT

25g / 1oz butter	salt
450g / 1lb cherry tomatoes	freshly ground black pepper
scant ½ teaspoon sugar	

Melt the butter in a frying pan, when it foams add the tomatoes. Keep them moving while they cook, about 2 minutes. Sprinkle over the sugar, toss the tomatoes and add salt and pepper, the coarser the better. Serve hot with French bread.

Summer Tomatoes with Cream and Chives

Allow 2 large or 3 medium tomatoes per person. Wipe them, slice them thinly and lay on a cold plate. Snip 2 fresh chives per person into tiny pieces and stir into some double cream, allowing 2 tablespoons per person. Season the cream with a little salt and a grinding of black pepper and spoon over the tomatoes. A surprisingly good dish.

Tomato Salad

In summer, and only when we have had plenty of sun, I like to make a salad with nothing more than underripe English tomatoes and a slightly sweetened olive oil and parsley dressing.

450g / 1lb tomatoes, ever so
  slightly underripe
salt
freshly ground black pepper
½ teaspoon sugar

1 tablespoon chopped fresh
  basil leaves
2 tablespoons chopped fresh
  parsley
3 tablespoons extra virgin olive
  oil

Slice the tomatoes, thinly or thickly, whichever you prefer. Sprinkle over some salt, pepper and sugar and scatter over the herbs. Drizzle over the olive oil and leave for as long as you can before eating, but at any rate more than 15 minutes. This way the tomatoes will marinate in the slightly sweetened dressing.

Eggs Baked in Tomatoes

An idea adapted from a recipe of Margaret Costa.

Cut some large tomatoes in half horizontally and scoop out the seeds. Sprinkle with salt and a little crushed garlic. Break an egg, very carefully, into each tomato, but don't use more than a very little of the white. Season with salt and freshly ground pepper.

Spoon 1 tablespoon double cream over each egg, season with salt and pepper and a few chopped fresh herbs, tarragon would be nice, if you have some.

Sprinkle over a little Parmesan cheese and bake in a preheated moderate oven, 180°C/350°F (gas mark 4), for 15–20 minutes, or until the egg has just set; they need careful timing. Serve, in Mrs Costa's words, 'on a croûton of bread fried crisp and golden in hot olive oil'.

Tomato Stew

I often make a double quantity of this juicy stew and eat it cold the next day.

50ml / 2fl oz olive oil	800g / 1¾lb ripe sweet peppers,
1 medium onion, diced	red and yellow, cored, seeded
2 cloves of garlic, sliced thinly	and cut into large pieces
1 bay leaf	salt
450g / 1lb tomatoes, chopped	freshly ground black pepper

Heat the oil in a heavy-based pan, add the onion and cook over a gentle heat until the onion is golden, about 5–7 minutes. Add the garlic and the bay leaf, continue cooking for 2 minutes, then throw in the peppers and cook for a further 10 minutes. Add the tomatoes, salt and pepper and cook, stirring occasionally, for 10 minutes. Serve hot or cold.

Basil, Tomato and Anchovy Dip

The credit for this addictive dip goes to Lynda Brown, author of *The Cook's Garden*. She uses it as a sauce for grilled fish. I like it spread on pitta bread or toast.

Combine 1 largish, skinned and very ripe tomato, a handful of fresh basil leaves and 1 anchovy fillet with enough olive oil to make a thick sauce.

Five Fast Tomato Sauces
A Fresh Tomato Sauce

50g / 2oz butter	1 tablespoon chopped fresh
1 onion, sliced	basil
900g / 2lb ripe tomatoes	freshly ground black pepper
salt	

Melt the butter in a pan, add the onion and cook gently until soft. Pour boiling water over the tomatoes, leave them to soak for no longer than 1 minute, then drain them and peel off the skins. Cut each tomato in half, scoop the seeds out with your fingers and discard. Chop each tomato roughly and toss into the pan with the softened onions.

Add 1 teaspoon salt and the chopped basil, then simmer gently for 10 minutes. Season with a screw or two of black pepper.

An Uncooked Tomato Sauce

900g / 2lb ripe tomatoes
½ small onion, chopped
1 clove of garlic, crushed
1 wineglass of olive oil

10 or so fresh basil leaves, torn
    into little bits
salt
freshly ground black pepper

Pour boiling water over the tomatoes and leave them to soak for 1 minute. Drain them, peel off the skins and cut the fruit in half. Scoop out the seeds and throw them away. Chop the tomatoes finely.

Put the tomatoes in a bowl and stir in all the other ingredients. Allow to sit at room temperature for a while before using; give it at least 20 minutes if you can.

Cherry Tomato Sauce

Cherry tomatoes are bursting with flavour, especially the ones that are speckled with green. They make a quick, if slightly extravagant, sauce.

450g / 1lb ripe cherry tomatoes,
    such as Gardener's Delight
1 wineglass of water
1 tablespoon olive oil

salt
freshly ground black pepper
a handful of chopped fresh
    parsley

Tip the tomatoes into a pan and cook until they start to burst. Pour in the water and leave them to bubble for 5 or 6 minutes.

Push the tomatoes through a sieve with a spoon, then stir in the olive oil, seasonings and herbs.

Tinned Tomato Sauce

Come winter, I make this sauce at least once a week. All the ingredients are in the storecupboard and it has been a life-saver on more than one occasion.

Peel and slice one large, or two small, onions. Put them in a pan with a generous knob of butter, cover with a lid and simmer gently until the onion is soft.

Chop a large tin of plum tomatoes and tip into the onions with the juice. Cook gently, uncovered and seasoned with a little sea salt, for 10 minutes. Grind over a bit of black pepper, add a further knob of butter, and use at once.

Tomato Chilli Sauce

This is the ubiquitous tomato sauce of Mexico. I make it when I have bought tomatoes that do not taste as good as they look.

4 large ripe tomatoes
1 small onion, chopped finely
2 fresh green chilli peppers,
  seeded and chopped
a small handful of fresh
  coriander leaves, chopped
salt

Chop the tomatoes finely – there is no need to remove the skins – and mix with all the other ingredients.

Grilled Tomato Sauce

Use this sauce with pasta or as an accompaniment to grilled vegetables, fish or meat, or serve it, blisteringly hot, in individual bowls with very crusty bread as a snack.

Place washed whole tomatoes on the grill pan. Place them under, or over (depending on your grill), and cook until they are soft and their skins are black and charred. They will probably have split too. Drop the tomatoes, skins and all, into a food processor or blender. Whizz till puréed, a matter of seconds, then add a little sea salt.

6

Grains, Lentils and *Beans*

*T*he most upwardly mobile of foods, these earthy, comforting foods are all the rage. It has been interesting to witness the way fashionable chefs have embraced the humble lentil, even mushy yellow polenta, for goodness' sake, and elevated them to such heights. Cous cous is appearing on all the smart restaurant menus, while rice pudding is moving in chic circles, sometimes rolled into croquettes and fried in butter. No doubt all these will suffer the same fall from grace as other chefs' toys such as kiwi fruit. Fortunately, home cooks are less fickle and those who have recently discovered these staples will hold on to them long after the trendy chefs have focused on some other mundane thing many of us have been enjoying for years.

For grains, read comfort food. A bowl of steaming porridge, a plate of risotto or a bowl of sweet rice pudding. Can there be a food that makes you feel more secure, more at peace with the world?

I rank lentils and beans, along with potatoes and pasta, as some of my very favourite foods. The fact they have to be soaked and take a good while to cook should exclude them from a book

on fast food. But I cannot think of life, or should I say meals,
without them. Lentils cook quickly and canned beans, though
not as good as home-cooked ones, are perfectly satisfactory.

GRAINS

Bulgar, bulghur, or burghul wheat is a favourite of mine. It has a nutty taste and grainy texture that I find a pleasing change from rice.

I have also learned to love polenta, the Italian cornmeal mush. Whether I would have had the chance had it not become so fashionable in recent years I do not know. Like lentils, it has become difficult to avoid in trendy restaurants. Quinoa is an ancient Andean grain that has a most fascinating bobbly texture in the mouth and a very slight bitterness I find refreshingly different. Buy it in health food stores.

How relevant are grains to the cook in a hurry? Wild rice and wholewheat take almost an hour to cook and are of little use unless they have been cooked earlier and can be incorporated into another dish. I have, though, cooked enough wild rice for two in just over half an hour, serving it with nothing but butter lest its very special texture and nutty flavour should be spoiled. Bulghur wheat, the grain cracked by boiling, needs only to be soaked before appearing with apricots, plums, lemon juice and masses of brilliant green parsley for a *tabbouleh*.

Oatmeal can be stirred into hot butter and seasoned with onions and black pepper for an earthy accompaniment. Some evenings after a taxing day I take solace in a warming bowl of rice, white, preferably the hugely fragrant basmati into which I stir whatever I have to hand. A lump of garlic soft cheese, a spoonful of *harissa* sauce or cooked lentils and a handful of fresh mint. It is not a question of needless frugality, I thoroughly enjoy eating so simply. It is often worth cooking a little extra to reheat the following day. Rice can be fried and tossed with beaten egg and almost all grains can be bound with beaten egg, spiced and patted into cakes for frying.

I always like to keep some sprouted grain in my fridge. Sometimes I grow my own: mung beans are the easiest and taste like tiny fresh peas. Although I have a salad sprouter, a series of perforated trays over a tray filled with fresh water, you can easily sprout them in a jam jar. A bag of alfalfa or radish sprouts is useful to have around. They are good sandwich fillers, particularly for those involving cheese, and are notoriously nutritious. For a fast fix they can be piled on to wholemeal bread and topped with thick yoghurt and a sliced avocado.

Porridge

I include porridge in this collection at the suggestion of Derek Cooper, of Radio 4's *The Food Programme*. The heat on which the porridge cooks is all important. It should not boil, but simmer peacefully, 'gently erupting and heaving like grey lava' writes Mr Cooper in *A La Carte* Magazine. 'Giving the familiar "plop" every few minutes just to show it is still cooking' is how Catherine Brown puts it in her book *Scottish Cookery*.

ENOUGH FOR 2

600ml / 1 pint water
100g / 4oz medium oatmeal (too fine a grain gives a pappy
   consistency)
salt

Put the water on to boil. A thick-based pan will help keep the mixture from burning. Dribble in the oatmeal with one hand stirring with the other. A spurtle, a tapered wooden stick, is the correct tool for this, but a wooden spoon will do. Tradition decrees porridge should be stirred clockwise.

Set the porridge over a very low heat and leave to reduce. The heat should be at a level where the surface hardly moves, giving only the occasional 'glop'. The consistency is determined by the length of time it cooks. Five minutes will give a sloppy texture, while 10 will ensure the oats retain some bite. Longer than 30 minutes and you will be able to cut it with a knife.

Taste and salt the porridge once it has reduced to your liking. Any earlier and the salt may cause the grains to harden. Eat hot, according to Ms Brown, by dipping each spoon of hot porridge into cold milk, thus ensuring the porridge in your bowl keeps warm.

Good things to put in your Porridge

I make the following suggestions, some stolen and some unorthodox. Taste the porridge first, then add salt and any of the following. Do not omit the salt even though you may also be adding sugar. The salt is important to bring out the flavour of the oatmeal.

* Heather honey and butter

* Blackberries, honey and cream

* Heather honey and whisky

* Thick natural plain yoghurt and molasses

* A warm compote of raspberries, blackberries and blueberries with a spoonful of buttermilk

* Ground cinnamon and toasted hazelnuts

Bulghur Wheat and Black-eyed Beans

I often use this earthy mixture, with its unusual texture of grain and bean, as a tool for soaking up the juices from a runny stew. Add shredded vegetables, dark green cabbage, crinkly spinach leaves, sliced courgettes or florets of broccoli and you have a feast.

FOR 2 AS A MAIN DISH, 4 AS AN ACCOMPANIMENT

2 tablespoons groundnut oil
1 medium onion, roughly chopped
225g / 8oz black-eyed beans, pre-cooked or tinned and well-rinsed

100g / 4oz bulghur wheat
salt
freshly ground black pepper

Warm the oil in a deep pan, add the onion and cook for 5–10 minutes, stirring occasionally, until soft and transparent.

Add the black-eyed beans, drained of their liquor, and the bulghur wheat. Stir in 300ml / ½ pint water, or cooking water from the beans if you have cooked your own. Simmer for 15 minutes. Taste and check the seasoning.

Bulghur Wheat and Aubergine Pilaf

A hearty main dish with half an eye to the Middle East. It is also an excellent accompaniment to grilled lamb or spiced chicken.

If you can remember to soak the bulghur wheat before you leave the house in the morning, you can cut down the cooking time. Remove the bulghur wheat from its water, wringing it out with your hands, and stir it into the aubergine and onion mixture, heat through for 2 minutes and then add the seasonings. The consistency should be slightly runny, like a risotto. Add a crushed clove of garlic with the onion if that takes your fancy.

FOR 4 AS AN ACCOMPANIMENT, 2 AS A MAIN DISH

4 tablespoons olive oil
1 bay leaf (optional)
1 small onion, sliced
2 small aubergines, cut into
   2.5-cm / 1-inch cubes
225g / 8oz bulghur wheat

300ml / ½ pint vegetable stock
   or water
2 tablespoons pine nuts
1 tablespoon fresh mint,
   finely chopped, about
   12 leaves
salt

Warm the olive oil, with a bay leaf if you have one, in a large pan. Add the onion and cook till it starts to soften, about 3 or 4 minutes. Add the aubergine cubes and cook, over a medium heat and adding a drop more oil if necessary, until tender, about 4 minutes.

Tip in the bulghur wheat. Stir. Pour in the vegetable stock or water. If you are using fresh stock or water you should add salt too. Simmer for 10 minutes, or until the water has evaporated. As soon as the liquid has disappeared stir in the pine nuts and mint, taste for seasoning, and serve.

Bulghur Wheat with Mushrooms

I use Gruyère here because I particularly like its flavour and texture when slightly melted. It is far from essential, though, and sometimes I use Cheddar or whatever comes to hand. A warming, frugal dish this, and a great favourite of mine with a glass or two of red wine.

FOR 4 AS A MAIN DISH

225g / 8oz brown mushrooms
2 tablespoons groundnut oil
225g / 8oz bulghur wheat

100g / 4oz Gruyère cheese, cut
   into 2.5-cm / 1-inch cubes
salt
freshly ground black pepper

Cut the mushrooms into quarters and cook them in a shallow pan with the oil for 3 or 4 minutes, until they are soft and golden brown. Remove them from the pan with a slotted spoon into a bowl. Keep warm.

Add the bulghur wheat to the pan, tossing the grains in what remains of the oil. Pour in 300ml / ½ pint water and add a pinch of salt. Simmer the grains gently for 6 minutes. Taste the bulghur to see if it is tender, if not cook for another couple of minutes.

Stir in the mushrooms and cheese, and season with black pepper and more salt if needed.

Fresh Plum Tabbouleh

The sumptuousness of ripe plums, the nutty bulghur grains and the refreshing notes from the mint and lemon produces a salad of myriad flavours and textures.

75g / 3oz bulghur wheat	salt
50g / 2oz (a good handful) fresh flat-leaf parsley	freshly ground black pepper
	4 small spring onions, trimmed
25g / 1oz fresh mint	225g / 8oz (about 6) perfectly
juice of 2 lemons	ripe juicy plums
2 tablespoons olive oil	

Cover the bulghur wheat with cold water and leave for 15 minutes. Chop the parsley and mint finely. Place in a salad bowl with the lemon juice, olive oil, salt and a few grinds of pepper. Chop or snip the onions into small pieces.

Halve each plum, pull or cut out the stone, and toss them into the herbs and dressing. Squeeze the water from the bulghur wheat with your hands. Drop the grains into the salad bowl and then mix gently with the plums and herbs.

Bulghur Wheat with Mango and Mint

I tend to eat tropical fruits, mangoes, pawpaws and passion fruit for breakfast rather than chopping them up into after-dinner fruit salads. Finding hungry friends on my doorstep one summer lunchtime there was little in the house other than the contents of the fruit bowl and the usual storecupboard stuff. Mint in the garden was sheer luck, but I could have done without it. As an accompaniment this goes rather well with grilled chicken.

FOR 2 AS A MAIN COURSE SALAD, OR 4 AS A SIDE DISH

100g / 4oz bulghur wheat	25g / 1oz (a good handful) fresh mint
1 large mango, ripe and fragrant	
juice of 1 lemon	4 spring onions or 1 small sweet red onion
2 tablespoons olive oil	

Soak the bulghur wheat in cold water for 15 minutes. Peel the mango, over a serving bowl to save the rich, sweet juice, then remove the flesh from the stone with a small knife. Cut the flesh into small dice.

Pour in the lemon juice and the oil, then chop the mint and add it to the mango. Chop the onion(s) in small dice and add to the rest of the ingredients. Wring the water from the bulghur wheat with your hands, then fold the ingredients together gently. Leave for a few minutes for the flavours to marry.

Bulghur Wheat Pilaf with Butter and Almonds

The simplest imaginable winter supper. A perfect antidote to over-indulgence, and reassuringly frugal. Lift the spirits by serving with a fruity, peppery salad of watercress and blood orange.

FOR 2 AS A MAIN DISH, 4 AS AN ACCOMPANIMENT

225g / 8oz bulghur wheat	freshly ground black pepper
300ml / ½ pint water or	50g / 2oz butter
vegetable stock	4 tablespoons flaked almonds,
salt	toasted

Put the bulghur in a pan with the vegetable stock or water. Add salt – I think the grain needs it when served hot – and a few turns of the peppermill. Let it simmer over a low heat for 8 minutes, by which time most of the water will have been absorbed. Taste it; if it is not tender, then cook it for a minute or two longer.

Remove the pan from the heat, stir in the butter and the flaked almonds and leave, with the lid on, for a further 10 minutes to absorb the butter. Taste the mixture, add more salt and pepper if you think it needs it, then serve.

Onion Skirlie

I was reminded of this simple accompaniment by Catherine Brown in her book, *Scottish Cookery*. It makes a fine side dish for roast game or grilled oily fish such as mackerel.

50g / 2oz dripping or butter	salt
1 large onion, finely chopped	freshly ground black pepper
100g / 4oz coarse oatmeal	

Melt the dripping or butter in a shallow pan over a medium heat. Add the onion and cook until soft, about 5 minutes. Sprinkle in the oatmeal, and season with the salt and pepper.

When all of the fat has been absorbed, which should take a couple of minutes, the skirlie is ready. Serve hot.

Date and Pistachio Cous Cous

I love cooking cous cous the traditional Berber way: washing and soaking the grains of semolina, then drying and steaming them, separating the grains, then steaming them again.

I don't often have time to faff around with all that though. Here is a quick method.

FOR 4 AS AN ACCOMPANIMENT TO A SLOPPY, SPICY STEW

225g / 8oz cous cous	75g / 3oz fresh dates, stoned
75g / 3oz dried apricots	and chopped
75g / 3oz prunes, stoned	knob of butter
50g / 2oz shelled pistachio nuts	

Cover the cous cous in a bowl with an equal volume of water. Stir occasionally until the grains have absorbed all the water, which will take about 15 minutes.

Cut the dried apricots and prunes into quarters. Rub the cous cous through your fingers smoothing out any lumps. Mix the grains and all the chopped fruit with the pistachios. Dump the whole lot into a shallow dish, cover tightly with foil, and bake in a preheated oven, 220°C/425°F (gas mark 7), for 20 minutes till hot.

Remove the foil, fluff up the cous cous with a fork while stirring in a good knob of butter.

Quinoa with Grilled Peppers and Oregano

This comforting grain, available from health food stores, makes a fine supper when cooked with onion and garlic, and then tossed with grilled sweet peppers. If you don't have the oregano, use marjoram, either fresh or dried. I have served it with Baked Feta and Thyme, see page 269, with some success.

FOR 4 AS AN ACCOMPANIMENT

2 red peppers, halved, seeds removed and cut into long strips
4 tablespoons olive oil
150g / 5oz quinoa
1 medium onion, finely chopped
2 cloves of garlic, sliced
1 bay leaf
2 teaspoons dried oregano
2 tablespoons chopped fresh parsley

Put the pepper strips on the base of the grill pan, drizzle with half the olive oil and cook under a preheated grill for about 5 minutes on each side, turning once, till sweet, very tender and black at the edges.

Pour the quinoa into a fine-mesh sieve and rinse under cold running water. Warm the remaining oil in a shallow pan or high-sided frying pan and fry the onion and the garlic till soft, 8–10 minutes, on a medium heat. Add the bay leaf, oregano and quinoa. Pour over 450ml / ¾ pint water and simmer for 8 minutes. Almost all the liquid will have been absorbed.

Remove the peppers from the grill, stir them into the quinoa and onion mixture with the parsley and serve.

Quinoa with Thyme and Taleggio

The pleasure of this substantial supper is the mixture of textures; the tiny bobbles of quinoa and the melting cubes of hot cheese. Almost any cheese, but particularly Gruyère, Cheddar and Mozzarella, will work well too. Save a few thyme leaves for scattering over the top as you serve it.

2 tablespoons olive oil	100g / 4oz quinoa
leaves from 4 sprigs of fresh thyme	1 wineglass of dry white wine
1 bay leaf (optional)	300ml / ½ pint hot vegetable stock
1 medium leek, trimmed and shredded	100g / 4oz Taleggio cheese, sliced
1 clove of garlic, sliced	

Warm the oil with the thyme leaves, and a bay leaf if you have one, in a pan over a gentle heat. Add the leek and the garlic and cook for 5 minutes, covered, stirring from time to time.

Tip in the quinoa and the wine. Let the wine bubble away (you need its flavour not its liquid), then pour in the hot stock. Simmer, stirring occasionally for 10 minutes, watching that it does not catch on the bottom. When the stock has been absorbed by the quinoa grains, stir in the cheese. Serve straight away.

Rice

My favourite rice is the fragrant basmati, which is pertinent to this book because it cooks quicker than some. I have had little joy from the boil-in-the-bag instant rices that I somehow manage to overcook even when I stick to the instructions like glue. I much prefer to wait slightly longer for basmati. Rice reheats reasonably well, at least better than pasta, and it may be worth cooking a little extra, cooling it quickly and keeping it in the fridge for the next day. I have reheated many a bowl of rice in a colander over boiling water then tipped it into a bowl and stirred in something savoury from the cupboard.

Plain White Rice

Exactly what it says. Serve as an accompaniment or as a main course if you are feeling decidedly delicate.

175g / 6oz long-grain white rice
1 teaspoon salt

After weighing the rice, tip it into a measuring jug. Note the quantity, then pour it into a heavy-based saucepan. Add the salt, then add exactly twice the quantity of cold water. This will probably be 400ml / 14fl oz.

Bring to the boil, turn the heat down to a simmer, then cover with a lid. Cook for 12 minutes, no longer. Lift the lid: there should be no water left and little steam holes should have appeared in the rice. Lift a few grains of rice out with a fork, taste them to see if the rice is tender. It probably is. Replace the lid and remove the pan from the heat. Leave for 2 minutes.

Good things to stir into Rice

There are times when a bowl of steaming rice, perfumed basmati or pure and comforting white, is simply enough. When this is the case try stirring in one of the following aromatic mixtures.

* Lots of butter and Parmesan cheese

* Sliced mushrooms, sautéed in butter with a teaspoon ground coriander

* A handful of toasted pine nuts

* A tin of lentils, drained, well-rinsed and warmed with a knob of butter

* Hot spinach, shredded and cooked beforehand in butter

* Shavings of Pecorino cheese and shredded raw fennel

* A spoonful of black olive paste and a couple of finely-sliced, sun-dried tomatoes

* Fresh tarragon leaves and a spoonful of tarragon vinegar

* Shredded carrot, toasted flaked almonds and raisins

* Thin shreds of ham, Italian Parma or Spanish *serrano*, or cubes of cooked smoked pancetta

* Cubes of smoked bacon, cooked crisp, stirred in with their hot fat

* A tablespoon extra virgin olive oil and a dash of balsamic vinegar

* A lump of commercial garlic and herb soft cheese

* Herb butter and a squeeze of lemon juice

* A handful of fresh mint, chopped, and half a cucumber, peeled and diced

* A rich, buttery cheese, such as Brie or Taleggio, cut into cubes

* A spoonful of basil pesto from a jar

* Finely-chopped chilli peppers and chopped fresh coriander leaves

* A spoonful of spicy *harissa* sauce

Fragrant Brown Basmati Rice

Nutty brown rice scented with turmeric, cloves and cinnamon is the perfect accompaniment for grilled meats, spicy stews and runny vegetable casseroles. The cooking method here is entirely unorthodox – but it works. The first boiling cuts out the long soaking and the slightly reduced cooking time gives a chewy bite to the rice.

FOR 4 AS AN ACCOMPANIMENT

225g / 8oz brown basmati rice
1 tablespoon groundnut oil
½ teaspoon ground turmeric
3 whole cloves
½ stick of cinnamon

8 green cardamom pods
2 bay leaves
salt
juice of ½ lemon
25g / 1oz butter

Put the rice in a deep pan and pour in enough water to cover the rice by about 2.5cm / 1 inch. Boil hard over a high heat for 5 minutes. Meanwhile, warm the oil in a saucepan and fry the spices and bay leaves for 2 minutes till fragrant.

Pour the rice into a sieve over the sink. Tip the rice into the pan containing the spices, cover with fresh water, salt, and bring to the boil.

Turn down the heat, clap on a lid, and cook slowly for 15 minutes. By this time the rice will have absorbed all the water. Turn off the heat and allow the rice to stand, still covered, for a full 10 minutes.

Remove the lid, add the lemon juice and the butter and fluff the grains of rice up with a fork. Fish out the bay leaves. Tip into a warm bowl and serve.

Risotto with Parmesan Cheese

The risotto only just makes it into this collection. It requires half an hour of your undivided attention. Even so, I find it perfectly possible to throw a salad together while keeping a very close eye on the rice. Radicchio and fennel or mushrooms would be my choice. You will need Italian *arborio* rice if your risotto is to have an authentic consistency.

FOR 4 AS A MAIN DISH

1 small onion, finely chopped
50g / 2oz butter
275g / 10oz arborio rice
1 wineglass of dry white wine

1 litre / 1¾ pints hot vegetable or chicken stock
50g / 2oz butter
50g / 2oz Parmesan cheese, grated

Cook the onion in the butter over a medium heat until soft, about 5 minutes. Add the rice, stir, then pour in the wine. Continue cooking until the wine has reduced by half, then pour in a ladleful of stock.

Let the risotto simmer gently, adding another ladle or two of stock each time the liquid is absorbed into the rice. Stir, almost continuously, ignoring the ringing telephone or anything demanding attention, until the rice has taken up all the stock. If you intend to follow with a salad, make it near to the cooker, so that you can keep a watchful eye on the rice.

After 25 minutes' cooking time, stir in the butter and grated cheese. The risotto is ready when the rice is *al dente*, that is, when tender but retains some bite, and the consistency should be creamy.

Good things to put in a Risotto

Add to the above recipe:

Asparagus
450g / 1lb freshly-boiled asparagus can be added after the onion has been sautéed. Half the stock should be replaced with the asparagus cooking water. Pass Parmesan cheese at the table

Courgettes
Add 4 medium courgettes, sliced into thin rounds and cooked till golden with the onions

Celery
Add 4 sticks of celery, sliced as thick as coins, when the onions are soft. Include some of the leaves, a small handful, which add a delightful aroma

Artichoke Hearts
Probably the best use for bottled or tinned artichoke hearts is to cut them into quarters and toss them in a risotto. You will need at least 12 for 4 people. Add them when the onions are soft. Throw in lots of fresh parsley too

Fennel
The loveliest of all. Add finely-shredded raw fennel and the merest hint of Ricard if you have some, after the onions. Throw in a handful

of very finely-chopped fresh parsley. Oh, and be generous with the Parmesan

Basic Fried Rice

I have watched Shanghai-born chef Kam-Po But make this in his restaurant kitchen. Traditionally, it is more likely to be eaten at home than in a restaurant where the savoury dishes are better for being eaten with plain boiled rice.

FOR 2 AS AN ACCOMPANTMENT

350g / 12oz cooked white rice
2 tablespoons groundnut oil
2 spring onions, trimmed and
   cut in fine rounds

1 egg, beaten with ½ teaspoon
   salt
salt

If the rice is very cold, fork it through to separate the grains. Heat the wok or frying pan, pour in the oil and swirl it round the pan. Lower the heat and drop in the onions. Fry for 30 seconds, stirring constantly.

Tip in the egg all at once, leave for a few seconds, then stir to break up the setting egg. (Chopsticks are easiest for this.) Add the cooked rice. Toss the pan, pushing the egg and rice around the pan for 3 minutes. Taste, and add salt if necessary. Serve hot.

LENTILS *AND* BEANS

Lentils take mercifully little time to cook, and few need soaking. The fashionable *lentils de Puy* are the ultimate pulse. Their slate-blue-green flesh has a deep spiciness and an earthy, nutty aroma. In summer I add redcurrants to sharpen a bowl of brown lentils. In winter I toss them into a tomato sauce spiced with chilli if I am feeling too lazy to do more, or serve them as a side dish with a Middle Eastern mint dressing.

Beans, though lacking the bite of home-cooked ones, emerge from a tin relatively unharmed as long as you rinse them thoroughly of their emetic brine and cook them only briefly to keep them *al dente*. I have made a dish of rich creamy beans by warming tiny haricot beans from a tin with cream, thyme and tarragon, which is now a great favourite.

Pale green flageolet, tiny white haricot and motley pink pinto beans all come in tins, and are an invaluable storecupboard staple. Drained, rinsed and stirred into a spicy tomato sauce then topped with grated cheese they make a comforting winter supper that needs no recipe. Warm them with your best olive oil and a handful of fresh green beans and you have a multi-textured side dish.

Tinned chick peas are virtually indistinguishable from the home-soaked and cooked ones. Open a tin and you will save hours in soaking time and a fortune in gas. I turn to them for whizzing up a garlicky dip for warm pitta bread when I need a snack in seconds.

Much is made of the bean family's ability to induce flatulence. There are all sorts of methods for reducing this property, and I have even heard of research into producing beans that have had their remarkable phenomenon bred out of them. Personally, I am amazed at all the fuss. So, beans give you wind. And what is wrong with that?

Lentils with Tomatoes

This storecupboard supper is a life-saver when the fridge contains nothing but the cat's milk and an old packet of Japanese soya paste.

100g / 4oz brown lentils
1 bay leaf
3 tablespoons olive oil
1 onion, chopped
1 fresh red chilli pepper,
   chopped

1 × 400g / 14oz tin plum
   tomatoes, chopped
salt
freshly ground black pepper

Wash the lentils in a sieve under running water. Cook them with the bay leaf and a tablespoon of the oil in boiling salted water for 15 minutes. Drain them in a colander.

Meanwhile, fry the onion in the remaining oil for about 5–7 minutes, until soft and golden. Add the chilli and cook for a further minute or two. Add the drained lentils and the tomatoes with all their juice, salt and pepper. Simmer gently for 10 minutes and serve hot.

* Once associated with slow-cooking, the lentil, which cooks to perfection in 15–20 minutes and sometimes less, is good snack material. Sometimes I boil them with a bay leaf and a little oil, then just drain them and smother in soft butter and black pepper. How to feel indulgent on 30p

Hot Brown Lentils with Mint Vinaigrette

Small brown lentils will cook in about 20 minutes. Tinned ones make for a quicker salad but are somehow less toothsome and seem to lack the natural spiciness of freshly-cooked ones.

FOR 2

225g / 8oz brown lentils
1 bay leaf
a sprig of fresh mint
leaves from 2 sprigs of fresh
   mint, chopped
salt

freshly ground black pepper
1 shallot, finely chopped
2 tablespoons white wine
   vinegar
6 tablespoons extra virgin olive
   oil

Wash the lentils in a sieve under running water. Cook them, there is no need to soak them, in boiling salted water with the bay leaf and the mint until tender, about 20 minutes.

Meanwhile, make the dressing. Crush the mint leaves with a little salt in a small bowl. Add the chopped shallot and pour in the vinegar. Mix in the oil with a fork. Season with pepper.

Drain the lentils and pour over the dressing while they are still warm.

Lentil and Redcurrant Salad

Redcurrants have a short season during June and July. I like the different textures in this salad with its spicy, nutty lentils and tart, fresh currants. Snap up whitecurrants if ever you see them, they are even better.

FOR 2

175g / 6oz lentils, *de Puy* or small brown
100g / 4oz redcurrants
4 fresh chives, chopped

2 tablespoons extra virgin olive oil
juice of 1 lemon or lime
salt
freshly ground black pepper

Wash the lentils in a sieve under running water. Cook them in boiling salted water for 12 minutes; they are cooked when tender but still firm to the touch. Drain and place in a bowl.

Top and tail the currants and add to the lentils. Snip the chives into 1-cm (½-inch) lengths and add them with the olive oil, lemon or lime juice and salt and pepper to the lentils. Mix all the ingredients gently so as not to crush the currants.

Warm Two-bean Salad

Inspired by David Scott, who runs the Everyman Bistro in Liverpool, the warm flageolet beans are given bite by the addition of a few crisp French beans. A good way to use up leftover beans. The better the olive oil the more fragrant the dish.

FOR 2

100g / 4oz flageolet beans, cooked

100g / 4oz French beans

2 tablespoons extra virgin olive oil

juice of 1 lemon

salt

freshly ground black pepper

Place the cooked flageolet beans in a saucepan and add just enough water to cover them. Put them on a low fire and bring gently to a simmer. Top and tail the French beans, and cook for 3 minutes in boiling salted water. Drain both types of beans and mix, while still warm, with the olive oil, lemon and salt and pepper.

White Beans with Tarragon and Cream

A comforting dish of herby, creamy beans. You will need some bread to wipe up the juices from the plate, or serve it on toast.

FOR 2

a knob of butter

1 small onion, finely diced

1 bay leaf

1 small carrot, finely diced

2 sprigs of fresh thyme

leaves from 4 branches of fresh tarragon

1 × 400g / 14oz tin white haricot or flageolet beans

150ml / ¼ pint single cream

salt

freshly ground black pepper

Melt the butter in a saucepan and fry the onion gently, until it is soft and golden. It must not burn, or it becomes bitter.

Add the bay leaf, carrot, thyme and tarragon. Tip in the beans, well-rinsed and drained. Pour in the cream and slowly bring to the boil. As soon as the mixture starts to boil remove it from the heat, correct the seasoning – it may need a good grinding of pepper – and serve hot.

Hummous

An earthy-tasting purée of chick peas that can become addictive.

SERVES 5–6 AS A STARTER

225g / 8oz tinned chick peas
6 tablespoons tahini paste
2 cloves of garlic, peeled
6 tablespoons lemon juice
3 tablespoons olive oil

cayenne pepper
freshly ground black pepper
salt
olive oil, for drizzling

Whizz the chick peas in a food processor or blender with a little of the liquid from the can until they are smooth. Add the tahini, garlic, lemon juice and olive oil and work in the processor or blender until very smooth. Season with the peppers and salt. Turn into a dish, scraping out all of the hummous from the mixer bowl with a rubber spatula. Flatten the top slightly, then drizzle over some olive oil and serve with warm pitta bread.

Michael's Beans

I am always suspicious of recipes that 'tart-up' commercial products, remembering the maxim about the uselessness of throwing good after bad. That said, I have found several tinned or frozen products can be useful as a springboard for your own invention and whim. Tinned beans are one of them. I prefer not the bland sweet beans that sell in their millions, but the ones available from health food shops. These contain no added sugar; have a lightly spicy sauce and no weird preservatives. This recipe is named after the friend whose idea it was.

FOR 2

2 tablespoons groundnut or
   olive oil
6 rashers of smoked streaky
   bacon, diced
2 medium onions, thinly sliced
2 × 400g / 14oz tins best-quality
   baked beans, such as 'Whole
   Earth' brand

2 medium-hot fresh red chilli
   peppers, split, seeds removed
   and chopped
4 tablespoons molasses
salt

Heat the oil and fry the bacon for about 3–4 minutes, till the fat turns golden in colour. Add the onions and cook over a medium heat till they soften and sweeten, about 5–7 minutes. Tip in the beans. Add the chillies and simmer until the beans are thoroughly hot. Stir in 2 tablespoons of the molasses, taste, then add more molasses and some salt if you wish. Serve hot.

Grilled Lamb with Flageolet Beans and Coriander and Parsley Sauce

I admire those who know what they will be eating the following day. They are the sort who remember to soak the beans overnight. I rarely have a clue what will be for supper tomorrow, which is why tinned flageolet beans intrude into my recipe for lamb with beans.

FOR 2

4 plump cloves of garlic, peeled
2 large chump chops, 2.5cm / 1
   inch thick
salt
freshly ground black pepper
75ml / a good 3fl oz extra virgin
   olive oil, plus 1 tablespoon

1 × 400g / 14oz tin green
   flageolet or white haricot
   beans
1 onion, thinly sliced
1 bay leaf
1 small handful each of fresh
   parsley and coriander leaves

Put the garlic cloves in a small pan, cover with water and simmer for 15 minutes. Season the chops and brush them with a little olive oil.

Drain the beans of their liquid, rinse them well, tip them into a medium saucepan with a little salt and simmer with the onion, bay leaf, a sprig of the parsley, the tablespoon of olive oil and enough water to cover. They are already cooked and need only gentle simmering for 5 minutes to heat through.

Grill the chops until brown on both sides, about 3 minutes per side; they will be pink in the middle. Drain the garlic and whizz in the food processor or blender with the coriander, remaining parsley and a little salt. Pour in the rest of the olive oil. Transfer to a small saucepan and warm through, but do not bring to the boil. Meanwhile, drain the beans, stir in half the garlic and parsley purée and divide between 2 warm plates. Put a chop on each plate and spoon over the remaining purée.

7

Chicken

*C*hicken is the most versatile meat for the quick cook. Any cut – thigh, drumstick or whole leg and breast – is both accessible and easy to deal with. There is no need to embark on any butchery yourself; the butcher will cut exactly the pieces you need from a fresh bird. Prepacked joints are available from any supermarket. Chicken also has the added advantage of being extremely low in fat compared to red meats.

There are broadly two types of chicken available. The best of these is free range, where the birds have been allowed to forage for at least part of their own food and have daytime or permanent access to both grassland and shelter. Free-range chickens are available in all decent supermarkets and butchers and are only slightly more expensive than the alternative, for those who have no conscience about how their food is reared. The intensively-farmed or 'broiler' birds live their short lives in large windowless sheds, a more uncomfortable existence than that of free-range birds, as they grow from chicks to full-sized chickens. Their feed is laced with antibiotics to guard against disease, though many birds die before slaughter. The flavour of these chickens is much blander (some would describe it as tasteless) than that of free-range birds.

Free-rangers mature more slowly without the growth

promoters added to intensive birds' feed and are therefore sold at a premium. These birds are hardier breeds than those used in intensive farming, which combined with their opportunity to feed naturally and take some exercise, results in a better-flavoured bird. Unfortunately the free-range system is open to abuse, so it is best to buy from a reputable supplier. The black-legged Poulet Noir and the French Poulet de Bresse are especially flavoursome breeds, the latter being marked with a stamp of authenticity, rather like a bottle of wine's 'appellation contrôlée'.

Birds described as 'corn fed' have been kept on a maize diet, which makes their flesh slightly yellow. Their flavour is rich and a little gamey, more like pheasant, which is, of course, how chickens used to taste.

The chicken recipes that follow were all developed using free-range French chickens. The meat is matched with its natural partners, such as garlic, olives, butter, spices, cream and fresh herbs like tarragon and parsley.

One final point, when buying chicken, beware of the pieces in the shops that have had their skin removed. The skin is a valuable asset, crisping deliciously and keeping the flesh moist during cooking.

Chicken with Orange and Black Olives

One of my favourite recipes in the book, this simple supper uses kitchen staples to brighten up a plate of chicken pieces. Use any cut of chicken you like, though I have also tried this recipe with duck breasts and found it even better. Sautéing the chicken pieces till golden brown before adding the stock is essential to the flavour and character of the dish. It looks smart served on a plain white plate with a deep rim.

FOR 2

2 tablespoons olive oil
50g / 2oz butter
2 whole chicken legs
225ml / 8fl oz chicken stock
1 teaspoon dried thyme leaves
12 black olives, stoned

1 orange, cut in half then into thin slices
1 tablespoon freshly chopped parsley
salt
freshly ground black pepper

Heat the oil and half the butter in a shallow pan. Brown the chicken pieces on both sides, then add the chicken stock. Stir in the thyme, olives and the orange slices. Cover and simmer gently for 20 minutes.

Check that the chicken is cooked – when pierced with the point of a knife the juices should run clear – then remove the pieces to a warm serving plate. Taste the sauce, add the parsley and season it with pepper, and very carefully, if at all, with salt. Turn up the heat, reduce the liquid by bubbling down to 150ml / ¼ pint, then whisk in the remaining butter. The sauce will be shiny and slightly thickened when it is ready. Plate the chicken pieces and pour over the sauce. Serve with a starchy accessory, such as wide noodles or steamed potatoes or, even better, with the quick bulghur wheat and lemon used in the lamb pitta on page 239.

Mozzarella Chicken with Pesto Gravy

I have given two methods for the same dish. The first gives a neater result, while the second, which I think the more interesting, is not for the faint-hearted. It includes turning the chicken over in the pan so that the cheese topping melts into the pan juices, resulting in a deeply savoury finish.

FOR 2, AS A MAIN DISH WITH SALAD

2 large boneless chicken breasts
50g / 2oz butter
2 tablespoons groundnut or
    vegetable oil
3 tablespoons pesto from the jar

1 ball / 100g / 4oz of
    Mozzarella cheese, cut into
    5-mm / ¼-inch slices
freshly ground black pepper

Cut each breast in half lengthways and flatten with a rolling pin between two sheets of clingfilm, until they are 5mm / ¼ inch thick. Be gentle, you don't want a purée. Cook the chicken in the melted butter and oil in a shallow pan for 1–2 minutes on each side.

Without removing the chicken from the pan, spread each piece with a tablespoon pesto sauce, place a slice of mozzarella on top of the pesto and sprinkle with pepper. Now, EITHER:

Pick up the chicken with a fish slice and place it in a grill pan. Flash under a preheated hot grill till the Mozzarella melts. Add the remaining pesto to the pan with 2 tablespoons water and stir. Remove the chicken from the grill and pour over the pan juices, OR:

Turn the chicken over with a palette knife so that the cheese is on the bottom. As soon as it starts to melt and sizzle, scoop each piece up with a fish slice, making sure that the melted cheese is not left behind. Turn the chicken over, the cheese and pesto now tantalisingly melted, and place in a warm serving dish, easing the cheese from the slice with a palette knife. Add the remaining pesto and 2 tablespoons water to the pan, in which some of the pesto and cheese will be left behind, and stir, scraping up all the crusty bits in the pan. Pour the pesto pan juices over the chicken and eat immediately.

Chicken in Hoisin Sauce

An approximation of a dish I ate in a Chinese restaurant in Paris. I asked for the recipe, but was none the wiser after they had told me. Ask the butcher to chop the chicken through the bone, or do it yourself if you are good with a cleaver, but take care not to leave any sharp splinters of bone in the chicken.

FOR 2

2 tablespoons groundnut oil
2 cloves of garlic, peeled and
   crushed
100g / 4oz chicken pieces,
   chopped through the bone
   into 2.5-cm / 1-inch pieces
100g / 4oz brown mushrooms,
   cut into quarters
2 tablespoons dry sherry

100g / 4oz broccoli, split into
   large florets
300ml / ½ pint chicken or
   vegetable stock
1 tablespoon light soy sauce
2 tablespoons hoisin sauce
2 teaspoons cornflour mixed
   with 2 teaspoons water

Heat a frying pan or wok until hot, pour in the oil and add the garlic. Stir quickly, with chopsticks or a large spoon, so that the garlic cooks for 20 seconds without standing still. It must cook without burning. Add the chicken, brown lightly, then the mushrooms and broccoli. Fry for 3 minutes, stirring all the time.

Add the rest of the ingredients except the cornflour. Cook until the chicken is tender and the broccoli cooked but still crisp, about 4 minutes. Add the cornflour mixture, and serve when the mixture thickens. Serve with rice or noodles.

Chilli Chicken Pitta

A wonderful snack, spicy and substantial, of chicken pieces with chilli, dribbled with mint-flecked yoghurt, then stuffed into Middle Eastern pitta bread. Don't be put off by the long list of ingredients, you will probably have most of them.

1 small onion or 4 spring onions,
    chopped
4 cloves of garlic, crushed
3 tablespoons groundnut oil
juice of 1 lemon
½ teaspoon salt

1 tablespoon runny honey
1 teaspoon paprika
½ teaspoon mild chilli powder
1 small fresh red chilli pepper,
    seeded and finely chopped
225g / 8oz boneless chicken

FOR THE SAUCE:

6 tablespoons plain natural
    yoghurt
1 tablespoon chopped fresh
    mint
1 teaspoon paprika

2 spring onions, trimmed and
    chopped
crisp lettuce and hot pitta bread
    or baps, to serve

Mix together the onion, garlic, oil and lemon juice. Add the salt,
honey, paprika and chilli, dried and fresh. Cut the chicken into lumps
about 2.5cm or 1 inch or so square, and stir into the above ingredients.
Leave as long as you can, but at least for 20 minutes. Mix the
ingredients for the yoghurt sauce.

Heat the grill, which should be red-hot. Scatter the chicken over
the grill pan and cook till the pieces are crisp and shining golden
brown on the outside, yet still juicy within – about 8 minutes, turning
once. Cram the lumps of chicken into hot pitta bread with the spiced
yoghurt and some shredded crisp lettuce.

Spiced Chicken with Brown Butter

Ground coriander, cumin and both mild and hot chilli are used here
to lend warmth to a simple grilled chicken. Use an ovenproof dish
that will hold the spicy brown butter, which is an integral part of the
dish and can be spooned over any accompanying rice or perhaps
some bulghur wheat with mint.

FOR 2

2 teaspoons paprika

½ teaspoon cayenne pepper

1 teaspoon ground cumin

½ teaspoon coriander seeds, crushed

3 cloves of garlic, finely chopped

salt

50g / 2oz butter, at room temperature

4 chicken thighs

Mix together all the spices, garlic and salt and beat them into the butter. Spread the butter all over the chicken skin and put each piece in a heatproof dish that will fit under the grill. Drizzle over the oil. Cook under a preheated, moderately hot grill some 12.5cm (5 inches) away from the flame, till the skin is crisp and slightly blackened, about 10 minutes on the first side and 6 on the other.

Spoon the nutty brown butter over the chicken regularly as it cooks. The chicken is cooked when its skin is crisp and golden brown, and the flesh is moist and just short of being undercooked. Serve hot, with boiled rice and the butter and juices from the dish.

Chicken with Spices and Cream

Nothing raises purist eyebrows quite like the mention of curry powder. I will say in its defence that I have eaten some delicious meals where the main dish was spiced with a commercially-blended powder. I prefer to toast and grind my own spices but when short of time I use a 'proprietary' powder, then add a few spices of my own.

FOR 4

4 chicken pieces, breasts or thighs

salt

freshly ground black pepper

25g / 1oz butter

1 tablespoon groundnut oil

2 medium onions, roughly chopped

3 plump cloves of garlic, crushed

2 tablespoons curry powder, from a recently opened tin

½ teaspoon ground cinnamon

4 medium tomatoes, seeded and chopped

250ml / 8fl oz chicken stock

100ml / 4fl oz double cream

juice of ½ lemon

Rub salt and pepper into the chicken. Heat the butter and oil in a shallow pan, add the chicken and cook till the skin is golden. Add the onions and garlic and cook over a medium heat until soft, about 7 or 8 minutes.

Stir in the curry powder and cinnamon. Cook for 4 minutes until the spices are cooked. Add the tomatoes and the stock, then simmer until the chicken pieces are tender and cooked right through, about 15 minutes.

Stir in the cream. Taste the sauce. Add salt and pepper and the lemon juice, a little at a time, tasting as you go. Simmer for 1 minute, then serve hot, with basmati rice.

Tarragon Chicken

Make sure that the tarragon you are buying, or picking, is the French variety, which has a refined aniseed smell and flavour. There is also a Russian tarragon that has a coarser flavour and a light aroma only. You can spot it by its narrower leaves, and its slight bitterness. Avoid at all costs those skinned chicken breasts; you need the skin to keep the moisture in the flesh as it cooks.

FOR 4 WITH A GREEN SALAD OR HARICOT BEANS

4 large boneless chicken breasts	250ml / 8fl oz double cream
50g / 2oz butter	salt
8 healthy sprigs of fresh tarragon	2–3 teaspoons wine or tarragon vinegar or lemon juice

Slice the chicken breasts into strips about 1cm (½ inch) wide. Melt the butter in a shallow pan over a medium heat. Strip the tarragon leaves from their stems.

When the butter starts to sizzle, add the chicken pieces and tarragon. Cook until the chicken has coloured slightly, about 3 minutes. Move the chicken around the pan but remember that the skin must turn golden in order to give a good flavour. Check that it is almost cooked through by cutting a strip in half. Pour in the cream and let it simmer until it thickens slightly, about another 3 minutes. Add salt and a teaspoonful vinegar or lemon juice, taste, then add a second, then taste again and add a third if you wish.

Half-a-dozen sublime Chicken Sandwiches

Chicken with Watercress and Mushroom Sandwich
Slice a boneless chicken breast into thin strips about 1cm (½ inch) wide. Season with salt and pepper and sauté in butter in a frying pan. Remove the chicken when it starts to brown, after about 1 minute, and set aside to keep warm. (On a plate with a glass bowl on top will do.) Add a little more butter or a drop more oil to the pan, then cook a handful of sliced mushrooms until softened, about 2 minutes. Lift them out with a draining spoon and add to the chicken. Soften a few shredded lettuce or watercress leaves and stems in the butter left in the pan, lift them out and stir in a couple of tablespoons of mayonnaise. Spread two soft baps or crusty rolls, split and toasted, with the mayonnaise and then pile on the chicken, mushrooms and leaves.

Hot Chicken with Cream and Garlic Sandwich
Slice a chicken breast into 1-cm (½-inch) strips. Sauté with a sliced clove of garlic in a little butter till the strips start to brown, about 1 minute. Stir in some chopped fresh herbs, whatever you have, and enough double cream to make a thick 'glop'. Check for seasoning, then spoon over split, toasted rolls or slather into hunks of French bread.

Yesterday's Roast Chicken Sandwich
Stir-fry small strips and hunks of roast chicken in a little oil, butter or dripping in a frying pan. Shred any cooked greens such as broccoli, spring greens or spinach, and throw in with the chicken. Season generously (these are leftovers remember), and cook for 2 or 3 minutes. Scoop in any leftover gravy and pan juices, then when very hot, pile into halves of French bread or muffins. Eat while still steaming.

Chicken with Basil Mayonnaise Sandwich

Make a basil mayonnaise, either by stirring shredded basil leaves into mayonnaise or mixing bottled pesto with an equal amount of a good-quality, ready-made mayonnaise. Spread it over thick slices of good white bread, then top with thick slices of well-salted cooked cold chicken and spicy salad leaves such as rocket. Crisp iceberg lettuce will do if there is nothing else.

Hot Garlic Butter Chicken Sandwich

Lay thin slices of cooked chicken on toasted English muffins or bread. Spread with garlic butter, then flash under the grill until the butter melts.

Grilled Blue Cheese Chicken Sandwich

Cream a little blue cheese (anything will do) with some butter at room temperature. Add a few chopped walnuts if you have some (a spoonful of Cognac wouldn't go amiss either). Spread this mixture on thick slices of cold chicken. Lay the chicken on crisp toast, grill till bubbling, then top with another slice of hot toast. Occasionally you come across people who mutter darkly about eating meat and cheese at the same time. Ignore them, they don't know what they are missing.

Chicken Po' Boy

The po' boy, or poor boy, is the classic New Orleans snack of French bread stuffed with fried fish or meat. Oysters, fried in cornmeal, were the original main ingredient, though the really poor boys had only fried potatoes. Good mayonnaise, and plenty of it, is essential. This is the basic chicken version.

FOR 2

2 small baguettes
1 skinned chicken breast
fine cornmeal or plain flour
a little groundnut oil for frying

mayonnaise
shredded lettuce, iceberg or Cos
½ lemon

Split the baguettes lengthways, put the halves together and warm them in a hot oven. While they are heating, slice the chicken breast into six pieces and roll them in the cornmeal or flour. Alternatively, put the cornmeal or flour in a bag and shake the pieces in it.

Fry the chicken in hot shallow oil till crisp, about 4 or 5 minutes, turning once. Remove the bread from the oven and spread all the cut sides generously with mayonnaise. Add some shredded lettuce to the bottom half of each baguette, then pile on the fried chicken pieces. Squeeze over the lemon juice and fit on the top halves. Press down firmly and eat while still warm.

Grilled Chicken with Muscat Wine and Thyme

These chicken pieces will be especially delicious if you let the sweet wine caramelise slightly on the skin as they grill. Use an orange muscat wine, such as Essensia or Brown Brothers for a change, drinking the rest of the bottle with nuts and fruit afterwards. I serve this dish with sautéed potatoes and a blood orange and watercress salad.

FOR 2

1 small carrot
1 small onion
a stick of celery
4 cloves of garlic, lightly
   crushed

the leaves from a few fresh
   sprigs of thyme
2 wineglasses of muscat wine
4 chicken pieces, breasts or
   thighs

Dice the carrot, onion and celery. The pieces should be about the size of dolly mixtures. Toss them together in a bowl with the garlic cloves, thyme leaves and muscat wine. Put in the chicken pieces and turn them over in the wine. Set them aside whilst you prepare the rest of the meal.

Heat the grill, place the chicken pieces on the grill pan and set them about 10 or 12 cm / 4 or 5 inches from the heat, a little further if they have a bone in them. Spoon over plenty of the herb and wine juices and grill for about 12 or 15 minutes, turning once and basting with the wine. They are ready when the juices from the chicken run clear and the skin is golden and crisp. Spoon the wine and herb juices over the chicken as you serve it.

Plain Grilled Chicken

I find it difficult to think of anything I would rather eat than a piece of chicken that has been grilled over an open fire. I wouldn't choose a breast, much more likely a boned and flattened leg. It will have been brushed with a little olive oil, seasoned with coarsely ground black pepper and grilled over embers, its flesh juicy and its skin slightly charred. The only addition would be half a lemon on the side of my plate.

In the summer, when I can cook and eat my food out of doors, something as simple as grilled chicken is a popular supper. In the winter I have to resort to cooking on my grill indoors. Like most domestic grills I guess, this is one where the heat comes from above. It does not give quite the same effect as this most ancient of cooking methods; the food lacks the smoky tones from the aromatic embers, and great care has to be taken to stop the food drying out. I find that continually basting with an aromatic oil or butter keeps the food juicy and fragrant.

I am convinced chicken tastes better, and is somehow juicier, when cooked on the bone. Of course it takes longer to cook through. A little care is needed to avoid the skin being reduced to cinders in order to cook chicken right through to the bone. Set the meat a good 10cm / 4 inches from the heat source and almost double up on the cooking time; expect a leg or breast to take about 20–30 minutes to grill, turning once. To check whether it is cooked don't spear the flesh with a skewer as that method loses all the precious juices. You must pinch it, between thumb and forefinger. Firm and springy – it is probably ready, soft and squashy – almost certainly not.

Four ways with Grilled Chicken

Grilled Chicken with Herb and Shallot Butter

Mix together, in a food processor if you like, 75g / 3oz butter, a small handful of fresh breadcrumbs, 2 finely chopped shallots, 1 clove of garlic and 2 tablespoons fresh parsley. Spread the paste over the chicken 5 minutes before it is due to finish cooking. Baste regularly.

Grilled Mustard Chicken

When you brush the chicken with oil, brush it also with a couple of heaped tablespoons mustard, the crunchy Dijon variety for preference. Grill as usual.

Teriyaki Chicken

Before you grill the chicken pieces, leave them in the following mixture for as long as you have time for, then keep brushing them with it throughout their spell under the grill: 50ml / 2fl oz groundnut oil, 50ml / 2fl oz shoyu soy sauce, 1 finely chopped garlic clove, 2 tablespoons *mirin* (sweet rice wine) and the grated zest from a small orange.

Honey and Soy Grilled Chicken

Mix together 2 tablespoons runny honey with 1 tablespoon each light soy sauce and lemon juice. Sprinkle in a few drops of Tabasco sauce, and 1 crushed clove of garlic. Brush the chicken pieces with the honey and soy mixture and grill as before, brushing regularly.

Grilled Chicken with Garlic and Lemon

A quick way to liven up supermarket chicken pieces. A green salad, the sort you find ready-washed in bags in the supermarket, is a fair accompaniment. Even better is a bowl of lentils – well-rinsed tinned ones will do – dressed with a workaday vinaigrette and brought to life by a generous seasoning of chopped fresh mint leaves.

8 chicken pieces, a mixture of thighs and drumsticks

2 juicy lemons, halved

1 plump clove of garlic, sliced finely

4 tablespoons olive oil

salt

freshly ground black pepper

Put the chicken pieces in a shallow dish. Squeeze over the lemons, add the garlic and the olive oil and set aside while you prepare the rest of the meal.

Heat the grill to medium heat; it should not be too hot, which might cook the outside too quickly, leaving the chicken raw inside. Open the window or switch on the extractor. Season the chicken with salt and pepper. But the pieces in the grill pan, spoon over some of the juices and place under the grill. The chicken should sit between 10 and 15cm (4 and 6 inches) from the heat source. Turn once, basting with more of the juices.

The chicken is cooked when the skin is crisp all over, and caramelised in places, and the juices from the meat run clear when pierced with a metal skewer. Serve hot or cold, with the cooking juices poured over.

Grilled Chicken with Red Chilli, Garlic and Yoghurt

A flattering side dish for this spicy grilled chicken is courgettes with yoghurt. Stir-fry coarsely grated courgette, squeezed dry, with a little groundnut oil and a few mustard seeds until tender, about 4 or 5 minutes. Stir in a few spoonfuls of thick yoghurt and a sprinkling of paprika. Or try the Bulghur Wheat with Butter and Almonds recipe on page 195, with a dollop of thick yoghurt on the side.

FOR 2

2 cloves of garlic, peeled

a piece of fresh root ginger, about 2.5cm (1 inch) long, peeled and chopped

2 teaspoons paprika

150ml / ¼ pint plain natural yoghurt

salt

1 tablespoon ground cumin seeds	4 large chicken pieces,
½ teaspoon ground cardamom	breasts, drumsticks or
½ teaspoon chilli powder	thighs

Throw all the ingredients, except the chicken, into the food processor or blender and whizz till smooth. Put the chicken pieces in a shallow dish and smooth over the spicy 'glop'. Set aside for at least 15 minutes, longer if you can, while you prepare the rest of the meal.

Place the chicken under a preheated medium hot grill, about 10cm (4 inches) away from the flame, then cook until the juices run clear – about 15 minutes for boneless joints, 20–25 for those with the bone in – turning once. Let the ochre-coloured skin char a little.

Chicken with Chilli, Lime and Parsley and Quinoa Salad

I love this salad with chicken, and the lime's bright citrus notes lift the grain's earthy blandness. Use chilli oil, instead of the oil and peppers, if you have some, to marinate the chicken.

FOR 2

2 chicken breasts, preferably with the wing attached	2 small hot fresh red peppers, seeded and very thinly sliced
juice of 2 limes	salt
2 tablespoons olive oil	freshly ground black pepper

FOR THE QUINOA SALAD:

100g / 4oz quinoa, see page 225	2 tablespoons extra virgin olive oil
leaves from 2 handfuls of parsley	salt
grated zest and juice of 1 lime	freshly ground black pepper

To make the salad, rinse the quinoa, then cook it in boiling salted water until it is tender but has some bite to it. This will probably take about 15 minutes, but start tasting after 12. Drain and cool under running water. While the quinoa is cooking, chop the parsley, but not too finely. Mix together the lime zest, juice and oil and add salt and pepper to taste.

Salt and pepper the chicken, and cook with the peppers under a preheated medium-hot grill, well away from the flame, for about 7–10 minutes on each side, spooning over the juices. When you test the chicken for 'doneness', stick in the skewer nearest to the bone, to make sure it is cooked right through. Let the skin char a little.

Dress the grain with the lime and oil and mix with the parsley. Serve with the hot chicken.

Devilled Chicken

Buy a cooked chicken in France and you will get a juicy, savoury bird that will most likely still be warm when you get it home. The supermarkets here have those rather hard, cold, shrink-wrapped numbers. But they can be useful, so here is a way to perk one up quickly. The idea is far from new, but somehow particularly relevant today. Devilled cooked meat recipes can be found in early cookery books.

FOR 2 WITH GREEN SALAD
2 cold cooked chicken legs

FOR THE PASTE:
1 tablespoon Dijon mustard
2 cloves of garlic, finely crushed
2 tablespoons fruity chutney –
   apple, mango, whatever

1 tablespoon Worcestershire
   sauce or mushroom ketchup
a good shake from the Tabasco
   bottle

Mix the ingredients to a paste. Slash the skin and flesh of the chicken with a sharp knife and spread the spicy goo over the meat and inside the slashes.

Grill, 10cm (4 inches) or so from the flame, till sizzling and hot right through – about 10 minutes, turning once.

* Chicken cooked in this way makes a wonderful sandwich. Slice the meat from the bone while still warm and pile into a crusty roll or soft floury bap, then spread with lashings of mayonnaise and a few crisp green leaves

Chicken Marsala

Quick and creamy. The flour used here has two important tasks; it protects the chicken and seals in its moisture, and helps form savoury deposits on the base of the pan, which dissolve into the Marsala or sherry to deepen the flavour of the sauce.

FOR 2 WITH A SALAD

2 boneless chicken breasts	4 tablespoons double cream
50g / 2oz butter	salt
flour	freshly ground black pepper
1 wineglass of Marsala or dry sherry	

Put the chicken between two sheets of clingfilm and bat them out to a 0·5cm (¼ inch) thickness with a rolling pin.

Melt the butter in a shallow pan. Dust the chicken with flour on both sides and lay in the sizzling butter. The butter should be quite hot. Cook for 2 or 3 minutes – no longer – on each side until golden brown. Remove the chicken to a warm plate.

Tip away most of the butter, turn up the heat, and pour the Marsala or sherry into the pan. Let it bubble while you scrape away at the morsels of chicken that have stuck to the pan. When only half the Marsala or sherry is left, tip in the cream. Season with salt and pepper. Return the chicken to the pan. Taste, adding more pepper or salt if you wish, then cook for 1 minute more. Done. A fennel and raw mushroom salad dressed with lemon juice and a bland oil would be fine with this.

Grilled Chicken Livers with Mustard and Thyme Butter

A fine sandwich that will double as a light supper if you have eaten substantially earlier in the day. Muffins or soft floury baps are a doughier substitute for the crisp toast.

FOR 2 AS A SUBSTANTIAL SNACK

50g / 2oz butter, softened
1 shallot, chopped
1 tablespoon grain mustard
2 teaspoons chopped fresh thyme
  leaves
1 tablespoon chopped fresh
  parsley

225g / 8oz chicken livers,
  cleaned
salt
freshly ground black pepper
English muffins or toasted
  bread

Soften the butter so that it is sloppy but not liquid. Mix in the shallot, mustard and herbs. Lay the livers on the grill pan, skewered if you wish, and brush them with a little of the herb butter. Season them well with salt and pepper and cook them under a preheated grill, a very hot one, for 2 or 3 minutes, turning once, till crisp outside, pink within. Test a liver by cutting it in half. Pile them on split muffins or rounds of toast with a dollop of the remaining herb butter.

Warm Chicken Liver Salad

FOR 4 AS A STARTER OR LIGHT MAIN DISH

4 large handfuls of assorted
  leaves: spinach, batavia,
  dandelion, rocket or whatever
75g / 3oz mushrooms, thinly sliced
6 tablespoons vinaigrette, made
  with salt and freshly ground
  black pepper, mustard, red wine
  vinegar and olive oil

1 tablespoon olive oil
225g / 8oz chicken livers,
  cleaned
2 tablespoons red wine
  vinegar
salt
freshly ground black pepper

Wash the leaves, toss them with sliced mushrooms and vinaigrette, and divide between 4 plates.

Heat the olive oil in a frying pan. Add the chicken livers and cook until brown on the outside, about 3 or 4 minutes. They must remain pink in the centre. Tip the livers on to the salad leaves. Pour the vinegar into the pan, scrape up any crusty bits and add a little salt and pepper. Knap the contents of the pan over the livers.

Chicken Livers with Bacon, Capers and their Pan Juices

Nothing polarises opinion like a chicken liver. I love their crumbly texture, crisp outside and pink within, while others cannot even look at them. One thing is for sure: the quicker you cook the little morsels, the better they are.

FOR 2 AS A SUBSTANTIAL SNACK

75g / 3oz fatty bacon, cut into cubes

1 small onion, finely diced

2 cloves of garlic, crushed

a large knob of butter

350g / 12oz chicken livers, cleaned

6 tablespoons dry sherry or red wine

1 tablespoon capers, rinsed

salt

freshly ground black pepper

2 rounds of crisp, buttered toast, to serve

Put the bacon into a large frying pan over a medium heat. When some of the fat starts to melt, fry the onion and garlic till they soften, about 5–7 minutes. Add the butter, a piece about the size of a walnut will do, then toss in the chicken livers. Sauté them until they are crisp on the outside but still pink in the centre. Test a liver by cutting it in half after 1 minute's cooking.

When the livers are done remove with a draining spoon to a warm bowl covered with a plate. Pour the sherry or wine into the pan, scrape up any sediment with a spatula, and let it simmer for 30 seconds. Throw in the capers, return the livers to the pan and season with salt and pepper. Tip out on to rounds of hot toast with the precious pan juices.

Sautéed Chicken Livers

I am not sure whether garlic is better here or not, I have tried it both ways and feel that both are fine. Add a plump clove of garlic, sliced paper-thin, to the butter if you wish. Tart little seedless green grapes from the supermarket will be better here than something more sweet and winy which would be more suitable afterwards.

FOR 2 AS A STARTER OR SUBSTANTIAL SNACK

25g / 1oz butter
50g / 2oz bacon, smoked streaky for preference, diced small
225g / 8oz chicken livers, cleaned
100g / 4oz seedless grapes
1 tablespoon flour
100ml / 4fl oz double cream
salt
freshly ground black pepper
2 tablespoons chopped fresh parsley
2 handfuls of mixed salad leaves, to serve

Melt half the butter in a shallow pan and fry the bacon for a minute or two, add the livers, followed by the grapes. Sprinkle over the flour, cook for a minute till the livers have browned on the outside, then stir in the cream and cook until it is warmed through. Season to taste and add the parsley.

Pile the salad on to two plates, then spoon over the livers and drizzle the sauce on the leaves.

Cold Turkey Sandwiches

I do not believe the turkey was ever really meant to be eaten. What everyone sees in the wretched things is beyond me. It is impossible to cook the breast and legs to perfection at the same time. There are countless dotty suggestions from cookery writers on how to avoid dry legs or breasts, none of which I have ever found make the slightest difference.

Turkey really starts to interest me when it appears cold in a sandwich on Boxing Day evening. (And for the next six no doubt.) The secret is to make sure that the turkey is not cold from the fridge, but is at cool room temperature.

Roast Turkey, Apple and Cranberry Sandwich

Slice the cold roast turkey into pieces about as thick as a one pound coin, which is probably thicker than you would expect. Grate an apple or two, skin and all, and stir in a dollop of cranberry sauce. Scatter in a few walnuts (they can be freshly shelled ones at Christmas) and a drizzle of nut or sunflower oil. Season the sliced turkey, being enthusiastic with the salt, then pile on to unbuttered brown bread with the grated apple and cranberry.

Roast Turkey, Hot Bacon and Chutney Sandwich
Now we're talking. Butter two slices of hot toast. Cover one with thinly-sliced cold roast turkey. Spread the turkey with mango chutney. Cover the mango chutney with streaky bacon that is both hot and crisply-fried. Slap on the second piece of hot buttered toast.

Quick things to do with leftover Christmas Turkey

You have eaten the best bits roast with little sausages, nutty stuffing and proper gravy. You probably also had sprouts, though I cannot imagine why, and sweet roast parsnips and crisp roast potatoes. Here are some ideas for the rest of the bird:

* Cut the largest, flattest slices of breast you can. Lay them on a grill pan. Spread them with pesto sauce from a jar. Cover with thin slices of Gruyère cheese and grill till it starts to melt. Catch the cheese before it goes rubbery; it should be just melting

* Cut chunks of brown and white turkey meat into bite-sized lumps. Melt a little of the dripping from the turkey tin in a frying pan. Fry a handful of diced streaky bacon and button mushrooms till golden. Throw in 2 minced cloves of garlic and a handful of cooked broccoli florets. Throw in twice as much turkey meat as mushrooms and greens. Fry until everything is hot. Pour in a wineglass of red wine and let it bubble till syrupy. Taste it, you may need salt and pepper. Eat as it is or pile it over a plateful of salad leaves

* Strip the carcass. No, I don't know why you bought such a big bird. You will be left with lumps of brown and white meat of all sizes and some wonderful jelly. Melt a large knob of butter in a frying pan and gently cook a tablespoon dried tarragon, which you have reconstituted with an equal amount of boiling water. Stir in a 100ml / 4fl oz pot of double cream. Boil until it starts to thicken. Throw in the turkey scraps and the jelly. Warm through, then taste and add salt and pepper. A drop or two of lemon juice would not go amiss. Serve with hunks of bread and glasses of dry white wine

8

Meat

*T*raditionally, it is the meat recipes that form the bulk of a cookery book. In this one I have included approximately 40, which is somewhat less than those for chicken or fish. I feel that this is very much in line with modern eating patterns. I know of no one who eats as much red meat now as they did ten, five or even two years ago. Almost without exception people are eating more fish and poultry, and I feel bound to respect that trend. I suspect that meat's repositioning in our diet is due to a number of reasons.

It is now recognised that we should cut down on fat consumption to reduce the risk of heart disease. The healthy eating campaign has highlighted the World Health Organisation's recommendation that we should all eat less fat, particularly saturated fat – the type in meat. Their suggestion that no more than 30 per cent of our energy should come from the fat we eat in meat and dairy produce is way below the actual figure of 42 per cent. It is regrettable that in order to be really succulent meat needs a significant percentage of fat.

Secondly, many more people are now aware of the unpalatable side of intensive farming methods. More of us now understand that if we are to enjoy the benefits of cheap meat it is the animals who must pay. The majority of meat consumed in this country has been produced by intensive farming. My objection to this is that the animals are often kept in totally unnatural conditions. Intensive farming methods mean animals often never see the grass they traditionally live on, spending their time in situations that prohibit their normal behaviour. Most are confined, some shackled, and many never see the light of day, especially calves for veal, which are still kept tethered in total darkness with little more than concrete to lie on.

The food scares of recent years have also left their mark. Disease has become rife in intensive farming, whether of poultry and eggs (or fish for that matter), or cattle. I am sure that I am not alone in being amazed and appalled that cattle, who are, of course, natural herbivores, were being fed the processing waste of their own kind. It may sound simplistic but to rearrange an animal's existence so drastically is bound to lead to trouble of one sort or another.

The more adventurous we become in our eating and cooking the less likely we are to rely on meat as the most important feature of a meal. Many cuisines make more of fish, vegetables and grains than we historically do, and meat is often no longer such a prominent part of our shopping lists.

There is much talk about 'real meat'. This is a term used to signify meat from old-fashioned breeds, which have been reared in the traditional manner. That is to say the animals spend their lives on something nearer to what we imagine a 'story book' farm to be like, without being subjected to the degrading procedures of intensive farming. Most animals feed on pasture, with all the grasses, herbs and clover that go with it, and home-grown, often organic, feedstuffs. The animals have access to open air with shelter when needed, and are not given growth promoters or routine antibiotics. Pigs are kept in grass paddocks in summer and straw-filled pens in winter.

Such farmers are caring ones who often accompany their animals to the slaughterhouse to ensure that their animals suffer from as little stress as possible. 'Real meat' is usually produced by small-scale operations, often on family farms, and it is important to note that farmers producing meat in this way are a growing band, not a dying breed. As you would expect, meat produced in this way is more expensive, but it should come as no surprise when people say that it tastes like 'meat used to'. It is my hope that the trend away from quantity in favour of quality will mean that one day all meat may be produced this way.

At its best, meat can be a succulent and substantial addition to a fast meal; pork chops sizzling from the pan, lamb steaks charred crisp outside and juicy and pink within or a thin slice of liver glistening with savoury onion gravy.

LAMB

I am not convinced that slow-cooking or a cream-based sauce does much for lamb. Lamb should be cooked quickly by fierce heat so that the outside is crisp, with the edges very lightly charred. The inside must be sweet, juicy and pink. I have no doubt that this is best attained by cooking over a charcoal fire. Lamb offers itself to this type of cooking better than almost anything else. But few of us have access to a charcoal grill.

For most of us, myself included during winter months, a grill that cooks from above is all there is. A ridged, cast-iron grill that fits over the heat works to good effect, but is only practical when used with an efficient extractor fan. The recipes in this section contain instructions for those with grills where the heat comes from above. The result will be better if you have a charcoal grill, but timings must then be taken with a pinch of salt as I have no idea of how much heat you have harnessed in your wonderful charcoal brazier.

Lamb seems to me to be at its best when robust herbs, like thyme or rosemary, are involved. When lamb is not grilled with olive oil and these hardy aromatics then it requires a bold spicing from a sweet or hot pepper, or the warmth of ground cumin and coriander. I have enjoyed lamb best in Morocco and Greece, less in Italy and even less so in France. Roast lamb, which does not come within the realm of this book, cooked with garlic and herbs and served with pan juices and roast potatoes, is another matter.

For the quick cook there are several cuts to bear in mind. Cutlets from the best end, of course, and thicker chump chops from the rear of the saddle, are good for grilling and frying. Cubed lamb is best known for casseroles but is better spiced and grilled. If you thread the meat on to a skewer, choose a flat one so that the meat does not slip round when you turn it.

Minced or ground lamb often ends up in shepherd's pie and spaghetti bolognaise, which is a shame, as it makes the best meatballs, especially when spiced with mint and cumin. Choose meat that has been finely ground; it sticks together better during cooking. Generally, I avoid made-up lamb kebabs, as butchers are often too timid with their spicing for my taste.

Rack of lamb is the quickest of roast meats, cooked in 20 minutes or less. Steaks, cut from the leg, are fine pieces of meat and good value. Cut into strips for a stir-fry or grill them whole.

* Lamb discolours quickly once sliced. This means that you can often find it marked down in supermarkets at the end of the day. A good buy for a late shopper

* I have to say that I never buy frozen lamb. It looks so depressing in the supermarket freezers

* Good-quality lamb should have crisp white fat with a waxy feel to it. The flesh should be a soft pink in young lamb deepening to an orangey-red at one year

* Lamb is the one meat that has escaped the attention of the 'factory farmers'. The animals thrive on rough, often inaccessible pasture often made up of short grass, heather and herbs

Grilled Lamb Chump Chops

FOR 2

2 large chump chops, 2.5cm /	olive oil
1 inch thick	salt
1 clove of garlic, peeled	freshly ground black pepper

Lay the chops on a plate. Crush the garlic to a paste with a pestle and mortar or on a board with the flat of a large knife blade. Smooth a little olive oil over both sides of the chops with your fingers, spread over half of the crushed garlic, then set aside while you prepare the rest of the meal.

Heat the grill, and spread more olive oil and the rest of the garlic over the chops. Cook the chops under a hot grill, for a minute on each side, then turn the heat down a little and continue grilling for 4 minutes, without turning. Remove from the grill and season lightly on both sides with a little salt and a few grinds of pepper. Eat at once.

Serve with courgettes sautéed with mint, followed by a leafy salad.

Lamb Chump Chops with Yoghurt and Mint

There was a certain fashion for making chilled cucumber soup by grating cucumber into yoghurt, then tarting it up with spices and mint. Good as it was, it wasn't really soup. Made thick and without the cucumber it makes a spicy paste with which to anoint lamb before grilling.

FOR 2

4 small chump chops, about 2cm / ¾ inch thick, weighing 400g / 14oz in total

6 tablespoons thick, natural plain yoghurt

2 plump cloves of garlic, peeled

a small handful of fresh mint leaves

1 teaspoon ground cumin

1 teaspoon ground coriander

½ teaspoon cayenne pepper

¼ teaspoon each of salt and freshly ground black pepper

Mix all the ingredients except the lamb in the blender or by hand. Heat the grill to very hot.

Slather the spiced yoghurt over both sides of the lamb and grill till firm and ever so slightly charred at the edges. The lamb should be pink in the middle, about 4 minutes on each side.

Eat with:

* A cucumber salad dressed with white wine vinegar and chopped fresh dill

* Fragrant Brown Basmati Rice, page 200

* Grilled Potatoes, page 169

* The spice paste for this recipe can also be applied to cubed lamb to be grilled and stuffed into pitta bread

* It makes a spicy sauce as well for smothering on baked or grilled potatoes

Lamb Sandwiches

Britain is very good at country house hotels, full of ticking clocks and sleeping dogs. I have fond memories of working in one where the chef-patron was famed for his afternoon teas with home-made cakes. He knew nothing of the pranks we would get up to during his afternoon break. Two or three of us would rush through our duties, then make ridiculous fairy cakes, smothered with fluorescent pink icing topped with whole glacé cherries, which we would leave among the exquisite pastries on the elegant tea trays. They looked so absurd, rather like garden gnomes at Sissinghurst.

But these afternoon duties were punctuated with feasts from the larder. The cold roast local lamb made the best sandwiches. We spread dripping on the home-baked white rolls, then piled on sliced lamb spread with redcurrant jelly.

Lamb and Cracked Wheat Pittas

This recipe is one of the very few reasons for keeping a packet of dried mint in the house.

FOR 2 AS A SNACK

100g / 4oz fine bulghur wheat or 50g / 2oz sprouted wheat

225g / 8oz rare roast lamb, sliced 1cm / ½ inch thick, at room temperature

1 tablespoon dried mint

juice of 1 lemon

a handful of fresh English parsley, finely chopped

2 spring onions, trimmed and cut small

salt

4 pitta breads or brown rolls

Soak the bulghur wheat for 15 minutes in cold water. Toss the lamb slices with the dried mint, lemon juice, parsley and onions. Taste and season with salt. Squeeze the water from the wheat. Mix the soaked or sprouted wheat with the rest of the ingredients. Check the seasoning and pile into toasted pittas.

Lamb Noisettes with Thyme and Black Olives

FOR 2 AS A MAIN DISH

4 noisettes of lamb, about
  2.5cm / 1 inch thick
olive oil
1 tablespoon chopped fresh
  thyme leaves

75g / 3oz small black olives,
  stones removed
freshly ground black pepper
½ lemon, cut into quarters

Brush the noisettes of lamb with olive oil. Sprinkle both sides of the chops with chopped thyme.

Heat a small amount of olive oil in a heavy shallow pan, just a thin film on the bottom of the pan. When the oil is hot sear the noisettes on both sides, cooking them for about 3 minutes on each side.

Just before the lamb is cooked, toss the olives into the pan. Grind black pepper quite coarsely over the lamb, squeeze over a little lemon and eat immediately. Eat with:

* Wide noodles tossed in parsley and butter

* Tomato Stew, page 183

* Pasta with Whole Garlic, Goat's Cheese and Thyme, page 107

* Mashed Potatoes, page 168

Moroccan Spiced Grilled Lamb

The effect that the Moroccan-inspired spice paste has on the lamb here depends on the length of time the lamb spends in the marinade.

Some may like the light spicy notes you have when the lamb is marinated with the spices for 20 minutes or so. Others will prefer the deeper flavours of a 2-hour soaking. This is particularly good when the meat is seared on a hot ridged grill pan over a gas flame.

FOR 2

2 chump chops or 350g / 12oz cubed lamb

1 small onion, grated or very finely chopped

1 clove of garlic, crushed

½ teaspoon ground cumin

½ teaspoon paprika

a pinch of cayenne pepper

2 tablespoons each of chopped fresh flat-leaf parsley and coriander leaves

4 tablespoons olive oil

juice of ½ lemon

Put the lamb in a shallow dish. Mix the other ingredients and toss with the meat. Leave for as long as you wish before cooking. The flavour will become stronger the longer the meat is left in the marinade.

Shake any liquid from the meat and cook under a preheated grill till firm and lightly crisped on the outside and pink and juicy within, about 3–4 minutes on each side. Eat with:

* Fresh Plum or Apricot *Tabbouleh*, page 193

* Bulghur Wheat and Aubergine Pilaf, page 192

* Tomato Salad, page 182

Spiced Lamb Kofta with Pine Nuts and Red Cabbage

Crisp red cabbage, shredded really fine and lubricated with a good dollop of thick Greek yoghurt makes a change from lettuce as the ubiquitous pitta-stuffer. Throw in a few raisins too if you like. These are rather moist and may break up a little during cooking, but they are none the worse for that.

225g / 8oz minced fresh lamb
1 medium onion
1 clove of garlic; fresh and plump
1 teaspoon ground cumin
1 teaspoon cayenne pepper
1 small egg, lightly beaten
1 tablespoon pine nuts

¼ teaspoon each salt and
   freshly ground black pepper
groundnut oil, for
   shallow-frying
juice of ½ lemon
pitta bread, Greek yoghurt
   and red cabbage, to serve

Put the minced lamb in a large mixing bowl. Peel the onion and garlic and put in the food processor till finely chopped or grate them coarsely. Mix with the other ingredients and the salt and freshly ground pepper.

Knead with your hands until the mixture comes together. It will be quite wet. Roll into small rounds, no bigger than table-tennis balls. Flatten them slightly. Warm a finger's depth of oil in a shallow pan, and when it is very hot add the balls, in small batches, and fry till crisp and brown on the bottom – 4–5 minutes. Turn carefully and fry the other side for about 2 minutes. Drain on kitchen paper, then squeeze over the lemon juice.

Serve hot, in split warm pitta breads, with red cabbage, as above.

Lamb Grilled with Mustard and Lemon

A mild enough seasoning that does not overpower the flavour of the lamb. Steaks cut from the leg usually come nearly 2.5cm / 1 inch thick, for anything thinner or thicker alter the cooking time accordingly.

FOR 2

2 plump cloves of garlic, peeled
a good pinch of sea salt
1 tablespoon fresh thyme leaves
   or 2 teaspoons dried thyme
2 tablespoons grain mustard

2 tablespoons lemon juice
4 tablespoons olive oil
4 lamb steaks or chops,
   weighing about 100g / 4oz
   each

Crush the garlic with the salt in a pestle and mortar or in a small bowl with the end of the rolling pin. Add the herbs, mustard and lemon juice. Whisk in the oil with a fork, or small whisk, until the mixture is sparkling and has slightly thickened.

Pour one-third over the lamb, turn over the meat and anoint that side too with a second. Heat the grill to very hot. Grill the lamb for 3–4 minutes on each side, depending on how thick the meat is. Brush with the remaining mixture as you turn the meat. The lamb should be a little singed outside, and rare within.

Serve with:

* Tomatoes with Garlic, page 178

* Grilled Mushrooms, page 151

* any of the green salads, pages 175–6

Liver with Onion Chutney

You will need a chutney that is thick with onions and raisins, rather than a sweet fruity one. The coarser the pickle the better. Coriander seeds, which often appear in these products, are a bonus. Don't expect anything even vaguely edible from a dark-brown, vinegary, sugar-laden commercial product.

FOR 2

2 tablespoons olive oil
25g / 1oz butter
275g / 10oz lamb's liver, thinly sliced
1 wineglass of red wine

4 tablespoons coarse-cut oniony chutney (if you have a hot chutney use 2 tablespoons, plus 2 of a mild fruity one)

Heat the oil and butter in a frying pan. When it sizzles, fry the liver very quickly until brown on both sides, probably a minute on each side. Remove the liver to warm plates. Pour the wine into the pan. Scrape up any residue from the pan with a spatula as the wine reduces over the heat. Stir in the chutney. As soon as it bubbles, spoon over the liver.

If you have the time, mashed potato is good with liver cooked this way, or in any other for that matter. If not, I would serve a salad of floppy pale green lettuce, dressed with plenty of lemon, and bread to mop up the sauce.

Kidneys Cooked with Sherry

Most *tapas* bars serve a version of this recipe, some using flour in the sauce while others prefer breadcrumbs. In Spain, this recipe is made with veal kidneys, hardly the things you have just lying around or can pick up on a last-minute dash to the supermarket. Lamb's kidneys make an accessible substitute.

FOR 2, WITH MASHED POTATOES

8 lamb's kidneys, halved and cores removed
juice of 1 lemon
2 tablespoons olive oil
1 medium onion, chopped
2 cloves of garlic, crushed
1 tablespoon flour
1 wineglass of dry sherry
1 tablespoon fresh flat-leaf parsley, chopped
salt
freshly ground black pepper

Drop the kidneys into the lemon juice and mix well. Leave for at least 10 minutes.

Heat the olive oil in a shallow pan and cook the onion until soft and translucent, about 5–7 minutes. Add the garlic and cook briefly over a medium heat. Turn the heat up to boil away any liquid. Drain the kidneys, dry them on kitchen paper and add them to the pan. Brown the kidneys on all sides, stir in the flour and add the sherry with an equal amount of water. Bring to the boil, reduce the heat and simmer for 10 minutes. Add the parsley, taste and season with salt and pepper.

Souvlakia

For several years I spent much of each summer in Greece. It now seems as if I lived on these little lamb parcels bought from street vendors. I have better results when using a ridged cast-iron pan left over the gas until really hot, then brushed with a little oil, than when I attempt to cook under the domestic grill. Marinate the lamb for as long as possible.

FOR 2

1 medium onion, peeled
4 cloves of garlic, peeled
50ml / 2fl oz groundnut oil
½ teaspoon ground cinnamon
1 teaspoon ground cumin
1 teaspoon ground coriander
1 teaspoon ground paprika, and a little more
salt
350g / 12oz lamb, leg or shoulder, cut into 2.5-cm / 1-inch cubes

2 tablespoons loosely-packed, finely-chopped fresh mint
4 tablespoons natural plain yoghurt
4 pitta breads, toasted while the lamb cooks
a handful of crisp shredded lettuce
a little cayenne pepper, to sprinkle

Whizz the onion and garlic with the oil in a food processor till they are reduced to a slush (failing that, you will have to grate the onion and crush the garlic). Mix in the spices, adding a good ½ teaspoon salt. Stir into the cubed lamb, and set aside for as long as you can, tossing it around in the dry marinade from time to time.

Heat the grill to very hot. If the grill is not hot enough the lamb will cook through before the outside is crisp. Shake the cubes dry and grill until slightly charred without and pink and juicy within. It will take about 2 minutes on each side in a hot pan or 4 minutes on each side over charcoal or under a domestic grill. Sprinkle with salt.

Stir half the mint into the yoghurt in a small bowl. Split each warm pitta bread to reveal a pocket, pile in the hot lamb with the shredded lettuce. Spoon over the yoghurt and the rest of the mint, sprinkle lightly with cayenne. Eat with your hands.

PORK

Pork is not the meat it was. Cross-breeding and intensive farming have taken their toll, and the great drive to produce leaner pork has resulted in a loss of the meat's inherent richness and succulence. Pigs often spend their lives on concrete floors, never allowed out to forage for their own food, and sometimes permanently tethered. The stress of modern slaughter too can result in a bland and dry meat.

The good news is that some small-scale farmers are producing pork by conventional methods. This free-range pork is a different product altogether. Many of the old breeds renowned for their flavour are being used and are allowed to roam in the open air. The combination of humane rearing and traditional pure breeds gives a product which has a deeper flavour and more succulent texture. Free-range pork is available from better butchers and some food halls.

Cuts of pork suited to the short-of-time are steaks cut from the leg or tenderloin and chops from the loin. Steaks are sometimes batted thinly to form an escalope, which can be used in place of veal escalopes. Pork cuts such as these can be pan-fried or grilled, being served with their pan juices or a quickly-made cream sauce, or stir-fried.

* Friends of pork include garlic, lemon, fresh sage leaves, pears and apples, plums and apricots. Peppercorns, either soft green ones from a tin or crushed black ones, and aniseed notes from star anise, fennel or tarragon are flattering seasonings for pork too

BACON

Bacon, either green or smoked, back or streaky, can be a godsend to the quick cook. It plays a starring role in two of the great snacks of all time, the British bacon sandwich and the American BLT, and when grilled and chopped it adds savour if thrown into pasta and salads.

Buying bacon needs care: I avoid anything wrapped in plastic – it has little flavour and is always wet and slimy. It rarely tastes of anything but salt. My favourite bacon is streaky, which I think has a better flavour and texture. Pancetta from Italian grocers is my choice for any occasion where the bacon needs dicing; it has plenty of delicious fat, which is good for cooking. For all other uses I prefer a double smoked streaky such as that found at Messrs Paxton and Whitfield, the London cheesemongers.

* The colour of bacon depends on the cure, but expect the better-flavoured types to be quite dark. Smoked bacon will be slightly darker than green bacon, and drier to the touch

* I have found that loose bacon, stacked in piles in butchers and grocers, is often a better product than anything prepacked. Far from the supermarkets with their fancy packaging, the best seems to be found in the fast-disappearing country grocers which double as the local post office

* Bacon, particularly smoked, has a flavour that goes a long way. Use it as a seasoning rather than an ingredient; chop grilled bacon and crumble it over leafy salads such as *frisée* and spinach or chicory, and toss a handful into a broccoli or cabbage stir-fry

Pork Steaks with Lemon and Sage

Dried sage is the most pungent of herbs, having a bullying effect on any food. It belongs in the bin. By contrast, fresh sage, used a leaf at a time to scent cooking oils before frying meat, is a much more delicate affair.

FOR 2

flour, for dredging
salt
freshly ground black pepper
2 pork steaks, weighing about 200g / 7oz each and 1cm / ½ inch thick

25g / 1oz butter, plus a large knob to finish
2 tablespoons groundnut oil
10 fresh sage leaves
2 tablespoons lemon juice

Season the flour with salt and pepper, dip the escalopes in it and shake off any excess. Heat the butter and oil in a shallow pan with the sage leaves. When the butter is hot, slide in the steaks and fry quickly till browned. They will take 3 minutes per side if the butter is hot enough. Put the steaks on a warm plate. Pour the lemon juice into the pan and let it come to a boil. Scrape away at any crusty bits stuck to the bottom of the pan with a spatula. Stir in the large knob of butter, about the size of a walnut, and let it melt. Return the pork to the pan for a few seconds. Serve the steak with its juices and eat while hot.

Serve with:

* Raw fennel, shredded and tossed in lemon juice and nut oil; lettuce hearts, quartered, and drizzled with the pan juices from the pork; plain wide noodles (*pappardelle*) tossed in butter

* Cherry Tomato and Watercress Salad, page 181

Porc au Poivre

A richly aromatic dish for an autumn or winter's night. The pork chops are best if cut thin, no more than 2.5cm / 1 inch, and the fat is allowed to crisp in the butter. Crushing the peppercorns coarsely is best done with a pestle and mortar where the process is marginally slower, but is easier to control than an electric mill. Ground too fine and the spice will burn.

FOR 2

50g / 2oz butter
2 pork chops, about 2.5cm /
    1 inch thick
2 tablespoons roughly-crushed
    black peppercorns
3 shallots, finely chopped

1 tablespoon Cognac
4 tablespoons red wine
100ml / 4fl oz tinned
    consommé or chicken stock
walnut-sized knob of cold
    butter, to finish the sauce

Melt half the butter in a shallow pan over a medium heat. Press the chops into the crushed peppercorns. Make sure that as many as possible stick to the chops. When the butter sizzles add the chops. Cook until the juices run clear, about 8–10 minutes, turning once during cooking.

Remove the chops from the pan and keep warm. Melt the rest of the butter in the pan and cook the shallots till soft, about 2 minutes. Pour in the Cognac. Stir. Cook for 1 minute at a good boil. Add the wine and bubble for a further minute. Pour in the consommé or stock and leave at an enthusiastic simmer until the liquid has reduced to 6 tablespoonfuls, about 4 minutes.

Stir in the cold butter. This will give a shine and richness to the sauce. Pour the sauce over the chops. Serve with mashed potatoes and a plate of salad afterwards.

Pork Steaks with Fennel

The lemon in this recipe is quite pronounced. To enhance the aniseed notes you could add a teaspoon, but no more, of Pernod with the lemon juice. Serve with a dish of white mushrooms, buttons or large cups, sliced thin and dressed with a little olive oil and lots of chopped fresh parsley.

FOR 2

2 tablespoons olive oil
2 thick pork steaks, about 1cm /
   ½ inch thick
salt
freshly ground white pepper

1 medium fennel bulb, weighing
   about 300g / 11oz, thinly
   sliced, green fronds saved
juice of 1 large lemon

Warm the olive oil in a sauté or frying pan. Season the meat with salt and pepper. When the oil is hot, add the pork, and fry quickly on one side to a proper golden brown, about 1–2 minutes. Then turn over, without piercing the flesh, and seal the other side. Turn down the heat, throw in the fennel, apart from the fronds, and cook until it has softened and browned slightly. Check that the meat is cooked through, but still juicy. It will take about 7–9 minutes.

Remove the meat to warm plates with a draining spoon. Throw in the fennel fronds and the lemon juice, scrape any crusty bits from the bottom of the pan with a spatula, boil for a couple of minutes, then pour over the pork.

Pork and Pears

The garlic is used here purely to scent the cooking oil. A faint whiff more than anything. A fluffy pile of puréed potatoes, mashed without butter or oil, and a few sharp leaves would be my choice for a side dish. It is important that the pears are ripe.

FOR 2

2 loin pork chops, about 2.5cm / 1 inch thick
salt
freshly ground white pepper
2 tablespoons groundnut oil
2 cloves of garlic, crushed flat but unpeeled

2 ripe pears, cut into eights and cored; peeled if you wish
75ml / 3fl oz / ½ wineglass of dry white wine
75ml / 3fl oz vegetable or chicken stock or water

Season the chops with salt and pepper. Heat the groundnut oil with the crushed garlic cloves in a shallow pan over a high heat. Slide in the pork chops – take care, they will spit at you – and seal on both sides.

Turn down the heat, add the pears, and cook until both are tender and browned, about 10 minutes. Remove the chops and pears to a warm plate. Pour most of the fat from the pan and return to the heat. Pour in the wine, scraping away at the bits of pork and pear that are clinging to the pan. Add the stock, or water, and simmer until reduced by half, about 2–3 minutes. Pour the pan juices over the chops and pears.

Eat with:

* a salad of bitter leaves, such as rocket

* chicory leaves dressed with lemon and chopped walnuts

* spinach leaves, cooked for a few seconds with some drops of water, till they wilt, black pepper, no butter

Five-spiced Pork Buns

Not pork buns as in *dim sum*. Pork buns as in spiced grilled pork sandwiches.

ENOUGH FOR 2 AS A SNACK

275g / 10oz pork leg or shoulder, cut into 2.5-cm / 1-inch dice
3 cloves of garlic, crushed
2 tablespoons dark soy sauce
2 tablespoons lemon juice
2 teaspoons five-spice powder
2 tablespoons runny honey
freshly ground black pepper
2 handfuls of torn *pak choi* or watercress
4 soft baps, sesame seed buns or English muffins, for serving

Put the pork in a bowl and mix with the other ingredients.

Heat the grill to very hot. Line the grill pan with foil, put in the lumps of pork and grill till crisp on the outside, but still juicy within, about 5–6 minutes, shaking the pan regularly to turn the meat.

Split the baps, buns or muffins horizontally, dip their cut sides in the cooking juices in the grill pan then pile on the chunks of pork. Eat while hot.

VEAL

Veal is the meat of a four- to six-month-old calf. It is inclined to be lacking in flavour and dry. I choose not to buy veal, and have very few friends who cook it either. Neither of my local 'upmarket' butchers say there is much call for any cuts of veal beyond paper-thin escalopes, though both my local supermarkets sell a small amount of cubed meat for casseroles.

There are no recipes for veal in this book *per se*. Many of the pork recipes, particularly those for chops and steaks, and a few for lamb, such as the pan-fried or grilled steaks, are quite suitable for veal. The *Porc au Poivre* and Pork Steaks with Fennel would be especially suitable. You will find more about veal in the introduction to the meat chapter.

BEEF

Lean does not necessarily mean flavoursome. Beef needs a fair marbling of fat in among the meat if it is not to be dry. Little veins of creamy fat are a sure sign that the meat is likely to be succulent. Dark, almost purple meat means that the carcass has been hung for about a fortnight and should have some flavour.

There is a great deal of talk about breeds, and whether the Aberdeen Angus has a better flavour than the Hereford or the Charolais. The answer is, of course, the one you like best. The only way to discover which you prefer is to taste them all.

The recipes for beef here are all very simple. There is no need to cook beef beyond recognition or cover up its flavour with an overpowering sauce. Steaks are useful for those who have little time to cook. In the absence of a charcoal grill you may find a ridged cast-iron grill pan that sits on the heat a sound investment. The trick is to get them very hot before you add the (oiled) meat.

Carpaccio

In my youth I was a waiter at The Savoy. I watched with amazement and disgust as pallid businessmen lunched on steak tartare. To this day I still cannot stomach the mixture of minced raw beef and raw, barely beaten, egg.

Carpaccio is also raw beef, served with a sauce made from raw eggs. But somehow it is a very different beast. The paper-thin slice of beef, with its soft texture and gentle flavour, is drizzled with a mustardy mayonnaise. I like *ciabatta*, that floury flat Italian bread with it. And rocket leaves dressed with lemon juice, or a spinach salad.

FOR 4

225g / 8oz fillet of beef, scrupulously trimmed of fat

1 teaspoon lemon juice

1 teaspoon Worcestershire sauce

1 heaped teaspoon smooth mild mustard

200g / 7oz mayonnaise – bome-made or bought

a drop of milk

The beef is easier to slice when it is very cold. You can put it in the deep freeze for 15 minutes or so. Slice it very thinly with a long sharp knife. By thinly I mean as thin as you can go without the beef looking like a lace tablecloth. By sharp I mean like a razor. Lay the paper-thin slices on large cold plates.

Mix the lemon juice and seasonings into the mayonnaise. Thin to drizzling consistency with a little milk. Pour ribbons of sauce over the meat.

* An unsophisticated but equally good (better actually) way to eat this dish: split a piece of *ciabatta*, spread the bottom half with the sauce, then pile on the thin slices of meat with a few rocket or spinach leaves and more sauce. Cover with the top half of the bread

The Hamburger

This is the basic hamburger, made with ground beef and seasoned only with salt and pepper. Tomato purée, garlic, mustard, soy and Tabasco sauces are all worthwhile additions, but not really necessary.

The leaner the meat, the drier the hamburger. Choose beef that has a fair amount of fat, perhaps more than you would usually prefer. I suggest at least 10 per cent, which is not a lot. Chuck or neck usually provides the ideal amount of meat and fat. If you buy the meat cubed to mince yourself, beware of overprocessing it, which will reduce it to a sticky paste.

These basic burgers are fried so that you can make a gravy, but grill them if you prefer, and sacrifice the best bit.

FOR 2

225g / 8oz minced beef
salt
freshly ground black pepper

25g / 1oz butter
1 tablespoon groundnut oil

Mix the beef with the salt and pepper. Be frugal with the salt. Use your hands to form two loose but not untidy patties, and set aside.

Heat the butter and oil in a shallow pan. They must be hot and sizzling when you add the burgers. Fry them till crisp on each side, and springy to the touch, about 3 or 4 minutes if you like them rare. If you want to know exactly to what degree they are cooked inside, you will just have to cut one of them open.

Lift out the burgers and keep them warm. Sprinkle 4 tablespoons water into the pan, stir it round over the heat for a few seconds, scraping up all the bits of burger that have stuck to the pan. Let the gravy bubble for a minute, then pour over the meat and serve.

More Hamburger ideas

Consider these hamburger ideas too, all of which are fine, but hardly orthodox. Some may consider them pure heresy.

Add to the raw hamburger mixture:

* 2 teaspoons chilli sauce, Moroccan *harissa* or Indonesian *Sambal Olek*

* a walnut-sized lump of blue cheese stuffed into the middle of each burger

* 1 tablespoon double cream, a crushed clove of garlic and 1 small finely-chopped onion

* 2 teaspoons Dijon-style mustard and a teaspoon Worcestershire sauce

* 2 tablespoons chopped fresh parsley and 2 tablespoons grated mature cheese

* And for serving over the meat or for dipping the bun in, toasted or not:

* Cream Gravy: remove the hamburgers from the pan, sprinkle in a tablespoon flour and scrape up any crusty bits of meat clinging to the pan. Pour in 125ml / 4fl oz double cream, bring to the boil, then season with freshly ground black pepper

* Add 2 tablespoons seedy mustard and 6 of double cream to the pan juices

* Rinse the pan out with 2 tablespoons lemon juice, then throw in a handful of chopped fresh flat-leaf parsley

* Remove the hamburgers from the pan. Add a handful of quartered mushrooms and fry till tender, adding more butter if necessary. Scoop them out and add them to the burgers. Rinse out the pan with Cognac, not forgetting to scrape at the best bits. Spread the split and toasted buns thickly with some of that mushroom pâté that comes in a tube, pile on the burgers and mushrooms and knap over the boozy juices from the pan. Slam the other half of the bun on top and eat

Burger in a Bun

Buy the right bun for the job: no crisp baguettes here, thank you. A soft bun is crucial. I like floury, doughy ones, and have on occasion used an English muffin. Avoid the very airy sesame-sprinkled numbers in the local shop; they are like eating cotton wool.

To my mind, it is essential the bun should be split horizontally and toasted, then dipped in the pan gravy before it meets the burger. The unsophisticated gravy above is ideal. Extras layered between burger and bun are a matter of choice, but consider the following classics:

* Sliced unskinned tomatoes, seasoned with black pepper

* Tartare sauce instead of gravy, made by mixing capers, gherkins, mustard and lemon juice into mayonnaise, slathered copiously on to the toasted bun

* Gruyère, Cheddar or Roquefort cheese grilled on top of the burger

* Iceberg lettuce, cold and crisp, shredded and piled on the bread

* Tomato sauce, one of the quick ones on pages 184–6, spooned over the bread

* Sliced gherkins, like the ones you find all over the pavements outside McDonald's, fished out by horrified youngsters

* Tom Ketch (lots of it)

Sloppy Joes

I love messy food. The sort that runs down your chin or up your arms. This particular mess looks like a hamburger that hasn't worked. American friends assure me that my omission of chopped green peppers from the classic recipe is sacrilegious.

450g / 1lb minced beef

1 onion, chopped

200g / 7oz dark mushrooms, chopped

1 tablespoon Worcestershire sauce

Tabasco sauce

2 tablespoons tomato ketchup

175ml / 6fl oz tomato juice or chopped plum tomatoes from a tin

salt

4 hamburger buns

Heat a frying pan, nothing flimsy, over a high heat until it is really hot. Add the beef and cook until it starts to brown. Add the onion. Stir. Cook till the meat has browned properly; there should be no raw streaks. Add the mushrooms, Worcestershire sauce, a few shakes of Tabasco, the tomato ketchup and juice. Turn down the heat and simmer for 15 minutes. Taste and add salt. Add water if the mixture is at all dry.

Toast the hamburger buns. Sandwich the filling between the toasted buns as best you can. It will spill out all over the place, but that is the point of the whole thing.

Steak Cooked in the Tuscan Manner

The Tuscans know how to cook steak. They rub the raw meat with olive oil and then squeeze on lemon when it is cooked. On the very rare occasions I cook a steak, this is how I do it.

The steak should be no more than 3cm / 1¼ inches thick. It should be cut from the rump, which has more flavour. I suggest you allow 225g / 8oz per person. Rub the steak with olive oil. Not too much, but enough to make it shiny and slightly slippery all over. Grind a little black pepper over the meat, coarsely.

Heat the grill. The meat is best cooked over charcoal. When the grill is hot, cook the meat on or under it for 3 or 4 minutes on each side. A bit less if you like it very rare. Put the steaks on to warm plates. Squeeze a quarter of a lemon over each steak and grind over a little salt.

Steak Sandwich

Mayonnaise, ketchup or mustard often lurk in steak sandwiches. None of them is necessary. The juices from the pan are good enough.

MAKES 2 LARGE SANDWICHES

4 small sirloin steaks, weighing about 75g / 3oz each, cut 1 cm / ½ inch thick

a little olive oil

salt

freshly ground black pepper

2 small baguettes, about 20.5cm / 8 inches long

Fry the steaks in just enough oil to stop them sticking to the pan. They will need barely 2 minutes on each side. Salt and pepper the cooked steaks and add a tablespoon or two of water to the pan. Slice the baguettes in half horizontally. Scrape any crisp sediment from the meat into the liquid as it bubbles. Dip the soft sides of the bread into the meat juices and pile the steak on to the two bottom halves. Press on the lids.

* A variation that seems to be exceptionally popular is to spread the halved baguettes with garlic butter, then warm them in the oven as you would garlic bread (that is, wrapped in foil). Lay the sliced steak on the garlic bread and pour over the pan juices

* A dab of mustard, rather than a dollop, can be a good addition, as is a thin spreading of anchovy sauce or *Patum Peperium*

Beef Stroganov

This late-nineteenth-century recipe was created for, and named after, the famous Russian family by their chief. The recipe found its 15 minutes of fame in the 1960s, when it became, along with coq au vin and profiteroles with chocolate sauce, standard bistro fare. Perhaps it was then that tomato purée, chopped tomatoes and tarragon found their way into the recipe. They are not in this one. Quartered mushrooms, rather than sliced, are unorthodox, but juicier. You will need two pans.

FOR 4

225g / 8oz beef tenderloin,
   trimmed of all fat
1 teaspoon paprika
salt
freshly ground black pepper
75g / 3oz butter
1 tablespoon olive oil

175g / 6oz onions, sliced
175g / 6oz brown mushrooms,
   quartered
1 tablespoon smooth French
   mustard
100ml / 4fl oz (1 small pot)
   soured cream

Cut the beef into fingers 5cm / 2 inches long and 0.5cm / ¼ inch wide. Roll the strips in the paprika, salt and pepper. Heat half the butter with the oil in a shallow pan, add the onions and cook till soft but not coloured, about 5–7 minutes. Add the mushrooms, and cook till tender, around 2–3 minutes.

In another similar pan melt the remaining butter. When it sizzles add the beef strips, cook over a high heat until the outsides are browning and the inside is pink, a minute or two is all it takes. Stir the mustard into the onion and mushroom mixture. Transfer the beef and its spicy buttery juices to the first pan and stir in the soured cream. Taste, add salt or pepper, bring to the boil and serve with wide, plain noodles.

Stir-fried Beef with Broccoli and Mushrooms

I claim no great knowledge of Chinese cooking. I scribbled the recipe down during a demonstration by a visiting Chinese chef. I have probably forgotten a few things, but I think it tastes good enough to set down here. Assemble all the ingredients in little bowls and cups before you start.

FOR 2

350g / 12oz beef, chuck or rump
2 tablespoons thick soy sauce
2 tablespoons medium dry
  sherry
2 scant teaspoons cornflour
4 tablespoons groundnut oil,
  plus 2 teaspoons
salt
freshly ground black pepper
2 tablespoons oyster sauce

1 × 5-cm / 2-inch lump of fresh
  root ginger, peeled and cut
  into matchstick-sized shreds
450g / 1lb broccoli, halved
  through the stalk and cut into
  large florets
100g / 4oz button mushrooms
3 cloves of garlic, thinly sliced
3 spring onions, trimmed and
  cut into 2.5-cm / 1-inch pieces

Cut the beef into pieces 1cm / ½ inch thick and 5cm / 2 inches square. Put them in a bowl with 1 tablespoon soy, half the sherry, 1 teaspoon cornflour, 2 teaspoons oil and 1 tablespoon water. Add a pinch of salt and a few turns of the peppermill. Leave for 15 minutes.

Mix the remaining cornflour and soy in a cup with the oyster sauce and 4 tablespoons water. Heat a work or light frying pan. Add 2 tablespoons oil. Over a high heat, add the ginger, broccoli and mushrooms. Fry and stir till the broccoli turns bright green. Add a pinch of salt and 4 tablespoons water. Cook for 3 minutes.

Remove, and wipe the pan clean. Reheat the pan and add the remaining oil. When hot add the garlic and the spring onions. Stir. Throw in the beef and cook till brown. Throw in the remaining sherry. Keep stirring. Stir the sauce in the cup and add to the pan. Stir till it thickens. Return the broccoli to the pan and serve.

Roast Beef Hash

The simplest form of hash is where yesterday's roast beef and potatoes reappear as a crisp fry-up. American friends who make it in my kitchen include other leftovers from the fridge. Sometimes this is not a good idea. My advice is to keep it simple, but most of all, crisp.

4 tablespoons dripping from the beef pan or 4 tablespoons butter

1 medium onion, finely chopped

450g / 1lb leftover cooked potatoes, cut into 5-mm / ¼-inch dice

1 level tablespoon flour

250ml / 8fl oz hot beef stock or leftover thin gravy

450g / 1lb cold roast beef and its fat, cut into 5-mm / ¼-inch dice

salt

freshly ground black pepper

Melt the dripping or butter in a large non-stick frying pan and sauté the onion until soft, 5–7 minutes. Turn up the heat and brown it lightly. Add the potatoes to the onion and fry for 10 minutes, till golden and crisp at the edges. Stir in the flour and cook for a further minute. Pour in the hot stock or gravy and simmer for 2 minutes, then add the diced beef.

Cover and simmer until a crust forms on the bottom, stir it in, then simmer again, tasting and adding salt; pepper and extra liquid if it appears dry. The hash is done when the bottom is crisp but there is a little liquid left too.

* A few greens, broccoli, spring greens or cabbage may be chopped and added with the beef

* Crumbled dried chilli pepper, or a chopped fresh chilli, can be stirred in when you add the beef

* A fried egg is a popular addition. Cook it in a separate pan and perch it on top of the hash when you serve

Cold Roast Beef Salads

When a joint is awkward to slice thinly for eating cold, I find it easier to hack lumps off the bone, then cut them into 2.5-cm / 1-inch squares. Again, it is important that the meat is not cold from the fridge. When too chilled the flavour is often dull. A lively dressing is most important if the salad is not to give you the feeling that you are eating leftovers.

Beef Salad with Orange Mustard Dressing
Toss 225g / 8oz diced cold beef in a dressing made from 125ml / 4fl oz natural plain yoghurt, 2 teaspoons mustard (a seedy honey one would be ideal), a teaspoon cider vinegar and the juice and a little of the grated zest of a small orange. Mix the beef and dressing with 1 large Cox's apple, cored and sliced into thin segments but not peeled, 1 small sweet onion, cut into thin rings and 2 handfuls of trimmed watercress.

Warm New Potato and Bean Salad
Boil 450g / 1lb new potatoes till tender. Drain and cut them in half. While still warm, mix them with 100g / 4oz cooked French beans, 1 × 400g / 14oz tin flageolet or haricot beans, drained and well-rinsed and 1 tablespoon rinsed capers. Toss with 225g / 8oz diced cold beef and 225ml / 8fl oz vinaigrette, see pages 175–6.

Double-walnut and Beef Mayonnaise
Whizz 225ml / 8fl oz mayonnaise in the blender with 6 medium leaves of baby spinach or sorrel, 8 fresh mint leaves, a handful of chopped fresh parsley and 1 tablespoon hot water. Scrape the mayonnaise into a bowl, stir in 3 pickled walnuts, halved and sliced, and a small handful of coarsely-chopped walnuts. Stir in 225g / 8oz diced cold beef.

Cold Roast Beef Sandwiches with Caramelised Garlic and Basil Sauce

A wonderful sandwich where the toasted bread is dipped in warm sweet garlic and basil dressing. *Poilâne*, that expensive, dense, sour bread sold in posh food emporiums, is just the thing for this. (Despite some wag once writing that it tastes like stale cake.) You may like to sharpen the dressing with lemon juice or wine vinegar to taste.

4 plump cloves of garlic, sliced
   in half
100ml / 4fl oz olive oil
a good handful of fresh basil
   leaves
1 tablespoon balsamic vinegar

salt
8 slices of interesting bread,
   sour dough, *ciabatta* or olive
lemon juice or wine vinegar
8 thin slices of rare, cold roast
   beef, at room temperature

Sauté the garlic cloves in half the olive oil in a small shallow pan till golden and soft, about 15 minutes. Shred the basil leaves and put them in the blender with the vinegar and a little salt.

Toast the bread lightly. Pour the soft garlic and its cooking oil with the remaining olive oil into the blender and whizz with the basil and salt. Taste and adjust the seasoning with salt, pepper and either lemon juice or wine vinegar. Spoon the dressing over the toasted bread. Lay the cold roast beef on the toast and eat.

Cheese

9

I would hate to live in a world without cheese. I particularly enjoy the artisan cheeses made by small producers, some of which are made with unpasteurised milk. These cheeses are becoming more accessible through dedicated grocers, delicatessens and, occasionally, butchers' shops. They are made on farms to traditional methods and have a far more complicated and interesting character than the modern 'block' cheeses. Each artisan-made cheese will vary according to the milk and the production methods, lacking the boring standardisation of the big dairies.

Cheeses made in this way have a far deeper flavour and more interesting texture than their factory-produced pasteurised counterparts. The French, whose taste in such matters is more adventurous than our obsession with blocks of Cheddar, have many hundreds of cheeses made in this way. Here in Britain we must rely on the enthusiasm of a small group of cheese-makers who are willing, against enormous odds, to come up with a finer product than that of the 'cheese giants'. A cheese of this quality is especially appropriate for those with little time. The better the cheese, the less you need to do to it. Try eating a thick piece of Mrs Appleby's pinky-orange Cheshire with a slice of pear or russet apple and you need not much else apart from some decent bread.

Particularly worth hunting out are Keen's Cheddar from Somerset; Montgomery's Cheddar from North Cadbury and Mrs Kirkham's Lancashire. I love the British and Irish blues such as Beenleigh and soft and tangy Cashel, either with bread or oatcakes or in a salad which includes radicchio and frisée. A trip to a cheese specialist is well worth the effort for the delights of soft creamy Wigmore, vegetarian Sharpham and a rich and spicy Milleens.

Goat's cheeses have become popular of late. It is a smart cook who has learned to grill rounds of soft white goat's cheese and toss them in a bowl of green leaves with a mustardy dressing for a five-minute supper dish. They marry surprisingly with sweet beetroot and dark rye bread too.

Where unpasteurised and artisan-made cheeses are not available, then go for a farmhouse pasteurised one. The last resort is the shrink-wrapped blocks of bland hard cheeses that sometimes seem to differ in colour only. Although uninteresting they are regrettably often the only alternative. Even unpromising blocks such as white Greek Feta can come to life when sprinkled with thyme and baked in a hot oven, and the solid Swiss cheeses are perfect for melting and scooping up with soft doughy muffins.

Although cheese prefers a cool place to live, the fridge is too severe. The flavour of cheese is dulled by cold storage; a cool room with good air circulation is best. Clingfilm and a cold fridge sound the death knell for a cheese that has been made with love.

Cheese Suppers

Of all fast suppers 'Cheese and Something' is the one that I turn to more than any other. A piece of cheese, a little salad and some fruit and I often need nothing more. It would not sustain everyone. But it is enough for me. Granted, it satisfies only if all the parts are fine. Good cheese is not difficult to locate, though you had best forget most of the supermarkets, which store their cheeses in too cold a cabinet and refuse (with one or two exceptions) to have any truck with cheeses made from unpasteurised milk.

Go to someone who will let you taste their cheese before you buy. With rare exceptions is a vast display of cheese a good sign. My local butcher carries hardly more than six cheeses, all sold in pretty near perfect condition. His wife may up the choice at weekends to include a couple of soft fresh goat's cheeses. A lovely summer combination is white goat's cheeses, with their grey coating of ash, sharing a plate with a pile of fresh cherries on their stalks.

I have had problems finding a perfect Camembert lately, but similar British cheeses such as Bonchester fill the gap admirably. I have eaten those funny little triangles of Camembert rolled in cornmeal or breadcrumbs and fried in hot oil. The crunchy coating hides a warm oozing mess of cheese. I have so far avoided the addition of a jammy purée such as cranberry or gooseberry which seem to have found favour lately.

Match the salad to the cheese. Sweet tomatoes with salty Feta, nutty russet apples with Cheshire and sweet winey grapes with sharp rich blues. A bowl of soft green lamb's lettuce (*mâche*) works nicely alongside cheeses such as milky Taleggio and Cantal. A gentle, wet-textured Ricotta is a gentle stuffing for mild tinned jalapeño chillies; you don't even have to stuff them, just serve a slice of Ricotta along-side the hot fat chilli pepper.

Occasionally I throw cheese into a salad. Cheese coleslaw can be good, especially if you use bitingly crisp white cabbage and a blue cheese, perhaps a Stilton. I make red cabbage coleslaw tossing in toasted pumpkin seeds, bite-sized lumps of Irish Cashel Blue, Italian Gorgonzola or French Roquefort, and huge dark raisins. I then pour over a warm dressing of hazelnut oil and cider vinegar. Or even simpler, spinach and rocket leaves with huge flat shavings of Parmesan drizzled with some very smart olive oil.

Ploughman's Lunch

I am sure most ploughmen would be horrified to see what is served nowadays in their name in some pubs. But the cheese need not be a slice from a sweaty block, sitting next to a pool of sweet caramel-brown pickle. Neither does the bread have to be a hunk of hard French bread or cottage loaf. Sticky coleslaw, lurid rice salad and potato crisps have helped this snack to sink to new depths.

A ploughman's lunch needs nothing more than good white or brown bread, cut from a fresh loaf or individual rolls, a lump of farmhouse cheese, not necessarily Cheddar, and a spoon or two of sharp pickle. An apple is a welcome addition in the field, less so as part of a pub lunch.

Choose a Caerphilly, Cheshire or Cheddar cheese and break off one large lump. Thin slices just curl up and laugh at you. A pickle or relish, pickled onions (if they are crisp), pickled walnuts or a spicy pickle is fine. A sweet pickle is most unsuitable. It goes without saying that the apple should be an old-fashioned variety, and not one of those polished, waxy numbers that shine lime green or red from greengrocers' shelves. A russet apple with a lump of unpasteurised Cheshire is a favourite of mine. I prefer cider to drink here, but beer of some sort is probably the most appropriate.

Deep-fried Mozzarella

Use the less expensive Mozzarella for this, rather than the more fragile and flavoursome *Mozzarella di Bufala*. Serve with a salad of bitter leaves such as radicchio or chicory.

2 balls of Mozzarella cheese	50g / 2oz fresh breadcrumbs
1 egg, beaten	groundnut oil, for deep-frying

Cut the cheese into slices, 1cm / ½ inch thick. Dip each slice in the beaten egg, then into the breadcrumbs. Heat the oil in a large deep pan or in a deep-fat fryer, slide in the breadcrumbed cheese slices and fry till lightly browned, about 2–3 minutes.

Deep-fried Camembert

Camembert, the sort that comes not just in a wooden box but also cut into triangles and wrapped, can be deep-fried too. Egg and crumb in much the same way as above, then fry in hot oil till crisp and golden with the molten cheese bulging at the seams. Remove from the oil and eat immediately with salad leaves and a handful of green olives. Reckon on about 3 per person, that is, 2 portions to the box.

Baked Feta with Thyme

Even the most mundane of corner shops seem to stock plastic-wrapped planks of Feta cheese, more sophisticated stores may also sell Halumi, a similarly salty white cheese most often found in Cyprus. Although firmer and saltier than the norm found in Greece, they can be turned into a good supper with a little olive oil, some crusty white bread and a glass or three of red wine, as rough as you like.

FOR 2

200g / 7oz block of Feta or Halumi cheese
1 tablespoon olive oil
2 healthy sprigs of fresh thyme leaves

Cut the cheese into 2 thick slices using a large knife. Place each slice on a piece of kitchen foil, dribble over the olive oil and scatter over the thyme leaves.

Put the cheese under a preheated hot grill or in a hot oven, 220°C/ 425°F (gas mark 7), very loosely wrapped round the foil, and cook until the cheese is warm and soft and slightly coloured here and there, 7–10 minutes. Eat with crusty bread and perhaps a tomato and cucumber salad.

Oven-melted Gruyère or Cheat's Raclette

Butter an ovenproof dish, preferably ceramic or glass, and quite shallow. One of those brown earthenware dishes would be perfect. Place a 450g / 1lb block of Gruyère cheese in the dish and place in a very hot oven till it melts, about 15 minutes. Scoop up the molten cheese, spreading it over crusty bread or boiled new potatoes. Return any unmelted cheese to the oven for second helpings. To drink: beer.

Cheese on Toast

The best thing about cheese on toast is that it is cooked almost as quickly as you can think about it. A good example is one where the bread is cut thickly from a proper white loaf and the cheese is sliced from a sharply-flavoured mature Cheddar. The trick of turning a good cheese on toast into a sublime one is to char the edges of the bread while melting the cheese to a patchy golden brown without it overcooking and turning to leather. This is how to do it.

Cut slices from a white loaf, you can use brown but I think white is better here, about 2cm / ¾ inch thick. Toast the bread on one side under a preheated hot grill till pale brown. Turn the bread over and toast again. Spread with butter if you wish, though I am not con-vinced it makes that much difference. Pile at least 2cm / ¾ inch high with thin slices of cheese, a good sharp Cheddar or a Caerphilly is probably best, then return to the grill. Cook under a medium heat until the cheese has melted and starts to brown in patches and the crusts of the bread have charred. Eat immediately.

Welsh Rabbit

I have had a number of minor disasters with traditional recipes for this savoury little delicacy, mostly involving mixtures that will not thicken or that turn irretrievably lumpy. This is not a particularly authentic version but it is the one that never fails for me, and is far quicker than the norm. The best flavour will come from cheeses that have some bite to them, though virtually anything will work. Stilton or a very mature Cheddar have enough of a tang to be interesting, Caerphilly or Wensleydale slightly less so. Eat as a snack with the rest of the beer.

FOR 2 AS A SNACK

225g / 8oz cheese
30g / 1oz butter
1 tablespoon Worcestershire
  sauce

1 tablespoon English mustard
2 tablespoons beer
4 slices of toast

Grate or crumble the cheese and mix to a rough paste with the butter, Worcestershire sauce, mustard and beer. Spread over the toast and grill for a minute or so, till it singes in patches. If the toast is slightly charred at the edges then ever better.

Different Rabbits

Chutney Rabbit
Instead of butter, spread the toast under the cheese mixture with a thick layer of chutney. Tomato or apple chutney is particularly good sandwiched between the toast and cheese.

Bacon or Salami Rabbit
Strips of bacon, grilled crisp, or slices from a salami can be laid on the toast before pouring on the cheese mixture.

Poached Egg Rabbit
A poached egg lurking under the cheese, while being somewhat heavy on the cholesterol count, turns the snack into something

altogether more substantial. Serve with crisp salad leaves such as *frisée* or chicory.

Pesto Rabbit
A spoonful or two of pesto from a jar can be stirred into the cheese mixture instead of the mustard. Be generous with the basil sauce, and use dry white wine instead of ale.

Asparagus Rabbit
The late food writer Jeremy Round made a version of this for a secret snack. It is certainly almost the only use I can think of for tinned asparagus. Lay the spears, which will probably overhang a little, over the buttered toast and top either with Welsh rabbit mixture or just grated cheese à la Round, then grill till bubbling.

* Use crumbled ends of cheese, any sort will do nicely, instead of Cheddar. Blue cheeses such as Stilton work splendidly, but my experience with some Swiss cheeses is that they tend to go leathery and hard.

   If you prefer not to use booze, then use thinly-sliced or grated cheese as a blanket for toast loaded with:

* Thick slices of big browny-black pickled walnuts

* Bottled artichoke hearts, sliced and drizzled with walnut or olive oil

* A mash of chopped black olives and anchovies

* Cold leftover ratatouille

* A mixture of chopped ham, gherkins and a few capers

* Sliced very ripe pears scattered with chopped fresh walnuts and a drop of Kirsch

Croque Monsieur

According to the *Larousse Gastronomique* the first Croque Monsieur was served in Paris, in 1910, in a café on the Boulevard des Capucines.

This most popular of French fast foods comes in sandwich form, either toasted or fried, or as a rich cheese sauce on a round of toast. Either way, it consists of bread, cheese and ham. Frying produces a crisper result, but toasting offers the benefit of less fat. *Croquer*, incidentally, means to munch, which suggests to me that the snack could delight in the name 'Mr Munch'.

Butter two thin slices of white bread. Cover one with a thin piece of Gruyère or Cheddar cheese, add a slice of ham, another of cheese, then the second slice of bread, buttered side down. Press together the sandwich with the palm of your hand, then toast under a pre-heated hot grill. The sandwich is ready when the bread is golden and crisp and the cheese is oozing out from the join.

Grilled Goat's Cheese

Most goat's cheese does not melt, it just softens and oozes tantalisingly. Grilled goat's cheese on toasted French bread is now a rather passé *amuse-gueule*. A shame really, because sharp *chèvre* and crisp bread make such a good snack, and even better when served atop a salad of trendy little leaves such as oak leaf lettuce, chervil, rocket and *frisée*. Until the whirligig of food fashion comes round again you will just have to eat your grilled goat's cheese by yourself, on those black octagonal plates you seem to have been hiding recently.

FOR EACH PERSON

1 slice of brown or white bread or four slices cut from a French stick
1 small goat's cheese, about 100g / 4oz in weight
a little olive oil

Toast the bread under a hot grill. When golden on both sides, slice the cheese into 4 thick slices. Drizzle a little olive oil over the toast, cover with the cheese and place under the grill. When the cheese has browned a little, about 2–3 minutes, serve with a leafy salad.

Beetroot and Goat's Cheese Savoury

I was invited on a very smart Press trip to Paris, where I stayed in an enormous and impossibly luxurious hotel. As my holiday accommodation usually consists of a sleeping bag, I was most grateful to my absurdly generous hosts. The highlight of the visit was dinner at The Bristol, an understated hotel with an innovative chef, Emile Tabourdiau. The unlikely combination of beets and cheese, which he presented as an elegant-striped terrine, is his.

Cover a slice of wholegrain toast with slices of cooked beetroot (not the vinegary ones though), about the thickness of pound coins. Add a layer of goat's cheese slices cut from a log, and drizzle over a little walnut or olive oil. Toast under a preheated hot grill and serve with some floppy green leaves such as spicy rocket or tender *mâche*, sometimes known as lamb's lettuce, dressed with nothing more than lemon juice and nut or olive oil.

A Salad of Bitter Leaves, Blue Cheese and Walnuts

A crunchy salad of bitter leaves and salty cheese in a thick mustard dressing. Bold flavours indeed. Piquant leaves are a bonus, but make this salad with whatever ones you have. Use one or a mixture of blue cheeses, and make sure, if the walnuts are from a packet, that they are fresh; they become rancid shortly after opening.

FOR 2 AS A LIGHT LUNCH, SUPPER OR SNACK

1 tablespoon Dijon mustard
1 teaspoon red wine vinegar
salt
50ml / 2fl oz groundnut oil
2 large handfuls per person of:
   chicory leaves, radicchio and
   frisée, torn into bite-sized pieces

100g / 4oz blue cheese:
   Dolcelatte, Roquefort,
   Stilton or Beenleigh Blue
75g / 3oz walnut pieces

Mix the mustard, vinegar and salt in a salad bowl, pour in the oil and stir until thick. Add the bitter leaves, crumble in the cheese and drop in the walnut pieces. Toss the leaves, cheese and nuts in the mustard dressing.

Ricotta with Broad Beans

Ricotta has a texture rather like a smooth and crumbly cottage cheese and a mild and creamy flavour. This white Italian cheese is made from either cow's or sheep's milk. It must be very fresh if it is to be good, and there should be no yellowing around the edges, which indicates ageing.

For me it is at its best when eaten as an accompaniment to baby broad beans. Just put the beans on the table with a lump of the Ricotta, let everybody scoop up the cheese, and shell the beans themselves.

This snack becomes a celebration when eaten outside, with friends, sitting in the first summer sunshine.

Cheese Plates

Cheese counters, in supermarkets and delicatessens, are often the home of really good cheese. A slice or two cut from a whole cheese and picked up on the way home can make a substantial snack, especially if following a bowl of soup. Well-made farmhouse cheeses, as opposed to shrink-wrapped factory blocks, respond to careful matching of accompaniments and the right glass of wine.

Taleggio with Grapes and Walnut Oil
Taleggio is a delicate Italian cow's milk cheese, usually found in its red-and-white-paper-covered grey rind. It is slightly firmer than Brie. Choose a little more than you think you will need, as its rind is not good to eat, and anyway the paper sticks to it. Lay a slice, about 1cm / ½ inch thick, on a plate, scatter over a handful of halved and

seeded black grapes and then drizzle with a little walnut or gentle olive oil.

Gorgonzola with Warm Potato Salad

Lay a 1-cm / ½-inch slice of ripe Gorgonzola on a plate. Accompany it with a potato salad made by slicing warm boiled new potatoes in half, mixing them with a few torn rocket or spinach leaves, then tossing in a little olive oil and lemon.

Feta with Raw Peas

Cut a slab of Feta in half horizontally. Drop a handful of shelled raw peas (available ready-shelled from some major supermarkets) over the salty white Greek cheese and drizzle with extra virgin olive oil.

Farmhouse Cheshire with Walnuts and Pears

A good farmhouse Cheshire takes some beating. Put a wedge, large enough for one, on a plate. By its side lay a ripe pear, sliced into eight and the core removed. Chop a handful of freshly-shelled walnuts roughly, and sprinkle them over the pears. Season with a few crushed black peppercorns and a few drops of cider vinegar.

Mascarpone with Fruit

Scoop a large dollop of sweet creamy Mascarpone on to a plate. Surround it with sliced pears, russet apples and a small bunch of muscat grapes. Dip the fruit into the cheese.

Ricotta with Apricots and Amaretti

Go for the freshest Ricotta in the deli; it should be soft, crumbly and white. Put a slice in the centre of a plate and eat it with stoned fresh apricots and little Italian almond biscuits, *amaretti*.

10

Fruit

I often turn to the fruit bowl in search of pudding. Bananas can be baked with spices and butter or whipped into a yoghurt-based fool, oranges can be sliced and drizzled with melted chocolate while apples might be best pan-fried with brown sugar and thick cream.

Old-fashioned apples have become a retailing success story recently. Inspired by one of the major chains, many are re-discovering the selling power of the apple. For years the super-markets have insulted us with the shiny green and red imported numbers with their cotton-wool texture and utter lack of scent. Growers are now being encouraged to produce the less profitable but hugely flavoursome old varieties, many of which had died out commercially.

We can now enjoy the apple's true seasons, tasting the nutty yellow-fleshed Blenheim Orange, the heavily-scented, white-fleshed Egremont Russet and the aromatic Ashmead's Kernel. Matching these traditional fruits to cheese can be a joy; try a real Caerphilly with a William's pear, an eighteen-month-old Cheddar with a Cox's Orange Pippin or a tiny fragrant Discovery apple alongside a lump of Wensleydale.

Treats like pineapple should be handled gently. Just peeled and sliced, then spiked with alcohol. Grapefruit, especially the *dawn-toned pink variety, are a perfect partner for the crisp white fennel bulb, and orange works wonders with spinach. Orange has the added advantage of helping the iron in the spinach to be more easily assimilated. Remember too that bananas make a substantial sandwich filling with alfalfa sprouts, peanut butter or bacon.*

Steamed Apples with Butter Sauce

An unfiltered, cloudy apple juice is best for this. The taste is simply better than those thin brown clear juices. Use whatever apples are in the fruit bowl, but Cox's have a very good flavour when cooked.

FOR 2

250ml / 8fl oz unsweetened apple juice
2 dessert apples, such as Cox's
40g / 1½oz unsalted butter

Pour the apple juice into a non-corrosive pan and bring to the boil. Cut the apples in half, peeling them if you wish. Take out the cores and lie them flat in a steamer basket to fit the pan with the juice.

Steam them over the apple juice for 4 or 5 minutes, a minute or two longer for large ones. Remove the apples from the steamer basket with a fish slice or palette knife. Place in a warm dish. Remove the steamer basket and turn up the heat under the juice.

When the juice has reduced a little, cut the butter into small cubes and whisk into the apple juice, a couple of cubes at a time. As you whisk the sauce will start to thicken. Pour the apple sauce over the steamed apples.

Apples with Butter and Sugar

PER PERSON:

2 medium dessert apples
25g / 1oz unsalted butter
1 tablespoon caster or brown sugar

Peel, core and slice the apples into 8 pieces. Melt the butter and add the apples and sugar as soon as it starts to foam. Cook the apples till they are soft and golden, about 5–7 minutes.

Apples with Orange Sauce

Omit the cream if you wish, or serve it separately in a jug. Cox's, as for most things, are a good apple to use as they keep their flavour when cooked, but use whatever is around.

FOR 2

1 large orange	2 tablespoons brown sugar
2 dessert apples	150ml / ¼ pint double cream
50g / 2oz unsalted butter	

Finely grate the zest and squeeze the juice from the orange. Peel and core the apples and cut them into segments, about 8 per apple if the fruit is a good size.

Melt the butter in a shallow pan; when it starts to sizzle, add the apple pieces. Cook for about 5–7 minutes, until they are soft to the point of a knife and golden brown. Transfer to a warm shallow dish with a palette knife.

Add the sugar to the butter left in the pan and place it over the heat until the sugar starts to melt, about 2–3 minutes. Stir while it is caramelising to stop it burning. Pour the orange juice and zest into the pan, and stir in the cream. When the mixture bubbles and thickens, pour it over the apples.

Apple, Walnut and Carrot Salad

Use the salad as a base, adding crunchy, nutty things as you will. Pumpkin seeds are good, and so too are raisins, golden sultanas and poppy seeds.

FOR 4 AS A SIDE DISH, 2 AS A SNACK

2 carrots, crisp and hard	2 tablespoons nut oil, preferably
2 dessert apples	walnut
50g / 2oz walnuts, roughly	1 teaspoon cider or white wine
chopped	vinegar
juice of 1 small orange	salt

Scrub the carrots and grate them coarsely. Grate the apples, without peeling them, core and all. Stir the walnuts into the apple and carrot. In a cup, mix the orange juice, oil and vinegar. Season with salt and toss gently with the carrots, apples and walnuts.

Pan-fried Apple and Cheese Salad

A rather smart way to eat an apple and a lump of cheese. Orange crumbly farmhouse Cheshire cheese is the one I recommend for this salad, but a Caerphilly would be fine too. Or use whichever British cheese you have.

FOR 2 AS A SNACK OR LIGHT LUNCH OR SUPPER

1 large or 2 small dessert apples	50g / 2oz crumbly farmhouse
1 tablespoon walnut or	cheese, such as Cheshire or
groundnut oil	Cheddar
2 tablespoons broken walnuts	½ lemon
2 handfuls of salad leaves,	
perhaps oak leaf lettuce	

Wipe the apple(s), but do not peel. Cut in half and then into quarters. Remove the core and cut the fruit into thick slices, about 6–8 slices per apple.

Warm the oil in a large shallow pan; when it is hot add the apples and walnuts. Cook the apples for about 3–4 minutes, until they are golden, turning them once. Place a few salad leaves on each of 2 plates. Remove the apples from the pan with a palette knife and scatter them among the leaves. Crumble the cheese over the hot apples – it will soften rather than melt – squeeze the lemon juice into the pan and drizzle the resulting dressing over the salad. Eat immediately.

What to do with leftover Baked Apples

Finding a cold baked apple in the fridge in a hungry moment can be a good thing. Leftover baked apples look so sad, punctured and deflated, especially when you remember how good they were when hot and fluffy and straight from the oven. I often have a baked apple left over; in fact, sometimes I deliberately put in an extra one.

Scrape the fluffy chilled apple flesh away from the skin. Then either:

* Mash the flesh with a fork, then fold it into an equal amount of thick, cold, natural plain yoghurt, and eat it then and there

* Cream the flesh to a purée with a fork and place in a small dish, sprinkle a tiny pinch of cinnamon and a grating of nutmeg (go easy on the nutmeg) on top, stir it in, then pour over a spoonful or two of single cream

* Mash the apple flesh really well with a fork, toss in a few plump raisins and a spoonful Calvados or Cognac. Spread it on a hot English muffin, thick buttered toast, or best of all, on malt loaf

* For each teacup of apple purée you have, whisk 2 egg whites till stiff and shiny with an electric whisk, fold in the apple and continue whisking till the mixture holds its shape softly in a spoon. Serve with cream or, even better, a purée of blackberries or raspberries whizzed in the blender with a little lemon juice

HONEYED PEARS

FOR 4
3 ripe pears
75g / 3oz unsalted butter
2 tablespoons runny honey

Cut the pears in half and remove their cores. Chop the fruit into chunks, roughly 2.5-cm / 1-inch cubes, but don't be too precise about this – the uneven size of the pear pieces is part of the pudding's charm.

Melt the butter in a pan, add the pears and cook for 7–8 minutes over a medium heat, tossing gently without breaking the fruit to a mush. When the chunks are golden, dribble over the honey and serve hot.

BANANAS

Date and Banana Cream

The sweetness of the dried dates is important here as fresh dates do not give the same result. If you have the time, give the assembled fruits and cream an hour or two in the fridge before you eat. The preparation time is barely 5 minutes.

FOR 4

4 large bananas, ripe but still firm, peeled
225g / 8oz dried dates
300ml / ½ pint single cream

2 teaspoons orange flower water
2 tablespoons flaked almonds, toasted

Slice the bananas about as thick as one-pound coins. Stone the dates and chop them. Toss the fruits together in a serving dish. Stir the orange flower water into the cream and pour over the fruits. Scatter over the almonds. The dessert is best eaten after a good hour in the fridge, but it will still be good after 25 minutes or so.

Baked Banana with Cardamom and Orange

FOR 4

4 ripe bananas, peeled
4 tablespoons brown sugar
50g / 2oz butter

2 cardamom pods
the juice from 1 large orange

Cut the bananas into slices about 1cm / ½ inch thick. Put them into a baking dish, sprinkle with sugar and dot the butter, in little pieces, on top.

Bake the bananas for 7–8 minutes, depending on their ripeness, in a preheated oven, 200°C/400°F (gas mark 6). While the bananas are baking, remove the little black cardamom seeds from their husks and crush them roughly. If you do not have a pestle and mortar, then put them in a paper bag and bash them gently with the end of a rolling pin. When the bananas are hot and have softened somewhat, take them out of the oven, scatter with the crushed cardamom and sprinkle over the orange juice. Return to the oven for a minute. Serve immediately.

Grilled Banana with Lime and Honey

FOR 4
4 ripe bananas
2 limes
2 tablespoons runny honey

Peel the bananas and place them in the base of a foil-lined grill pan. Squeeze the juice of one of the limes over the bananas and brush with the honey. Place the bananas under a preheated hot grill, rolling them over from time to time as they cook. They are ready to eat when they have turned golden but still hold their shape. Cut the other lime in quarters.

With a palette knife or slice transfer the bananas to plates, then pour over any juices from the pan. Eat while warm with a squeeze from the limes.

Hot Banana Brioche

Panettone, the open-textured Italian Christmas bread, is even better than the brioche, should you have some around after the festivities.

FOR 4
4 slices of brioche or *panettone*,   4 ripe bananas, peeled
   1cm / ½ inch thick   juice of ½ orange
rum, which is quite optional   thick yoghurt, to serve

Preheat the grill until it is very hot. Put the slices of brioche or *panettone* on the grill pan. Sprinkle with rum if you wish. Slice the bananas into pieces as thick as pound coins, and lay them, slightly overlapping, on top of the bread.

Squeeze over the orange juice and place the bread under the grill, until the banana starts to turn golden brown, about 5–7 minutes. Serve hot with thick yoghurt.

Banana Yoghurt Fool

FOR 2

4 soft, ripe bananas, peeled
300ml / ½ pint thick creamy natural yoghurt

Drop the bananas in the blender and whizz till smooth, but stop before they turn gummy. Add a spoon of yoghurt if they refuse to move, or use a food processor. Scrape into a bowl with a rubber spatula, fold in the remaining yoghurt, which should be chilled and thick, spoon into wineglasses and chill till you are ready to eat.

Banana Sandwich

The banana sandwich, of which there are many versions (I recently found one with cheese and jam), seemed to start life with the fruit mashed to a sticky pulp. I think this is a shame as the banana's texture is quite unlike anything else, being meaty and delicate at once. To my mind a banana sliced for a snack should be a firm one, on the underripe side even, and should be cut into pieces at least as thick as a pound coin.

Bacon and Banana Sandwich
The bacon must be crisp and the bananas ripe. This is one of those sandwiches that should be filled to capacity, even if the filling does sound a little eccentric. The sort of sandwich to devour alone.

streaky bacon rashers, sliced
thin
a little fat, for frying
crisp lettuce leaves, iceberg or
Cos

bread, sliced from a white or
wholemeal loaf
mayonnaise
mango chutney
bananas, peeled and sliced as
thick as pound coins

Fry the bacon rashers, with a little fat if necessary, until they are crisp. Grill them if you prefer, it really does not matter, but they must end up crisp. Shred the lettuce finely. Spread the bread with mayonnaise, then with mango chutney. Pile on the shredded lettuce followed by the bacon and the sliced banana. Cover with another slice of bread.

Banana, Cream Cheese and Walnut Sandwich

bread, sliced thickly from a
wholemeal loaf
cream cheese such as
Mascarpone, Philadelphia or
curd cheese

bananas, slightly underripe and
peeled
walnut halves, freshly chopped
(prepacked chopped nuts are
often stale)

Spread the bread with the cream cheese, as thickly as you dare. Add the banana, sliced, and cover with the chopped walnuts. Top with another slice of bread.

Banana, Alfalfa, Cottage Cheese and Date Sandwich

bread, brown and thickly sliced
cottage cheese
alfalfa sprouts

fresh dates, sliced or roughly
chopped
bananas, ripe, peeled and sliced

Spread the cottage cheese on the bread with extreme generosity. Cover with a layer of alfalfa sprouts, scatter the dates and sliced bananas and cover with another slice of wholemeal bread.

Banana Split

Some people come over all superior about ice cream sundaes. Their loss. A sundae made with the best ice cream, fresh fruit and thick cream is fast food of the first order, and not to be sniffed at. Reckon on 1 banana, 1 large scoop of ice cream, and 100g / 4oz berries per person.

bananas, ripe but firm
vanilla ice cream, the real thing

raspberries, or better still blackberries, whizzed in the blender with a little lemon juice

Forget the traditional presentation, who can seriously eat ice cream off a plate?

Peel and slice the bananas into thick chunks. Place a large ball of vanilla ice cream in a small dish, place the sliced banana around the side, then pour over the raspberry or blackberry purée, sieved if you must.

CITRUS FRUITS

Grilled Grapefruit

I was a child of the 1960s, and I can assure you that grilled grapefruit was the height of sophistication in Wolverhampton. (It probably still is.) Almost as a joke, I prepared it the other night, and, dare I say, rather enjoyed it. To remind:

Cut a yellow grapefruit (the whirligig of fashion being what it is, I feel obliged to insist upon the colour) in half across the horizon. Sprinkle it with sugar – white will give a thin crisp crust – and dash it under a very hot preheated grill. Don't give it long enough to heat the fruit through, just to caramelise the sugar – barely a minute.

Perfumed Pink Grapefruit Juice

FOR 1

1 teaspoon orange flower water
1 tall glass of pink grapefruit
    juice, either freshly-squeezed
    or from a carton

ground cinnamon
crushed ice cubes

Stir the orange flower water into the grapefruit juice, dust with a very little cinnamon and serve over plenty of crushed ice.

Grapefruit, Beetroot and Watercress Salad

Slice small cooked beetroot into discs as thick as pound coins. Put them in a bowl with the grated zest and the juice of an orange. Peel a grapefruit with a small sharp knife and cut into segments. Pour a spoonful of olive oil into the bowl with the orange juice and beets. Toss gently – this is not a dressing which needs to be emulsified – then add the grapefruit segments and a few good handfuls of trimmed watercress or *mâche* (lamb's lettuce). Salt or pepper is unnecessary. Serve with cold meat, duck is good, or with a sliced goat's cheese.

Pink Grapefruit and Fennel Salad

The sweetness of the grapefruit, the aniseed notes of the fennel and the creamy dressing work together to surprising effect. The colours are pretty too.

FOR 4 AS A SIDE DISH

1 pink grapefruit	salt
1 large fennel bulb, fat and round	freshly ground black pepper
4 tablespoons double cream	a small handful of green olives

Peel the grapefruit with a sharp knife, taking care to remove all the pith. Slice the peeled fruit crossways, putting the slices into a china bowl. Catch all the juice in a second smaller bowl; you will need it for the dressing. Slice the fennel into quarters and then into thin strips. Add them to the grapefruit. Scatter over the olives.

With a fork, mix together the grapefruit juice, cream and seasoning. Drizzle over the fennel, grapefruit and olives and serve.

Citrus Fruits with Honey

A salad made from the Christmas fruit bowl, with a dressing of the fruits' own juices sweetened with honey. A neat starter, or the perfect accompaniment to pork, roast hot or cold. When the salad is chilled, a few sprigs of fresh mint would not go amiss.

FOR 4 AS A SIDE SALAD
3 satsumas, clementines and tangerines
3 small oranges
1 grapefruit

the juices from the fruit **juice of 1 lemon**
2 tablespoons light, fruity olive **2 tablespoons runny honey**
  oil

Peel the fruits, taking care to remove all the pith, and slice them into rounds. Collect any juice which runs from the fruit in a bowl. Whisk the oil into the collected juices, add the lemon juice and stir in the honey. Dress the sliced fruits with honey, oil and fruit juice and chill for as long as you can.

Chilled Oranges

Leave firm Navel, Shamouti or Valencia oranges in the fridge. When they are thoroughly chilled (we are talking hours rather than minutes), slice them through into quarters from stalk to flower end. Eat them with your hands.

Spinach and Orange Salad

FOR 4 AS A LIGHT LUNCH DISH WITH CHEESE TO FOLLOW

4 handfuls of small spinach **freshly ground black pepper**
  leaves, washed **a small handful of tiny black**
4 oranges, small and firm **olives**
3 tablespoons virgin olive oil

Remove the stalks from the spinach, but leave the tiny ones. Peel the oranges with a knife, taking care to remove the pith and to collect the juice for the dressing. Cut the oranges in half, then each half into thin semicircular slices.

Stir the olive oil into the orange juice and season with the freshly ground black pepper and the tiny whole olives. Toss with the spinach and oranges.

An Orange Plate

Peel and slice 1 blood orange per person, taking care to remove all the pith. Serve the slices in little mounds on plates, arranged with an assortment of sweet and sticky dates, squares of darkest chocolate or little chocolate truffles, strips of crystallised orange and lemon peel and crisp biscuits such as brandy snaps. Set before your guests on your most beautiful plates, as an instant dessert, with hot dark roast coffee.

An Orange Snack

Slice a large juicy orange, or whatever orange you have in your fruit bowl, scatter over a spoon or two of muesli and a spoon of roughly-chopped dark chocolate. A bizzare-sounding snack perhaps, but it works.

Foil-baked Oranges

Peel 1 large orange per person with a small sharp knife, removing all the pith. Slice the orange into segments, then place on a square of foil. Sprinkle with a little orange flower water, or Cognac if that is more to your taste, and pull the slices together to reform the orange. Wrap up in the foil, scrunching and twisting it at the top. Bake in a preheated fairly hot oven, 200°C/400°F (gas mark 6), until heated through, about 10–15 minutes.

DAMSONS

Although damsons are hard to come by nowadays I include them here as I think a bowl of hot poached damsons, with a jug of cream, is one of the finest and fastest of fruit desserts. Damsons share with red peppers the almost magical ability to be transformed from the hard and tasteless to the sensuously rich and sweet by the application of heat. I must also declare a probably slightly romantic memory of the huge damson tree at home, when we would harvest the slightly overripe fruits on wet and misty autumn mornings, all around the smell of rotting leaves and mushrooms.

Hot Damson Compote

If you have spotted a wooden chip of damsons at the greengrocers, and plan to use them for a fast dessert then I suggest you make sure they are ripe. Some of them can be like purple-black bullets, and need a long, slow cooking to be good.

Remove the little stalks from the fruit, discarding any squashed ones. Put them in a saucepan, stainless steel for preference, and add a small amount of water to come no more than a third up the side of the pan, and a generous quantity of sugar. Bring quickly to the boil, turn down the heat and simmer gently till the fruits have burst their skins and their juices have worked with the sugar to produce a rich purple sauce, about 15 minutes. Serve hot with cream.

FIGS

The best figs I have ever eaten were in a national park in Yugoslavia, straight from the tree in a meadow filled with hummingbirds and butterflies. Figs appear in the shops in this country during the autumn, mostly imported from Italy and France. Although there are many varieties, it is the fat round purple ones and the pointed soft green variety that we see most often. Eaten as a snack they are good enough, but they make a fine end to a meal when served on a plate with freshly-shelled almonds and hunks of jewel-like pomegranate.

For me, along with the peach, they are the most sensual of fruits, and I can make an entire meal of a few figs and some flat floury bread such as Italian *ciabatta*. Try them split and dressed with a dollop of thick natural yoghurt or scattered with thin slivers of air-dried ham.

Check the fruit for ripeness by pressing very, very gently with your fingers – if they are soft they are ready. If they are oozing very slightly at the base, then eat them soon. To ripen them quickly, store in a paper bag at room temperature.

Dried figs, with the possible exception of dates, are the sweetest of all the dried fruits. I prefer the loose-packed ones that you find in greengrocers and Cypriot shops to the bags of smaller ones from health food stores, good though they are. Snack on them instead of sugary sweets, or add them to winter fruit salads with bananas, purple grapes and sweet Moroccan Navel oranges.

Purple Figs with Warm Honey

A snack to share with someone special, in bed, on a cold winter's night.

Split two bulging purple figs per person. They must be seriously ripe. Gently warm a small pot of runny honey, thyme or orange blossom if you have it, in a pan of simmering water. Carefully remove the pan from heat, twist off the lid, using oven gloves or a tea towel, and spoon the warm honey over the ripe figs. Eat with your fingers, sucking the purple-red flesh from the skins.

Figs with Parma Ham and Walnuts

FOR 2 AS A LIGHT LUNCH OR STARTER

6 ripe figs, green or purple
3 tablespoons chopped walnuts
150ml / ¼ pint thick natural
  plain yoghurt

2 paper-thin slices of air-dried
  ham such as Parma,
  shredded

Wipe the figs, then cut a cross in the top of each one, to go at least halfway down the fruit. Squeeze gently to open the fruit like a flower. Fold the chopped walnuts into the yoghurt, and stir lightly.

Spoon the dressing over the opened figs. Scatter the shredded Parma ham over the yoghurt.

Hot Poached Figs

SERVES 2

6 figs, green tinged with purple
450ml / 16fl oz red wine
4 tablespoons runny honey

Put the figs into a stainless steel or enamelled pan. Pour over the wine and spoon in the honey. Bring gently to the boil. Simmer until the figs are hot and tender, about 15 minutes. Serve tepid.

Figs with Navel Oranges

Cut 2 figs per person into quarters. There is no need to peel them, provided you have taken the trouble to wipe them. Place them in a bowl.

Peel a small orange per person, catching the juice as you cut away the peel and pith in the fig bowl. Cut the orange thinly into round slices, then add to the figs. Chill for as long as you can before eating.

A Plate of Dried Figs

Choose the plumpest, softest dried figs you can. You will probably find them in Cypriot shops and good greengrocers. Slice them in half across to produce two seedy rounds. Sprinkle them with a few fennel seeds. Arrange on plain white plates with new season fresh walnuts and a sprig of muscat grapes. Serve with strong black coffee.

Tinned Figs with Pernod

Figs come from a tin relatively unscathed, and are actually rather good if served very cold. Try not to think of fresh figs when you eat them.

SERVES 2

1 × 400g / 14oz tin whole green figs in syrup
½ teaspoon Pernod

Place the figs in a plain china dish with a draining spoon. Tip the Pernod into the syrup in the tin. Stir the syrup or shake it gently, then pour it over the figs. Serve with cream.

PEACHES

Late June, July and August see trays of scarlet, vermilion and yellow peaches in greengrocers and delicatessens. Enterprising supermarket chains may also have blushed white peaches, altogether too good to miss.

A ripe peach is a fragrant one. There is no need to squeeze, just sniff. Their aroma is rich and sweet, and some varieties, particularly white peaches, have a deep fragrance of roses and raspberries. Unforgettable. Carry them carefully, and bring them gently to ripeness in a brown paper bag. Only the very ripest need refrigerating, but bring them back to room temperature before you eat them, for it is then that they are at their most fragrant.

I have never had the same fondness for the nectarine, whose smell I find flat and the flavour not up to that of the peach. Many prefer them, disliking the fuzzy skin of the peach. For me that is one of the delights of the fruit, first the fluffy skin, then the sweet flesh with its juices that dribble down my chin. The choice is yours, and they are interchangeable in all recipes.

In savoury form the peach grills well. Try stuffing a stoned peach with soft cheese such as Dolcelatte and Mascarpone, then flashing it under the grill till the cheese melts. Or tossing a few crisp Cos lettuce leaves with sliced peaches and dressing them with a lemony vinaigrette.

And what faster food is there than a ripe peach sliced into the last glass of the red wine that accompanied dinner?

Dolcelatte, Mascarpone and Peaches

The blue- and white-striped cheese in your deli counter is a layered concoction of mild blue Dolcelatte and sweet Mascarpone, called Torta Dolcelatte. Although this first appears bizarre, it makes good eating. Try breaking off chunks of the creamy cheese and placing them in the hollows of stoned peach halves. Scatter over a few roughly-chopped walnuts and serve as a snack or starter.

Peaches with Basil

Slice fresh peaches, peeled if you wish, into a china dish. Squeeze over a little lemon juice, then toss very gently with a few shredded fresh basil leaves. Allow 4 leaves of basil per peach, and 2 teaspoons lemon juice.

Grilled Peaches with Honey

Both the fragrance and flavour of a truly ripe peach seem to be retained by cooking them quickly under the grill.

FOR 4

4 tablespoons runny honey   4 ripe peaches
juice of 1 lemon   4 teaspoons butter

In a small bowl mix the honey with the lemon juice. Cut the peaches in half and remove the stones. Lay them, flat side up, in a shallow baking dish.

Dot half a teaspoon butter on top of each peach. Brush the lemon and honey mixture over the peaches and place under a preheated, medium-hot grill. They are done when the honey starts to bubble and the peaches turn golden brown in patches, about 5–7 minutes. Serve hot with thick natural yoghurt.

Grilled Stuffed Peaches

Follow the previous recipe but forget the butter. Before you spoon over the honey and lemon, stuff the peach halves with the following filling.

50g / 2oz Ricotta cheese
6 *amaretti* biscuits, crushed in their papers with a rolling pin

Spoon over the honey and lemon and place under the preheated grill until the almond cheese filling begins to brown, about 5–7 minutes. Serve hot, spooning the syrup from the baking dish over the peaches.

White Peaches with Beaumes de Venise

A white peach, fragrant and warm from the windowsill rather than cold from the fridge, is a perfect partner for a glass of chilled Beaumes de Venise. You could, of course, slice the fruit into the chilled wine, then eat the wine-soaked peach with a teaspoon, and drink the rest.

A White Peach Plate

Make a dessert plate to end a high summer meal. Arrange deeply-perfumed white peaches on a pretty plate with a handful of fresh almonds, shelled but not skinned, and a little pile of deep-red logan-berries or raspberries.

PINEAPPLES

I cannot think of pineapples without transporting myself, just for a few minutes, to the beach in India. There, every morning of my holiday, I watched an awesomely dextrous man peel and slice a ripe pineapple for me. He would offer me one slice, then bag the rest in blue plastic and send me off along the beach.

* Tinned pineapple is usually very sweet, but I have eaten a perfectly passable pudding made by chopping up tinned pineapple, first drained of its juice, then put into a shallow dish. Thickly-whipped double cream was spooned over and spread level to the top of the dish. Sugar was dusted over the top and it was grilled under a very hot flame till the sugar caramelised – 3–4 minutes. There was probably a drop of Kirsch in among the fruit, now I come to think of it. I have heard of the same being done with tinned peaches

* I don't know why this is so good; spread cream crackers, quite ordinary ones are fine, with a thick swirl of cream cheese. Add a slice of fresh pineapple. That's it

* Pineapple with Kirsch is still one of the most popular desserts in the less pretentious Parisian restaurants, though it has long disappeared in Britain. No doubt in favour of 'a symphony of fruit sorbets with a purée of their fruits'. It is very important that the pineapple is ripe and chilled. Peel and slice the fruit and place it on a plate. Upend a measure of Kirsch, or rum if you prefer, over the fruit

PLUMS

Hot Buttered Plums

I enjoyed this dish as a child, although I remember it as plums on toast. Elizabeth David recorded it forty years ago, and I think it so good as to give my version here.

Make sure the plums are ripe; they should dribble juice (which you will catch in the dish) if they are ready. If your plums are not yet ripe, but for some reason you must use them, then you had better make a crumble instead.

FOR 2 AS A PUDDING OR SNACK

2 slices of white bread   **4 ripe plums, dark and juicy**
butter   **4 tablespoons sugar**

Butter the bread thickly. Remove the crusts. Halve and stone the plums. Lay the bread in a shallow dish, and sprinkle it with most of the sugar.

Place the plums, flat sides up, on the bread and dot over a few bits of butter. Sprinkle over the remaining sugar. Bake in a preheated fairly hot oven, 200°C/400°F (gas mark 6), for 15–20 minutes, until the butter has melted and the juices from the plums are bubbling. Serve hot, with cream.

SCARLET FRUITS *AND* BERRIES

Raspberries, mulberries, loganberries, redcurrants, blackcurrants and strawberries form the backbone of fast summer fruit puddings. Nothing good will come of fancy recipes for these glorious fruits. Raspberries with blackberries and soft white Petit Suisse cheese, blackberries crushed and folded into double cream with toasted hazelnuts, or a hot crumble made with blackcurrants and mint is sophisticated enough.

I try not to add anything to these fruits that will interfere with their fragrance. I see little point in adding *framboise*, the raspberry liqueur, to the fresh fruit, though blackcurrants are assertive enough to benefit from a touch of cassis. A sharp cream such as *crème fraîche* or *fromage blanc* is a favourite accompaniment, though even better, I think, is a half-and-half mixture of thick natural yoghurt and softly-whipped cream. The cream should barely hold its shape and the yoghurt must be a thick Greek one, perhaps a strained sheep variety. Sweet wines, especially the muscats and Sauternes, and a few peppery herbs such as basil and mint are other natural partners for red fruits.

With figs, muscat grapes and peaches, I think of the raspberry as among the finest fruits we have. I often eat a handful balanced on fresh white bread spread with soft fresh cream cheese such as Ricotta or Mascarpone. At their most heady and luscious, raspberries need no sugar or cream, just a white bowl and a spoon.

Strawberries need more help than the softer berries. Deeply-flavoured berries are a rare find nowadays. A squeeze of lemon juice or a splash of rose water will lift a slightly dull berry though there is little that will improve an out-of-season berry if it is really not ripe. The fact strawberries can be eaten with cucumber in a salad is hardly news, but have you ever thought of giving them a richer flavour with a sprinkling of precious balsamic vinegar or sharpening their edge with the juice and seeds of a passion fruit?

On a sunny day there can be few better ways of eating these deeply-perfumed rich scarlet and purple fruits than setting them out on the table under the shade, in their punnets, with a bowl of *crème fraîche* and a glass of muscat wine for those who wish for it.

Cherries

I am sure that cherries, yellow- and red-tinged, are at their best eaten straight from the greengrocer's brown paper bag. I remain unconvinced that their flavour is better for the application of heat. Crumbles are better made with plums, pies with apples and blackberries, and tarts are surely the vehicles for soft scarlet fruits. The stones, which take up most of the cherry, drive me quite mad.

I find the next best way to eat this fruit is: stone a handful of slightly sour cherries per person. Put half of the fruit in the bottom of a large wineglass. Two-thirds fill the glass with a soft fresh cheese such as a French *fromage frais*, then pile on the remaining fruit. Toast a few flaked or shredded almonds until they smell nutty and turn light brown in colour, and sprinkle them over the top.

Strawberries with Orange and Fromage Frais

Choose plump red strawberries, wipe or quickly wash them, then remove their green leaves and stalks. (To do so before would allow water to enter the berries.) Pile into a bowl and squeeze the juice from an orange over the fruit. Serve with a separate bowl of *fromage frais*.

Strawberries with Red Wine

Slice washed strawberries into a china bowl. Sprinkle with red wine, a light and fruity Beaujolais would be ideal, and set aside in a cool place for as long as you can. Half an hour is about long enough.

Strawberry Fool

A fool, lumpy with chunks of fruit and sharpened by *fromage frais*, is I think preferable to the usual concoction of a smooth, sweet, pink paste.

FOR 2
225g / 8oz strawberries
225g / 8oz *fromage frais*
100ml / 4fl oz *crème fraîche* or thick double cream

Crush the berries in a pudding basin with a fork. Fold in the *fromage frais* and the *crème fraîche*, slowly but thoroughly. Spoon into glasses or small pots and chill before serving – leave it for as long as possible. An almond biscuit or shortbread would make a flattering accompaniment.

Strawberries with Orange Juice and Grand Marnier

Cut the berries in half. Place them in a china bowl. Pour enough freshly-squeezed orange juice over the berries just to cover them. Stir in enough Grand Marnier to be interesting, then set aside to macerate for as long as you can, but half an hour should do it. If you get the chance to leave them overnight, though the berries will soften, they will taste even better.

Little things to wake up a bowl of out-of-season Strawberries

* A very light grinding of black pepper

* A squeeze of lemon

* A shake from the balsamic vinegar bottle

* A spoonful of orange flower or rose water

* A little shredded fresh mint

* The juice and seeds from a passion fruit

Raspberries

It is difficult to imagine that there could be anything more fragrant than a bowl of warm and perfectly ripe raspberries, eaten without the gilding of cream or sugar. Perhaps, though, at the height of the season, you may want to try something more adventurous.

Raspberries with Ricotta

FOR 4, WITH SECOND HELPINGS

450g / 1lb Ricotta, very white and fresh
3 tablespoons runny honey or 25g / 1oz icing sugar
2 tablespoons Grand Marnier
75ml / 3fl oz double cream, softly whipped
450g / 1lb raspberries

Push the Ricotta through a sieve, or whizz it in a food processor. Stir in the honey or icing sugar and Grand Marnier. Blend well. Fold in the whipped cream.

Pile the Ricotta cream into a glass or china dish and scatter raspberries around. Serve with a bowl of extra raspberries.

Scarlet Fruit Mess

Eton Mess, sometimes called Clare College Mess, is in its simplest form a concoction of strawberries and cream made by mashing the two together with a fork. Purists would say that it does not need the grated orange zest, crumbled meringues or other foreign bodies that appear in recipes from time to time. Although I like the idea of simply whipping cream and folding smashed strawberries into it, I do think that shop-bought meringues are a sound addition.

The best Mess to my mind is one where raspberries, rather than strawberries, are crushed gently with a fork until they bleed, next folded into lightly-whipped cream, then the whole mixture lightened and sweetened with a couple of meringues, broken up into little pieces.

The crucial point lies in the whipping of the cream. It should be full-fat cream, none of that whipping variety, and should be gently half-whipped, that is, until it is just about capable of holding a little shape, but by no means stiff enough to form peaks. Oh, and it really must be eaten quickly if it is to be good.

Hot Raspberry and Mascarpone Brûlée

Pile raspberries into a shallow ovenproof dish (a half soufflé dish or gratin dish is fine). Dot scoops of Mascarpone over the fruit and sprinkle with caster sugar. Place under a very hot preheated grill until the Mascarpone has started to melt and the sugar begins to caramelise, about 2 minutes. Serve hot.

Raspberry Fool

Whizz raspberries in the food processor till smooth. Squeeze in a little lemon juice, then fold in some softly-whipped cream. Reckon on an almost equal volume of whipped cream to berries.

Vanilla Ice Cream with Raspberry Sauce

Whizz a punnet of raspberries in a food processor, or push them through a nylon sieve. Stir in a squeeze of lemon juice. Serve over the best vanilla ice cream you can find.

Raspberries in Wine

Drop a handful of ripe luscious raspberries into a glass of chilled sweetish wine, preferably a Gewürztraminer.

Raspberry Compote

2 × 225g / 8oz punnets of raspberries
2 tablespoons sugar
1 teaspoon Kirsch

Tip the berries into a china or glass bowl. Sprinkle with sugar and Kirsch. Leave in a warm place such as the back of the cooker or in the airing cupboard for a few minutes, then serve with a jug of cream.

Ten-minute Trifle

Real trifle, made with home-made sponge cake, syllabub, and a gallon of sherry must be one of the most delicious puddings known to man, but it takes an age to make from scratch. The commercial alternative contains lurid orange jelly topped with a substance akin to shaving foam, only sweeter. It is topped with rainbow-coloured sugar-strands, or if you are really unlucky, those teeth-breaking silver balls.

The following recipe is almost as quick as its name and has some of the alcoholic creaminess of the former without any of the horrors, not to mention the E numbers, of the latter. I serve it unadorned, just a soft creamy mass in a plain bowl, scattering crystallised violets or rose petals over the surface only if I am feeling tacky.

FOR 4, AND IT IS EVEN BETTER THE NEXT DAY

10 sponge fingers, broken into 2.5-cm / 1-inch pieces
250ml / 8fl oz chilled sweet white wine, such as Moscato or half sherry
100g / 4oz raspberries, loganberries or juicy blackberries
2 ripe bananas, peeled and sliced
2 eggs, separated
50g / 2oz caster sugar
225g / 8oz Mascarpone cheese
a little vanilla extract or brandy

Put the sponge fingers in a 1.1-litre / 2-pint dish. You can use that cut-glass thing Auntie Connie gave you if you must, but the trifle looks far more elegant in a plain white china bowl. Pour over the wine, gently pressing the fingers down into the liquid, then throw in the raspberries or other berries and the bananas.

Cream the egg yolks with the sugar, add the Mascarpone and beat with an electric whisk till light and creamy. Tip in the vanilla or brandy. Whisk the egg whites till they form stiff peaks and fold gently but throughly into the cream. Tip the Mascarpone cream over the fruit and sponge. Shake the bowl gently for a few seconds. Set aside for as long as you can. A minute should suffice.

Blackberries and Raspberries with Petit Suisse

The most charming of all the cream cheeses must be the little pots of Petit Suisse. Unwrap one of the cheeses and place it in the centre of a small plate. Scatter a handful of raspberries and blackberries around the cheese, then pour over a dash of single cream. The effect of the sharp white cheese, the sweet yellow cream and the scent of the purple fruits is positively ambrosial.

Blackberry Fool

Crush, or rather bruise, the blackberries with a fork. Stir in a little caster sugar (reckon on 50g / 2oz sugar to 450g / 1lb), then fold gently into 150ml / ¼ pint softly-whipped double cream. Scatter over halved and toasted hazelnuts, if you like. It is most important that the cream is not overwhipped; it should barely stand in peaks, or perhaps drifts, and should fall lazily from the spoon.

Blackberries in Cassis

If you find any blackberry liqueur, *crème de mûres*, at the back of the cupboard then it would be just perfect. Cassis, blackcurrant liqueur, turns a bowl of berries into a wonderfully heady treat.

Tip the blackberries, which will probably be the large and juicy cultivated ones, into a glass bowl. Pour over a few glugs of cassis and sprinkle with sugar. Leave for as long as you can. Serve with a jug of yellow cream.

Blackberries with Melon and Muscat

If you have come home with some wild blackberries, ones that have missed being eaten en route or squashed on the carpet in the back of the car, try them the following way. Serve them, free from their prickly grey stems, in a simple bowl of china or glass, with cubes of ripe golden and fragrant Charentais melon, macerated for a little while in Beaumes de Venise or other chilled deep golden muscat.

Blackberry Yoghurt Burnt Cream

You will need either those sweet little white ramekin dishes or a shallow dish similar to a quiche plate. Two-thirds fill the dish with blackberries, or other berries if that is what you have. Cover with a layer of thick Greek-style yoghurt and smooth flat with a knife. Sprinkle a thin layer of caster sugar over the yoghurt and put under a preheated very hot grill till the sugar caramelises to a golden crust, around 2–3 minutes.

Fruits Brûlée

This summer pudding really excels when it is made with soft fruits, berries (black, blue and rasps), peaches if they are really ripe, and bananas. Redcurrants look like glistening jewels if a sprig or two is laid on top of the peaks of cream. Sheer indulgence, this fruit and cream mess has been known to seduce even confirmed pudding-haters.

FOR 6

225g / 8oz sugar

700g / 1½lb mixed soft fruits, to include bananas, peaches and raspberries

350ml / 12fl oz chilled double cream

Put the sugar in a heavy pan and pour in enough water to cover. Set over a high flame to boil, while you prepare the fruit. Peel the bananas, stone and slice the peaches and remove the stems from the raspberries. Put all the fruit in a serving bowl. Whip the cream until it forms soft peaks. If it starts to look grainy, then you have overwhipped it. Spoon the cream in waves over the fruit.

The sugar in the saucepan will start to turn to a pale golden caramel after about 10 minutes – watch it carefully as it is prone to burning, but do not stir it, which would make it crystallise. The caramel is ready when it turns a rich golden brown. Take off the heat before it starts to smoke, or it will turn bitter.

Immediately, taking care not to splash or burn yourself, pour the caramel over the cream and fruit. It will at once set to a crisp shiny coat. Serve within 30 minutes.

Blackcurrants

Blackcurrants, topped and tailed and sold in neat plastic boxes, are to my mind the most successful of frozen fruits. They are probably the only ones I ever really use.

Hot Blackcurrant Bread and Butter Pudding

FOR 2

Butter 4 thin slices of white bread very generously. I think you had better remove the crusts. Lay half of them in the bottom of a shallow ovenproof dish. Cover with 250g / 8oz thawed blackcurrants, or fresh topped and tailed ones if you have them, and sprinkle rather lavishly with caster sugar, about 2 tablespoons. You can use raw cane brown sugar if it makes you feel better, but it will change the flavour of the finished dish.

Place the remaining buttered bread, butter side up, over the currants, sprinkle with a little more sugar and 2 tablespoons cassis, *eau de vie* or Cognac and dot with a bit more butter. Bake in a preheated oven, 220°C/425°F (gas mark 7), for 20–25 minutes, until the blackcurrants have started to burst and their glorious juices have stained the bread. The result is juicy bread reminiscent of summer pudding underneath the crisp top. Serve with pouring cream.

Vanilla Ice Cream with Hot Blackcurrant Sauce

Cook some blackcurrants with a very little water until they start to burst. Stir in enough sugar to make them palatable but far from sweet, simmer for a couple of minutes to melt the sugar, then pour into a jug. Serve hot with balls of vanilla ice cream, which will melt slightly at the edges and swirl beautifully into the steaming purple compote.

Blackcurrant Crumble

Plums probably make the finest crumble. Or perhaps gooseberries. This blackcurrant version is pretty serious stuff, and is just as good cold. A glug from the cassis bottle will not go amiss, nor will for that matter, a few fresh mint leaves tucked in among the fruit.

175g / 6oz plain flour
100g / 4oz butter, plus 25g / 1oz
50g / 2oz caster sugar, plus 2
  tablespoons

450g / 1lb blackcurrants, fresh
  or frozen, topped and tailed

Whizz the flour and 100g / 4oz butter in the food processor. When they look like breadcrumbs stir in the 50g / 2oz sugar. Pile the currants into a deep pie dish, sprinkle over the 2 tablespoons sugar, and dot with the remaining 25g / 1oz butter. Cover the currants with the crumble mixture and bake in a preheated oven, 200°C/400°F (gas mark 6), until the crumble is golden and the fruit is bubbling, about 25 minutes. Serve hot with cream or thick, creamy yoghurt.

Redcurrants

Redcurrants mean only one thing to me – Summer Pudding. Squashed with raspberries and a handful of blackcurrants between layers of bread, it really must be the most sublime of English puddings, though it takes too long to prepare to be included in this book.

Hot Red Fruits

Perhaps unexpectedly, these fruits retain their individual flavours if not cooked for too long. The ensuing syrup is tart and rich, and any left-over makes a good kick-start for breakfast, with yoghurt.

FOR 4
225g / 8oz redcurrants
100g / 4oz blackcurrants
4 tablespoons sugar

450g / 1lb raspberries or
  loganberries or tayberries

Put the currants and the sugar into a stainless steel saucepan with 2 tablespoons water. Bring slowly to the boil. When the currants start to burst and flood the pan with colour, then tip in the raspberries, loganberries or whatever. Simmer for 2 minutes, no longer, and serve hot in a white china dish, with a jug of cream.

Whitecurrants

You are extremely lucky if you can find some whitecurrants; I have not seen any for at least two summers. When I next see a punnet, I shall serve the sprigs with tiny crisp water biscuits, on pretty plates, surrounding small mounds of Petit Suisse. I shall put a little scoop of the sweet white cheese on to a water biscuit, pile on a few golden currants and eat them in the garden, in the shade, with a glass of chilled sparkling Moscato.

Incidentally, a well-made redcurrant jelly can make a delightful snack eaten with cream cheese and water biscuits.

Secret Snacks and The Quick Fix

Visitors from other countries must be amazed at Britain's selection of cheap sugar-laden confectionery surrounding the tills in shops. In France or Italy one might leave the office for a few moments to stand at a bar and swig an espresso or munch a toasted sandwich, while here in Britain it seems people are more likely to return with a chocolate bar or even a packet of biscuits. All that fat and sugar is bad news for everyone except the huge cookie and candy (I won't say chocolate) companies.

Here are some salty or sweet alternatives which will hit the same spot but are, for the most part, better for you, and whose flavour means there is some point in snacking on them.

* **Sun-dried Tomatoes**, for a deeply savoury nibble

* **Pumpkin and Sunflower Seeds**, for toasting or eating straight from the jar

* **Black and Green Olive Pastes**, for dipping bread into

* **Tahini**, a paste made from toasted sesame seeds: drizzle on dry toast

* **Scottish Oatcakes**, eat them as they are from the box, or dip them, in totally unorthodox fashion, into olive pastes, or spread them with honey

* **Caviar**, forget the silly accompaniments such as chopped onion, and eat in generous heaps on hot toast

* ***Patum Peperium***, a secret blend of anchovy and spices, for spreading in minute amounts on hot toast

* **Bottled Tomato Juice and Tins of Consommé**, for mixing with

Worcestershire and Tabasco sauces and making extra-thick Bloody Marys, see page 25, which are almost as good as a meal

* **Umeboshi Plums**, Japanese salted plums, will keep in the fridge for months, good for when only something simultaneously salty and sour will do. Buy them from health food stores or Oriental shops

* **Yoghurt**, keep a tub of thick natural yoghurt in the fridge for sprinkling with nuts and honey; try it with thickly-sliced bananas too

* **Condensed Milk**, boiled in its tin for 1 hour till thick. It will keep for weeks in the fridge. An index finger is preferable to thin biscuits which break in the thick sweet gunge

* **Marshmallows**, toast till soft and warm. For serious sugar attacks

* **Chocolate**, the dark and fruity Manjari or Carré de Guanaja from Valrhona is pure chocolate with very little sugar and none of the fat and milk-powder padding of the cheaper varieties

* **Hunza Apricots**, tiny fawn wrinkly fruits from Pakistan, the wild Hunza apricot is chewy and addictive, available in health food shops

* **Turkish Delight**, make sure it's the real thing, rose- or pistachio-scented from Istanbul or the Lebanon

Select Bibliography

Andrews, Colman, *Catalan Cuisine*, Headline, 1988
Bareham, Lindsey, *In Praise of the Potato*, Michael Joseph, 1989
Beard, James, *American Cooking*, Hart-Davis Macgibbon, 1972
Bissell, Frances, *A Cook's Calendar*, Chatto & Windus, 1985
Bissell, Frances, *Sainsbury's Book of Food*, Webster's, 1989
Boxer, Arabella, *Mediterranean Cookbook*, Dent, 1981
Brown, Catherine, *Scottish Cookery*, Richard Drew, 1985
Brown, Lynda, *Fresh Thoughts on Food*, Chatto & Windus, 1986
Bunyard, Edward, *The Anatomy of Dessert*, Chatto & Windus, 1933
Child, Julia, *The Way to Cook*, Alfred Knopf, 1989
Christian, Glynn, *Glynn Christian's Delicatessen Handbook*, Macdonald, 1982
Costa, Margaret, *Margaret Costa's Four Seasons Cookery Book*, Nelson, 1970
Crabtree and Evelyn Cookbook, Barrie and Jenkins, 1989
David, Elizabeth, *A Book of Mediterranean Food*, John Lehman, 1950
David, Elizabeth, *French Country Cooking*, Purnell, 1951
David, Elizabeth, *French Provincial Cooking*, Michael Joseph, 1960
David, Elizabeth, *Summer Cooking*, Museum Press, 1955
Davidson, Alan, *North Atlantic Seafood*, Macmillan, 1987
Del Conte, Anna, *The Gastronomy of Italy*, Bantam Press, 1987
Freson, Robert, *Taste of France*, Webb and Bower, Michael Joseph, 1983
Gavin, Paola, *Italian Vegetarian Cookery*, Optima, 1991
Graham, Peter, *Classic Cheese Cookery*, Penguin, 1988
Gray, Patience and Boyd, Primrose, *Plats du Jour*, Penguin, 1957
Gray, Patience, *Honey from a Weed*, Prospect Books, 1986
Grigson, Jane, *Good Things*, Michael Joseph, 1971
Grigson, Jane, *The Mushroom Feast*, Alfred Knopf, 1975
Grigson, Jane, *Jane Grigson's Vegetable Book*, Michael Joseph, 1978

Grigson, Sophie, *Sophie Grigson's Ingredients Book*, Pyramid, 1991

Hambro, Natalie, *Particular Delights*, Jill Norman and Hobhouse, 1981

Hazan, Marcella, *Classic Italian Cookbook*, Macmillan, 1980

Heath, Ambrose, *Good Dishes From Tinned Foods*, Faber, 1939

Heath, Ambrose, *Good Sandwiches and Picnic Dishes*, Faber, 1939

Heath, Ambrose, *Good Savouries*, Faber, 1939

Heath, Ambrose, *Savoury Snacks*, Nicholson and Watson, 1939

Holt, Geraldene, *Recipes from a French Herb Garden*, Conran Octopus, 1989

Madison, Deborah, *The Greens Cookbook*, Bantam, 1987

Maschler, Fay, *Eating In*, Bloomsbury, 1987

Mellis, Sue and Davidson, Barbara, *The Born Again Carnivore*, Optima, 1990

Pomiane, Edouard, *Cooking in Ten Minutes*, Cookery Book Club, 1969

Rance, Patrick, *The Great British Cheese Book*, Macmillan, 1983

Roden, Claudia, *A New Book of Middle Eastern Food*, Viking, 1985

Roden, Claudia, *Picnic*, Jill Norman and Hobhouse, 1981

Ross, Janet, *Leaves from Our Tuscan Kitchen*, Dent, 1927

Round, Jeremy, *The Independent Cook*, Barrie and Jenkins, 1985

Sahni, Julie, *Classic Indian Vegetarian Cooking*, Dorling Kindersley, 1987

Scott, David, *The Demi-Veg Cookbook*, Bloomsbury, 1987

Seeber, Liz and Gerd, *Simple Food*, Dorling Kindersley, 1987

Spencer, Colin, *Colin Spencer's Fish Cookbook*, Pan, 1986

Stobart, Tom, *Herbs, Spices and Flavourings*, Penguin, 1987

Toklas, Alice B, *The Alice B Toklas Cookbook*, Michael Joseph, 1954

Waters, Alice, *Chez Panisse Menu Cookbook*, Chatto & Windus, 1982

Wells, Patricia, *Bistro Cooking*, Kyle Cathie, 1989

Acknowledgements

This book was unknowingly inspired by the late Jeremy Round, the much-missed food correspondent of *The Independent*. It was his 'admission' to eating midnight snacks of canned asparagus, piled on thick toast, covered with grated Swiss cheese and grilled until golden, that prompted me into collecting ideas for fast foods and secret snacks. That it has emerged as a book is due to Louise Haines of Michael Joseph.

Although I attempted a professional training and endured a wandering apprenticeship, I still remain very much an amateur cook. But I must thank the people who tried so hard to instill some form of discipline into my cooking, namely Kenneth Bell at Thornbury Castle, John Tovey at Miller Howe and the chefs at La Varenne in Paris and the Box Tree in Ilkley. I am grateful to Justin de Blank for encouraging me not to work at his grocer's shop for ever.

'Needs direction', 'needs encouragement' and 'works well if pushed' feature more than once in my school reports. I am grateful to Caroline Waldegrave and Arabella Boxer for their direction, and to Frances Bissell, Geraldene Holt and Delia Smith for their encouragement. I must thank my editor Louise Haines at Michael Joseph and Nancy Roberts at *marie claire* for their patience and for giving me the occasional push.

My thanks to Mike Georges who tasted everything but the fish, and to those who ate their way through the good, the bad and the downright indifferent, particularly Maggie Cowen, Adrian Barling, Jean-Louis and Jacqueline Bloche-Laine, John Zentner and Tony Richardson. I am grateful too to the many cooks I have shared kitchens with who will find their good ideas stolen and claimed here as my own.

Finally, I should like to thank Kevin Summers, and Digger, Magrath and Poppy for their constant company.

Index

All cheese recipes are indexed under *cheese* rather than the name of the particular cheese being used